St Monans

St Monans

History, Customs & Superstitions

by
Aitken Fyall

The Pentland Press
Edinburgh – Cambridge – Durham – USA

First published in 1999 by
The Pentland Press Ltd
1 Hutton Close
South Church
Bishop Auckland
Durham

ISBN 1-85821-670-2

Typeset in Bell 11/14
by Carnegie Publishing, Carnegie House, Chatsworth Road, Lancaster LA1 4SL
Printed and bound by Bookcraft Ltd, Bath

Dedicated to my wife June
and in happy memory of my granny
Jenny Easson.

Contents

List of Illustrations

Illustration Credits

	Picture Number
Bobby Anderson (late)	17
Lucy Boyter	12
C.W.R. Bowman	23
James Braid	32, 49
Joan Brown	30
John Davidson	42
Ivy and May Easson (late)	15
Fife Council	27
Annie Fyall	48
June Fyall	3, 5, 26
Philip Gay	31,41
Aese Goldsmith	1, 6, 11, 21, 24, 50
Henry Guthrie	16
John Guthrie	44
Ena and Tom Hughes	7
Jimmy Hutt	37
Jean Jenkins (late)	10
Janet Lindsay (late)	13, 14, 29
Peter Marr	43
Ruth and Bill Mathers	45
Jenny MacDonald	9, 18, 19, 20, 22, 33, 46
William P. Miller (late)	4
Robert Nee	39
John Ovenstone (Snr)	25, 28, 34
Lily Proudfoot	30
John Ritchie	40

Scottish National Portrait Gallery	2, 8
Nan & Humphrey (late) Tilbrook	47
Bill Webster	38
Jim Wilson	35, 36

Acknowledgments

THE PREPARATION and completion of this book would have been an impossible task without the kind assistance of many people, some of whom have contributed to the script, often suggesting new topics.

Hoping that I have included everyone, the following have my unreserved appreciation:

The late Bobby Anderson, Lucy Boyter, Joan Brown, Joan Clark (New Zealand), James Corstorphine, Sonny Corstorphine, John Cunningham, John Davidson, Ann Duncan, the late Ivy & May Easton, Fife County Planning Service, Annie Fyall, Jenny Gammon (Carmarthen Library), Philip Gay, Aase Goldsmith, Henry Guthrie, John Guthrie, Ena & Tom Hughes, Jimmy & Margaret Hutt, the late Jean Jenkins (Norwich), Mike King (Curator, Fife Museums), Nancy Latto, Sandra Linton (Fife County Economic Adviser – Policy), Jenny MacDonald (New Zealand), Ruth & Bill Mathers, Aileen McLaughlin (Fife County Community Libraries), Jessie Miller, Harry Montador, Roberta Montador, Robert Nee, Rev. Gilbert Nesbit, John Ovenstone (Snr.), Robert Ovenstone, Cathy Paterson (Pitlochry), Andrew Peddie, Donald Peddie (Kelso), Lily Proudfoot, John Ritchie, Vicki Salvage, Alex & Ena Scott (Melbourne), Elspeth Scott, Fiona Scott, Kenneth Smith, Mattie Stewart, James Tarvit (Scottish Fisheries Museum), John Thompson, Peter Thompson, the late Humphrey Tilbrook and Nan, Bill Webster, Tom Weir & Jim Wilson.

Jimmy Braid deserves a major mention for his experienced piloting of the project to endorsement by local government. I am also beholden to the members of the St Monans Community Council for their whole-hearted support of my efforts. I express my gratitude to Michelle Dixon, Deputy Editorial Director, and

Mary Denton, Publishing Manager of the Pentland Press and her staff, for their expert handling of the publication.

Finally, I must record special thanks to my wife, June, for her ever-helpful counsel, her eager and diligent research and her pains-taking production of the text but, most of all, for her unfailing patience.

Foreword by James Braid, OBE, JP.

It is an honour and a privilege to contribute the foreword to this excellent record of the History of St Monans, a village that both the author and I are so proud to claim as our birthplace.

I feel sure that it will give great pleasure to many readers, not only locally but also to others who have gone afar. Every chapter, over the wide coverage of our village life, has been well researched and covered in an historically factual and, at times, pawky manner.

Aitken, we are yet again proud of you in this new field of activity and thank you sincerely for being the first to record the history of our village.

I have thoroughly enjoyed reading this book and I am confident that there will be many others who will echo these sentiments.

West Shore
St Monans.
1st May 1998.

Introduction

SINCE BOYHOOD, I have been fascinated by the stories and legends of my native St Monans. My interest was first stimulated by the kindness of Andrew Allan, long-time Burgh Registrar, who lent me his treasured copy of John Jack's history of the village, published in 1844. Later, I had the good fortune to be given John Leighton's *History of the County of Fife*, published in 1840, by Mrs Christina Morrison and then, by Mrs Elizabeth Tarvit, a copy of the Charter of St Monance, a poster of Shore-Dues, Anchorages & Customs from 1817, the Income & Expenditure of the Parochial Board for 1876 and the *Handbook of the Brotherly Society* of 1884.

Apart from sundry information scattered through various books on the Kingdom of Fife, Jack's is the only publication, other than occasional guide books, devoted solely to St Monans. So it is that, after the passage of more than one hundred and fifty years, I have attempted to give a new account of my birth-place, from its beginnings to the present day.

The character of the village and its people has altered radically in the last fifty years. Modernisation and expansion often mean the loss of old landmarks. The almost total disappearance of the traditional pursuits of fishing and boat-building and the re-orientation of everyday life, occasioned by the impact of technology, transport and the mass media, has changed the complexion of the community irreparably.

The bustle of yesteryear, on the pier, in the boat-yards and on the streets and harbour, with their throngs of summer visitors, will not return, but the history and legends of those times should not be forgotten.

Inevitably, fact and fiction blur together, particularly in early accounts for, as ever, historians glean a great deal of their information from hearsay, much of it oft-repeated and, sometimes, misrepresented. I have therefore arranged my narrative in as chronological an order as possible but, because of the diversity of topics, it has often been difficult to decide where subject matter may best be placed. Many a true account of an event is, in time, expanded by some aspect that is simply and obviously folk-lore. I can only trust that my readers will find this practice acceptable.

My excursions into more general history have been made to set life and parochial events in St Monans into the broader framework of the Scotland and Europe of the times.

Rather than supply a glossary of little-used Scots words and tables of old weights, measures and money, I have given explanations and modern equivalents in the text. Again, except when quoting from original documents, I have adhered to the now accepted spelling, St Monans.

I believe that it is important to record, in detail, the architecture of the Auld Kirk. However, I have placed it in a separate appendix, so that the narrative is not interrupted for the general reader.

I have made my researches as comprehensive as possible but, as the story of a village over the centuries can be explored endlessly, I can only apologise for any sins of omission or commission.

I have asked Councillor James Braid, OBE, JP to provide a foreword. His long life of public service and dedication to St Monans and its people deserves no less. Jimmy, or Jas, as he is popularly known, was made a Freeman of the Burgh on St Andrew's Day, 1974, in recognition of his contribution as Magistrate, Provost, and Town and County Councillor. The one and only recipient of the Freedom, he has, at the time of writing, served for fifty-two years.

As the new Millennium approaches, I express the hope that we St Monans folk will continue to cherish and be proud of our heritage and that our village will enjoy a long and prosperous future.

Aitken Fyall
Bronwydd
Wales.
3rd June 1998.

Chapter 1

In the Beginning

ST MONANS came into existence as a fishing hamlet many centuries ago and the sea has been the way of life for generations of 'Simmininsers', as its inhabitants are known in the East Neuk of Fife.

Naturally, the site of the village goes back to the creation of the Earth itself, four thousand, seven hundred million years ago. Later, as a result of an asteroid hitting the planet, the Moon was formed, circling the Earth every twenty-eight days. Under its influence are created the tides, so vital to a seafaring community, ebbing and flowing twice in the twenty-four hours.

The motto of the village is '*Mare Vivimus*', 'We live by the sea', implying not only the geographical location but also the source of commerce and sustenance of its people.

The Coat of Arms depicts four fishermen in a boat, hauling their nets, with the additional motto, 'Grip Fast'. This secondary maxim has interesting origins. In 1067, Bartholemew, a noble Hungarian and founder of the Leslie family, who featured so prominently in the history of the village at a much later date, was Governor of Edinburgh Castle and also Lord Chamberlain to Queen Margaret. One of his duties was to carry her on the pillion of his horse, as there were many roads and footpaths entirely unsuitable for carriages. For her safety, he wore a stout leather belt on which she could secure a firm hold. On one occasion, crossing a stream, he cried 'Grip fast,' to which she replied, 'Gin the buckle bide.'

The establishment of a settlement at this particular location was dictated by the rock formation of the coast-line. The harbour lies in what is termed, geologically, the St Monans Basin, part of the St Monans Syncline. This 'fold' in the Earth's surface can be readily observed by following the direction of the ridges of rocks, or 'skellies'. From Pittenweem harbour, where they lie nearly at right angles to the braes, they then sweep almost parallel to the coast at St Monans, changing direction again, out towards Newark Castle. Thus is created a natural, safe harbour, with spring tides of eighteen to twenty feet depth of water and neaps of thirteen to fifteen feet. Again, importantly, the orientation of the rocks provide a natural breakwater against the prevailing easterly storms.

Fifty million years ago, the area was distinguished by active volcanoes, whose vents, as they are called, exist at present-day landmarks such as the hills, Largo Law and Kellie Law, the promontory, Kincraig Point by Earlsferry and at Ardross. In the triangle formed by St Monans, Largo and St Andrews, there are over one hundred such volcanic orifices. Magma or molten rock spewed out, covering the adjacent lands. The igneous layers formed when the lava cooled and solidified are visible in many areas of Fife. In particular, they are in evidence on the Auld Kirk's 'Witches' Hill', on the beach below, with seams of white crystals of calcite, and at Elie Ness. The David's Rock, on the West Sands, is a volcanic 'plug' of basalt, a very hard black stone. Much of the rest of the land is composed of coal, quartz, mica and limestone, the last being derived mostly from fossils and corals. Local varieties of limestone include 'Upper Ardross' at Pathhead, halfway between the village and Pittenweem, 'Hosie' from the end of Rose Street towards the swimming pool, 'White' at the Burnside, and 'Abercrombie' under the ancient dovecote by Newark Castle. Fine examples of limestone formations, worn over the centuries by the tides and the winds, are to be seen in the outcrop, jutting out to sea, just beyond the kirk. From the coastline, they are: the Lady's (formerly Our Lady's) Rock, Shank Craig and Long Shank. Originally, they were interconnected and joined to the mainland; the present separation from the shore is known locally as 'The Cut'.

For two and a half million years to 8000 BC, Britain experienced the Glacial Period, encompassing no fewer than seven Ice Ages, when mammoths roamed the Earth. Before glaciation, the present Firth of Forth was but a canyon, a slit in the Earth's crust, being some four hundred and sixty feet deep at the site of the Forth Road and Rail bridges at the Queen's Ferries. Glaciers, hundreds of feet in thickness, covered the land; by the west side of the

Lomond Hills, beyond North-West Fife, the ice reached over one thousand feet in depth. Eventually, a glacier from the Southern Highlands swept over the Ochil Hills, and moved slowly from west to east, scouring out the Clyde-Forth valley and onwards into the North Sea. Before the Glacial Period, the sea level was three hundred feet lower than today, but the weight of so much ice depressed the land, so that, by the end of the last Ice Age, the water level was one hundred feet higher than now. The ice melted, and the land recovered, resulting in the formation of 'raised beaches'; Miller Terrace is such a feature. Shells and fossils found there came originally from the sea bed, not, as has been popularly supposed, from the mussels, used in baiting fishing lines, which had been shelled there over the life of the village. A lower beach is the coastal walk to Pittenweem. The St Monan's shore-line is rich in fossils, the local favourite being the 'crowpie', or, more correctly, crinoid or encrinite. Fossilised skeletons, crowpies are often carried in the pocket or handbag for good luck. Indeed, a fisherman having poor catches was considered to have 'lost his crowpie'. Some of the sandstone ridges, particularly beyond Newark Castle, exhibit the entrapped fossilised remains of large tree trunks, one in particular measuring nearly three feet long and tapering in diameter from seventeen to fourteen inches.

A primary requirement of life is a bountiful supply of fresh water. In early St Monans, there were two main sources, the Inverie Burn, which rises in the reedy marshes in the Parish of Kilconquhar and runs down to the sea by the Auld Kirk, and the 'mineral' to the east of the windmill. There were also several perennial springs, but subsequent coal-mining drained the principal aquifers or wells. It was not therefore by chance that the bank of the main source of water was chosen as the site for the old shrine to St Monan and, eventually, for today's kirk.

Folk needed to keep warm and to cook. Early Fife was heavily afforested but, with no planned programme of replanting, the wood supply dwindled. Significantly too, King James IV, who ruled Scotland from 1488-1513, built the biggest 'ship-of-the-line' in the world, 'the King's gret schip', the 'Great Michael'. It was said that all the woods in Fife were felled to supply the timber. Measuring two hundred and forty feet in length, with a beam of thirty-six feet and with sides two feet in thickness, she carried, reputedly, a crew of three hundred, with one hundred and twenty gunners and one thousand fighting men. From the old accounts, she must have been a magnificent sight with her 'standaris, pinsalis and banaris in gold colouris, olye and vernesing' and 'the kingis ymagery, pinsalis and flaggis'. Captained by Admiral Sir Andrew Wood of Largo, the founder of the Scottish Navy, she was virtually useless in war and was eventually sold to Louis XII of France. By 1773, that great lexicographer Doctor Samuel Johnson was remarking: 'A tree might be a show in Scotland as a horse in Venice.'

In early times, the forests of Fife teemed with wild boar, wolves and herds of wild horses. The last, however, which were probably like today's garron, the sturdy horse of the Highlands, were too small and light to carry men in armour and the great war-horses favoured by the knights were imported from the Continent, particularly from Belgium.

Most farming used oxen but horses were required for the transport of goods over significant distances. Goats and poultry abounded and, in cultivated areas, ten milking cows were kept for each plough. Dairy produce was vital to the economy. A peculiar measure of that age was the 'tonegall' of cheese, a massive six stones or thirty eight kilogrammes.

Replanting of trees appears to have taken place subsequently, as John Leighton in his *History of Fife*, published in 1840, notes that 'of the parish acreage of one thousand and eighty four, some fifty seven are under wood.'

However, there was an alternative source of fuel. The St Monans Basin held coal, at Newark, Coalfarm and Abercrombie. In the *New Statistical Account of Scotland* (1845), the Reverend Robert Swann, minister of the Auld Kirk, gives the following description of the area:

> Coal. – There are said to be six seams of coal in the barony of St Monan's, splent and cherry. Those seams range in thickness from 18 inches to 7 feet. In former times the coal here was wrought to the depth of ten fathoms; but it had been given up for twenty-five years, when it was resumed, about nine years ago, the shafts being driven to the depth of 27

fathoms. For eighteen months, the working of the coal has been wholly abandoned, owing to the tacksman (lessee) not having been judiciously placed. Wrought in an effective manner, it might have afforded employment for one hundred persons. The number actually employed is said not to have exceeded thirty. It is believed that a person or company of capital and enterprise, might make the coal here a very profitable concern.

There are understood to be several seams of coal in the lands of Abercrombie.

Limestone. – There is abundance of limestone in the immediate vicinity of the village, and held to be of excellent quality. So rapidly, however, is it found to dip to the south-east, and so deep is the tirring [stripping] required, that the working of the limestone has not been found to pay. It was also much against the burning and sale of the lime, that the working of the coal came to be finally abandoned.

Thus, the early village had all the necessities of life, water, food from sea and shore and fuel for warmth and cooking.

Chapter 2

Who was St Monan?

THE NAME MONAN is first found in the history of the Guarani Tupians or Tupinambas, an Indian tribe of Brazil, whose religion was somewhat akin to that of the Incas of Peru.

Tupi mythology includes a series of civilising and creator heroes, the first of whom was Monan, in their language meaning ancient or old. He was the Creator of Mankind, who eventually destroyed the world with flood and fire. Then came Maire-Monan, the Transformer, who had the power of changing men and animals into other forms, in order to punish them for their sins. He taught the Tupinamba the arts of governing and of cultivating the earth.

The earliest form of religion practised in the locality of St Monans was pagan, following the rites of the Druids, with their sacred symbols of the mistletoe and the oak, and the worship of Nature and the Sun. Unlike the Aztecs of Mexico, who built great temples to the Sun and the Moon, the Druidical holy places were more basic. The Standing Stones of Lundy, which can still be seen near Largo, supposedly formed such a temple. The crude arrangement of the three megaliths, set in a triangle, constituted the judgement seat, the judiciary court of the Druids, who combined their priesthood with being educators and law givers. They were the civil and criminal authorities, wielding merciless power over the populace by superstitious fear and the threatened penalties of excommunication, outlawing and even death, as human sacrifice to their gods.

There are, however, conflicting views as to the origin of the stones. One authority claimed them to be Roman; another believed them to be the gravestones of Danish chiefs, who were conquered by Banquo and MacBeth and who fell in battle near the spot. Controversially, it has been asserted that the details of Banquo and the Danish invasion in the reign of King Duncan, are nothing more than the invention of the fertile brain of Hector Boece or Boethius, historian and co-founder and first Principal of the University of Aberdeen.

At Dunino, too, are fragments of a Druid's Circle, which once stood in a field on present-day Bailey Farm, this land being dedicated to Bel, the Sun God. Later, the pieces were incorporated into the porch of Dunino church, being consecrated and marked with the signs of the Cross. This was an old custom on the Continent, and probably also in Britain, where ancient rituals enacted beside them had given place to the holy mysteries of the Church of Rome. What is said to have been a Druid's sacrificial altar stone was converted, somewhat appropriately, into a sundial.

There are many references to Monan, especially in Scottish place-names and chaplainries, from Edinburgh to Kiltearn in Ross-shire, and even to a stream. Sir Walter Scott, in his poem 'The Lady of the Lake', wrote:

> The stag at eve had drunk his fill,
> Where danced the moon on Monan's rill,
> And deep his midnight lair had laid,
> In lone Glen Artney's hazel shade.
> But when the sun his beacon red,
> Had kindled on Ben Voirlich's Head …

Tom Weir, the well-known Scottish mountaineer and writer, confirms the existence of Monan's Rill, a well, bubbling out of the ground, as being on the east slope of Ben Voirlich, and being approached through Glen Artney, just as described by Scott. Weir believes that when Scott was writing about this area, a former hunting forest of the Stewart Kings, he had his information from a shepherd. The present shepherd, Pat McNab, still uses the name, although the connection with St Monan may be difficult to establish.

As a multiplicity of explanations and theories exist, the true origin of St Monan may never be known. Was he 'the fair, tall, smooth Moenon', a companion to Brendan the Voyager, who sailed from Ireland to preach Christianity on the British mainland?

Skene, in his *Celtic Scotland*, identified him with Moinnen, Bishop of Clonfert Brenain, again in Ireland, on the banks of the river Shannon. He died in AD 571. Boethius believed that Sanct Monanus was simply Moinnen, with the Latin masculine noun-ending '-us' added. Turgesius the Dane attempted to establish his national heathenism to replace the Christian faith, which he had found in Ireland. Systematically, he despoiled the country and, in AD 845, in addition to many fine churches and abbeys, burned and plundered the monastery of Clonfert Brenain. At this time, Kenneth MacAlpine was re-establishing his Scottish kingdom in Pictland and reclaiming for the Scottish clerics their old ecclesiastical foundations. Because of the state of the church in Ireland, Skene argued that a large body of Scots came to Fife from Ireland, bringing with them the relics of their saints.

St Monan's Day is given as 1st March, the same as St Moinnen in the Catholic Calendar and as Dewi Sanct, Saint David of Wales.

According to Cemerarius, in his *Account of the Scottish Saints,* St Monan was a martyr, celebrated for his miracles in Fife and on the May. The island of that name, lying at the mouth of the Firth of Forth, housed an important monastery, where, according to legend, in AD 874, the Danes massacred 6,000 Christians and Culdee monks, including St Monan and St Adrian of Pittenweem. Cemerarius called the village Inverny. One view is that the victim may well have been a hermit or monk, who guarded the relics of the saint in the shrine in St Monans.

The Breviary of Aberdeen and Bishop Forbes' *Kalendar of Scottish Saints* states 'Adrian and Monanus were natives of Pannonia in Hungary', who had come with 6,006 compatriots, and 'the Blessed Monanus preached the gospels to the peoples on the mainland and in a place called Inverry in Fyf'. This tradition was accepted by the noted historian Andrew Wyntoun, Prior of St Serf's monastery on Loch Leven. In his *Cronykil* of 1336, Wynton wrote that the saint first came to the village in AD 870, reputedly living on crabs and black bread.

In Invery, Saynct Monane,
That off that company wes ane,
Chesyd him sae nere the se,
Tae lede hys lyff; there endyt he.

Again to quote, 'The plenitude of caves in the sea-margin of Fife made it peculiarly available for eremite [hermit] practice. Many godly men chose to dwell apart in rocky oratories.' He instanced also St Rule at St Andrews, in the east of the county, and the solitary monk on the Island of Inchcolm in the west.

The Reverend Walter Wood, in his book of 1887, favoured St Munna or Fincan, founder of a monastery in Wexford, who died in AD 634. Two other versions are that he was known as Monan the Martyr or that he was Monanus, Archdeacon of St Andrews. Yet another Irish source is St Ethernan, identified with the Church of Kilrethen in nearby Kilrenny.

1. St Monans from the air

Chapter 3

St Monan's Shrine and Well

WHATEVER THE EXPLANATION as to the person of St Monan, there is no doubt that, in the ninth century, a shrine or chapel was built in his honour at the mouth of the Inverie Burn. With a supply of fresh water and a safe beach for landing from the Firth of Forth, it was an ideal location. Centuries before Bernadette Subirous reportedly saw the Virgin Mary at Lourdes in 1858, the Shrine of St Monan attracted thousands of pilgrims annually, especially on the Saint's Day of 1st March. They flocked into the village, seeking cures for their mediaeval ailments: small-pox, the Black Death, that deadly epidemic of bubonic plague that swept Europe and Asia in the fourteenth century, and leprosy. The last scourge struck down King Robert the Bruce, who contracted the disease during his Crusades in the Holy Land.

According to John Jack, a private teacher who wrote *An Historical Account of St Monance* in 1844, a friar lived at the shrine in the twelfth century. His good deeds were identified with healing, foretelling events and performing miraculous operations by word and by touch. This oracle was 'clad in the skins of reindeer', and 'never turned his eye towards the sun'. He was fed by an 'unkindness' of ravens, who nested in some stately elms behind his cave. Again, according to Jack, the chapel may have been erected in the middle of the eleventh century by Malcolm III, to commemorate the victory of the Caledonians and the expulsion of the Danes from Scotland. Local superstition claimed that, at the height of a terrible storm, the chapel was un-roofed, the walls shattered, the elms flattened and the oracle had disappeared, having been seized and carried off by kelpies.

The exact site of the chapel is not known but the cell of the hermit who attended the relics is on the right of the narrow lane connecting the Braehead to the Burnmouth.

It was described by a former minister of the Auld Kirk, the Reverend Doctor John Turnbull, as 'a snug recess, sheltered by the tiles and grey eaves of the byre, among the banks, walls, and ruinous tenements of the village, overhung by a dusky-coloured mass of high whinstone rock and a stair or gulley, winding past it in the front'. Tradition has it that St Monan's bones or relics are buried there or on the site of the original chapel. D. Hay Fleming, writing in 1886, claimed that it was called St Monan's stedd or site, that it had been used as a byre, but now functioned as a coal cellar and a shelter for ducks. Unwisely, in recent times, almost the entire site has been covered in concrete. At Crail, too, there was a chapel to St Monan. According to the *New Statistical Account*, 'there was no doubt a cell or chapel, dedicated to St Minin or Monan, at Kilminning Farm; the cornyards of which are still full of graves, like a regular burying ground.'

It was built, either by the saint himself or by one of his followers, at the end of the ninth or early in the tenth century. The little chapel probably fell into decay when the kirk in the town, the Collegiate Church of Our Lady at Crail, grew in importance, two hundred years later.

St Monan was also the Patron Saint of Kilconquhar Church, although that place name is supposedly derived from Conchobar or Conchar, giving the local surname of Connacher. There has long been a misunderstanding about the name Kilconquhar. In the East Neuk, Kinneuchar has been accepted as the rendering in the local dialects, but since time immemorial, there has been a clear distinction. Gordon of Rothiemay's map of 1645 shows that the different names referred to specific areas. He lists 'Kill Conquhair' as the church and 'Keanwchar' for 'the head of the loch'. Not only so, but he gives 'Lonhead alias Kinochar'. The Gaelic word *lon* means 'marsh'. Kilconquhar then is the *cille* or church of Conchobar, whose name in later Gaelic became Conchar. The *lon* seems to point back in time to when the loch was Redmyre, possibly Reedmyre, a sheet of water, little more than a marsh in summer.

To the east of the restored windmill on the East Braes can be seen some red-stained ground, crossing the coastal path, all that remains of the spring, called in an old Charter, the Well of St Monan. Pilgrims drank the water, its high chalybeate or iron-containing composition having supposedly curative power for all ailments from barrenness, through the diseases, to toothache and chilblains.

Local fishermen had their nets blessed there, washing them to enhance their strength and keeping qualities, before the introduction of 'barking' or waterproofing, by soaking in a hot solution of alum or cautch. The latter preservative is a resin extracted from the bark of the Indian or Burmese acacia tree. It was widely used by fishermen well into the twentieth century, before the introduction of synthetic fibres such as nylon or polypropylene, which replaced cotton.

Analysing the mineral water from St Monans in 1895, Doctor D.B. Dott declared it to be superior to that of famous spas. His findings are detailed in the following table.

St Monans Parish Magazine
No. 2233
104 & 106 South Canongate,
Edinburgh, 10th December 1895

Analysis of Water from St Monans, received 2nd December 1895	
Ammonia (saline)	0.08 part per million
Ammonia (albuminoid)	1.06 part per million
Nitrogen (as nitrate)	none indicated
Carbonate of Iron	6.70 grains per gallon
Manganese Sulphate	0.07 grains per gallon
Calcium Sulphate	15.30 grains per gallon
Magnesium Sulphate	12.36 grains per gallon
Alkaline Sulphate	4.87 grains per gallon
Alkaline Chlorides	10.00 grains per gallon
Silica	1.76 grains per gallon

Note: This is an interesting chalybeate water, containing more iron than some of the famous springs of the Continent. Unfortunately the amount of albuminoid ammonia is exceptionally high, indicating some objectionable contamination. If the water could be kept free from this impurity, it would undoubtedly be a valuable water.

D.B. Dott, FIC, FRSE

	Grains per Gallon				
	St Monans	*Harrogate*	*Tunbridge Wells*	*Spa*	*Schwalbach*
Ferrous Carb.	6.70	4.63	4.32	3.75	6.43
Manganese Sulph.	0.07	traces	traces	0.52 (carb.)	1.41 (bicarb.)
Calcium Sulph.	15.30	51.63 (chloride)	1.84 (chloride)	60.00 (carb. & phosph.)	17.0 (bicarb.)
Magnes. Sulph.	12.36	34.03 (chloride)	0.34 (chloride)	11.2 (carb.)	16.3 (bicarb.)
Alkaline Sulph.	4.87	—	1.76	1.0	0.6
Alkaline Chlorides	10.00	668.1	1.5	4.5	2.0
Silica	1.76	1.45	0.5	4.9	2.4

It is a little difficult to draw up a perfectly clear table, as the bases do not exist in all cases in the same state of composition. That, however, is a minor point. The results are quite sufficient to show the comparative medicinal value of the springs.

D.B. Dott.

It is likely that the good Doctor did not visit St Monans, but had samples sent to his laboratory in Edinburgh. His comment on the high amount of albuminoid ammonia as an objectionable impurity is interesting. The elimination of this single defect might have been easily achieved. He was probably unaware that effluent from Coalfarm's byres and cattle reeds ran into the spring. Albumin is a simple, naturally occurring protein, soluble in water and is present in milk as lactalbumin. The spring water would have exhibited excellent health spa quality, had the farm liquids been disposed of elsewhere.

In summary, it seems regrettable that such a potentially valuable asset to the community has been eliminated. The sale of natural spring waters is now a multi-million pound industry.

Chapter 4

Names of the Village

LIKE THE SAINT HIMSELF, the village has had many names. The land of Inverrin was gifted by King David I (reigned 1124–53), son of Robert the Bruce, to the Priory of the Isle of May, 'of Pednewem [Pittenweem] and Inverrin, which is Avernus's.' Avernus being the Latin name for Hell, it is not clear if the original owner gave it that title or if that was, indeed, his name! If Inverrin can be identified with Inverrinche, then a fishing hamlet existed here after David's death, firmly establishing the village as nearly 850 years old. At that time, Morgrund, Earl of Mar & Angus, and his wife, each gave two grants of half a carucate of land to the 'vill de Inverinnche to the Church of St Andrews'. A curious measure, a carucate was as much land as a team of oxen could plough in a season. A later measure was a plough-gang, taken to be 104 Scots acres (131 acres). This was the area that could be tilled by an eight-oxen plough in a year. These gifts were confirmed in 1228 by Alexander II, grandson of Ada, who was the daughter-in-law of David I and mother of Malcolm IV and William the Lion. She witnessed the original charters, but they were burned subsequently in a fire in St Andrews, where they had been stored. New ones were granted by Mary, Queen of Scots, on 4th October 1563. The oldest name of the division, as localities were then known, is the Parish of Abercrombie in the Priory of St Andrews. Alternative spellings were Abercrombin, Abbercrumbin or Abercrumbie. With a coastline of one and a quarter miles, the division was two miles long by one mile wide, and was bounded by the two burns, the Dreel and the Inverie.

Derived from the burn, an obvious name came from the Gaelic: *inver* meaning 'at the mouth of', and *rin*, 'a stream'. There have been many spelling variations e.g. Inverin, Inveryne, Inverny,

Inverroy, Inweerie, Inverye, Inverry, Innery, Inverey, Inverroy, Inverinnche, Finvirie and Fincan. An Irish version was Sanct Moinnen. Again, it is recorded that James IV of Scotland, embarking 'at Anster or Crail', was rowed around the coast of the East Neuk in a galley bearing 'Giftes tae the preists and Frères of Sanct Monanis'.

There were also: St Mounys (from a Dutch map dated 1580), St Monans (from a map of Fife dated 1645), St Minins (Church Records 1689), St Mynills, St Monnance (Church Records 1718), St Monance, St Monan, St Minan, St Munna, St Ninian, St Marianus, St Monan's, Sanct Minanis, Sanct Monnanis, Sanct Monanes, St Monane, St Mingans, St Menin, St Minin, Sanct Monnons, St Minnance (from a map of 1725 by the geographer, H. Moll) and Sanct Minnans. The last three versions are closer to the Simminins of the East Fife dialect in use today. With such a proliferation of versions, it is difficult to appreciate the controversy of the 1950s and 60s between St Monance and St Monans, with the latter being finally adopted. The argument seems to have been almost perennial. On 15th April 1933, the Minutes of the Town Council record: 'Baillie Miller referred to the spelling of the name of the Burgh. Baillie Guthrie moved and Councillor Marr seconded that St Monance be adhered to. Baillie Miller moved and Councillor Dunn seconded that St Monans be adopted. Three votes for the amendment and five for the motion, which was declared carried.'

Perhaps the most intriguing derivation is given by Forbes MacGregor in his book *The Salt-Sprayed Burgh – A View of Anstruther*. He writes:

> According to Archibald Scott, St Monance or St Monan's (locally pronounced S'mi-nins) was originally dedicated to an Irish lady of noble birth, educated at Candida Casa, or Whithorn, in Wigtownshire. Her christened name was Darerca, but her name of endearment, or pet name, such as those early missionaries rejoiced in, was Mo'enna or Mo'ninne. Clearly, the local pronunciation perpetuates this lady. There was also an early cill or small church devoted to this lady near Fife Ness. In a 1645 map, it is named Kilomonen.
>
> To prove that St Monance was a lady, one need only go

> back to the early records of Edinburgh. In the Old Town, St Monans Wynd was so named because a chapel there was dedicated to St Monan or Mennan and the Close was named Lady Minnan's or Lady Menzies or Lady Minnes Close ... St Monan is pure invention, if he is described as a man ... St Monan was a lady. I trust her claims will be strenuously supported by all of her sex.

An amusing latter-day reference to the saint is found in the story of St Trinnean's Boarding School for Young Ladies, which was started and run by Miss C. Fraser Lee in Edinburgh between 1922 and 1946. The names of the school houses were all connected with the early Scottish Church and, with Whithorn and Clag'rinne, was Monan.

The artist Ronald Searle's first pen-and-ink drawing of what was to become his hilarious *The Belles of St Trinians,* so delightfully portrayed in his books and in the famous Ealing Studio film, was inspired by conversations with some of the pupils.

Meanwhile, the old fishermen of Pittenweem will continue to call it 'Wast [west] Owerie'!

Chapter 5

Abercrombie Kirk

THERE WAS AN EARLY CHURCH AT ABERCROMBIE, which lies just north of the village of St Monans. The derivation of the name is 'upon the crook (or elbow)', as it is not far from where the Dreel Burn, as it runs down to Anstruther, turns sharply to the east in the estate of Balcaskie.

John Coquus, cook to the Royal Household of King Malcolm and his Queen, the saintly Margaret, had become 'Abercrombie of that Ilk'. He had two daughters, Mary and Margaret, named after the Queen of his church, the Virgin Mother, and the Queen of Scotland. Apart from their beauty, the two sisters were very rich in their own rights, owning vast tracts of land, so were much sought after by the young knights and nobles of East Fife. Among the most gallant of their admirers was Philip de Candelle, descendant of William de Candelle, who, as a member of the Royal Household, had received the estates of Anstruther. Philip had fought in France and in the Second Crusade to the Holy Land, in which Louis the Seventh of France and Queen Eleanor of Aquitaine had enlisted under the Cross. Margaret, who was gentle and timid when compared with the strong character of Mary, was wooed by the knight with tales of his prowess in the fight for the deliverance of the Holy Sepulchre from the Saracen Turks. To her, he sang passionate love songs of Provence and of Araby. Tradition has it that they were secretly married by St Monan, but more probably by a monk, who served in the early chapel. Their subsequent elopement engendered fierce jealousy in Mary. However, Margaret was widowed when Sir Philip fell at the Battle of the Standards in 1138 and the sisters were re-united. Piously, they worked hard together to establish a chapel at Abercrombie, and achieved their goal in 1160, when Arnold, Bishop of St Andrews, consecrated the building. The relics of St Andrew, three finger-bones, an arm bone and a kneecap, were paraded on their fertour, or bier, by four of the noblest laymen in the land. After the ceremony, the assemblage having dispersed, the sisters knelt in prayer at the altar. There was a fearful storm of thunder and lightning. The bishop, seeking them out to bid his adieus, to his consternation and horror found them both struck dead. In 1163, the Bishop of St Andrews passed the stewardship of the church on to the Abbot of Dunfermline.

From the possession of the adjacent lands, all the Abercrombies of Scotland sprang, their common ancestor, one Humphrey, having received a charter from King Robert the Bruce. Sir Ralph Anstruther was Treasurer of the Household of Her Majesty Queen Elizabeth, the Queen Mother.

Alternative history is quoted by Willie Miller. In his excellent pamphlet on the Auld Kirk, he avers that Abercrombie Church was consecrated, over a hundred years later, by David de Burnham on 20th October 1274.

In the days of the Resurrectionists, well remembered from the most notorious of the Edinburgh body-snatchers Burke and Hare, who were hanged in 1829, a special all-night guard was mounted after every burial.

Although still used as a graveyard, no part of the present ruin is original or older than the fifteenth century. Later research claimed that, based on the existence of crosses, one, the Irish cross, being built into the sides of the gateway, the building must have succeeded a Celtic place of worship of a much earlier time. Balcaskie House in whose grounds the church stands is still owned by the Anstruther family. With a fine terraced garden, it shows traces of French taste and ornamentation, reminiscent of a chateau of the Valois kings.

Chapter 6

The Auld Kirk

With the possible exception of the simple bridge, consisting of two massive stone slabs, giving access over the Inverie Burn to its front gate, the Auld Kirk is the oldest building in the village and that church in Scotland built closest to the sea. On days of high tides, gales or storm, spume, salt spray and waves force worshippers to use another entrance, further up the burn.

As ever, there are numerous questions about its origins. Was it founded by Alan Durward as national thanksgiving for victory over the Norwegians under King Hacon at the Battle of Largs in 1263? This was fought in the reign of Alexander III, who was killed in 1286, when his horse stumbled and fell over the cliffs at Kinghorn. Tradition has it that, in his youth, the King had stayed at Newark Castle as a guest of Alexander, Earl of Buchan who, at that time, held half the lands of St Monans; his brother-in-law, the Earl of Mar, was lord of the other half. Alan Durward was the Earl of Atholl, Chief Justiciary of the Realm and a Member of the Council of Regency during the king's minority years.

Many historians credit the kirk's erection to David II, son of Robert the Bruce, who died in 1374. The church had been preceded by the shrine or Royal Votive Chapel built to the memory of St Monan in the eleventh century.

In 1370, David gifted the lands of East Birns (identified as East Birnie in Crail) to 'God, the Blessed Virgin and to the chaplainries celebrating service in our Chapel of St Monan, which we have founded anew.' This information is reasonably consistent with that of Keith, who, in his *Scottish Monasticus,* includes St Monans in his list of the Houses of the Blackfriars or Dominican order of monkhood. He writes: 'the chapel was founded by King David II on the 3rd of April in the fortieth year of his reign [1369] and was served

2. King David II of Scotland
(by permission of Scottish National Portrait Gallery).

by an hermit.' He claimed that the original design had been cruciform or cross-shaped but that the nave had been destroyed. Sibbald also supported this view and Spottiswood refers to the chapel as 'a large and stately building of hewn stone in the form of a cross with a steeple in the centre'. No other source mentions that a nave was ever built, although an arch in the west wall suggests that one was intended. The steeple is of hewn stone, initially square in form and topped with an octagonal spire. The building was erected with the choir situated due east and west, as all places of divine worship were orientated like King Solomon's Temple.

At this time, the chapel was visited daily by a friar from the neighbouring monastery of Pittenweem. His duty was to offer up prayers of Thanksgiving for the safe preservation of the King and Queen. The latter was Margaret of Logie, whom David married in 1363 at Inchmurdach, present-day Kenly Green, by Boarhills. They had sailed from Leith to cross the Forth to Ardross Castle, where they were to dine with Sir William Dyschyntoun (Dischington), David's uncle by marriage. In a fierce storm, their ship was wrecked on Our Lady's Rock, so named after the Virgin Mary, who, with St Monan, had saved them. The King had an earlier reason to thank St Monan. At the Battle of Neville's Cross, near Durham, in 1346, he had been hit by two arrows, shot by an English bowman. The head of one had remained stuck fast in the wound for, reportedly, more than five years. In the battle, he had carried the Black Rood of Scotland, the Sacred Cross of St Margaret, in the belief that it would secure safety to his person and victory to his army. Prized by the English, the Black Rood formed the spoils offered up to the shrine of St Cuthbert in the Cathedral of Durham, where it hung until the Reformation, when all trace of it disappeared. David came, with a company of his nobles, to the shrine of St Monans to pray for help. According to Cemerarius, 'Proper oblations having been made to God and St Monan, the arrow dropped without more ado from its wound and did not leave any cicatrix behind.' This story may appear difficult to reconcile with the fact that he was captured and made a prisoner by Edward III for eleven years. Indeed, he was then only set free after the Scots promised to pay for his release, a ransom of 100,000 merks, a very large sum for such a poor country as Scotland at that time. However, the term 'imprisonment' might have been somewhat notional as David came to like the English and made many visits to the English court after he regained his freedom. There were therefore two reasons for the King wishing to build the church. Dates given for the foundation vary from 1362 to 1363-67, but obviously its erection took some considerable time.

3. The Auld Kirk from the fishing boat Reaper.

Also, King David would not forget that it was Isabel, daughter of the Earl of Fife, wife of John Cumyn, and thus daughter-in-law of Alexander Cumyn, Earl of Buchan, a lady who, in youth, would doubtless know every spot and the ways of the people in and around St Monans and who, when her brother, the young Earl of Fife, was in England with Edward (as was also her husband), claimed the family privilege, namely the hereditary right of conducting the King to the royal throne and of placing the crown upon his head.

> In the xxxiii. yere of Edward I. was a man of Scotland cleped Robert Brusse. He took upon him to be king of the land; and went to the Abbey of Scone to be crowned thare. The Countesse of Bowhan stol fra her lord all his gret hors, and with sweech men as she trusted, cam to that same abbaye, and thare sche sette the crowne upon Robardis head. Sche was take after of Englishmen, and presented to King Edward. He commanded sche schuld not be *ded*, but that there schuld be mad a hous al of tymber, upon the walls of Berwick, and there shuld sche be till sche deyed.

In the Register of the Great Seal, there is a Charter of Endowment of the chapel by David II, in 1369. It notices the chapel as having been already refounded by its granter. The charter does not refer to any objects of peculiar gratitude to St Monan, but is in the usual terms – 'for the safety of the soul of the endower, his progenitors and successors.'

Jack, however, avers that it was consecrated in 1343, by St Monan himself, who served as a priest for over thirty years, dying at the end of the fourteenth century and being interred in the East aisle. Yet again, Keith dates the building as 1369. Sir William Dischington, who also built and lived in nearby Ardross Castle, was appointed *'magister fabricae Sancti Monani'* i.e. 'the master builder of St Monans', in 1367. As the royal couple's host at the time of the shipwreck and, as kin through Robert the Bruce, it may be reasonably assumed that he was favoured with the overall supervision of the King's gift. Sir William is also the reputed architect or master mason of the square tower of Brechin Cathedral.

The architectural style is Gothic, and on completion was described thus: 'there arose under the hands of the masons, who were masters of their craft and laboured for love of it, a noble and large chapel in honour of St Monan, an hermite, who dwelt in this place called Inwearie.'

Despite the district being thinly populated, over one hundred and fifty men were employed in the construction. They were mechanics, labourers, masons, boatmen, carters and superintendents. Most of the materials were brought on site by sea in creers or rowing boats. The timber came from Inverness by sailing boat, the captain being one John Scott, a burgess of that city. The Coats of Arms in the ceiling are those of the Earl of Douglas, the Thane of Fife and the Lords of Annandale, of Dischington and of Leslie, with the Royal Arms of Scotland over the original high altar in the East. The entire building costs were £613 7*s.* (£613.35p.) plus £6 13*s.* 4*d.* (£6.66p.) to Adam, the carpenter.

James III, who died in 1488, was prevailed upon by Friar John Muir, then Vicar of the Scottish Province, to gift the church to the Friars Preachers and to have a monastery built alongside. A Bull of Pope Sixtus IV erected it formally into a convent at the King's entreaty. The papal mandate was addressed to the Archbishop of

St Andrews, and dated 18th March 1477. Amongst the Abstracts of Writs belonging to the City of St Andrews, there is (No. 53) a 'Decreet for Execution pronounced by William Schiver, Arch-Dean of St Andrews, sole executor deputed by the Apostolical See of a Bull granted by Pope Sixtus IV., under the Seal of the Holy See erecting the Oratories or Hospitals of the Predicant Order in St Andrews and St Monans, and to convert our places and houses, dated March 18th, 1477, and the Decreet is dated 14th December, 1477.' The history of the bestowal of this church on the Dominicans was narrated by Friar Andrew Leys to the Knights of Roslin. The foundation Bull pays a graceful tribute to the labours of the Friars Preachers of the time. The Bull clearly shows *two* Priories erected in the diocese of St Andrews – one in the city itself, another at St Monans. It was unusual to erect a Priory out of a Hospice, until after considerable lapse of time, to test its sincerity.

There is an interesting letter in the Roman archives of the Master General of the Dominican Order. It is a short statement of the names of Scottish Dominican Priories in 1557, written by the Provincial of Scotland, Friar John Grierson. He mentions St Monans and says he had then no subject residing there, for it had never proved satisfactory, and in his time, 1530–58, no more than two or three friars dwelt there. The full convent of Friars was suppressed in 1519, at the prayer of Friar John Adamson, Prior Provincial, as was also the convent at Cupar. The Priory can never have been anything but a small one; it lasted only from 1477 to 1519, with two friars in residence for a number of years later, and, about 1550, it lapsed altogether.

At one time, no part of the graveyard lay on the north side of the church. Constant tradition made the Priory to stand in a line with the north wall of the cemetery and further west. When the old cemetery wall was built, the foundation of what was supposed to be a wall of the Priory was encountered. The 'Christening Well' was situated a few feet inside the north-west corner of the cemetery. The grave-digger discovered, on opening the ground, a connected series of stones from that corner to the door in the north side of the choir. This might be the remains of a passage way – covered or open – from the choir to the Priory.

It is noted in entries in the Register of the Great Seal that

James III was in St Monans in 1482. The accounts of the Lord High Treasurer of Scotland show that King James IV, after he had been to Crail on the third day of June 1503, came the same day to St Monans:

> Item that samyn day thairefter in Sanct Monanes to the Kingis offerand xiiijs.
> Item to the Kingis offerand on the bred thair xiiijs
> Item to the priest that sung the mes, be the Kingis command xs.

The King was again in St Monans Church on two further occasions:

> 1505, 14th October. Item to the priest of St Monanes xiiijs
> 1506, 25th August. Item that day in Sanct Monanes to the Kingis offerand on the bred xjs. vid.
> Item to the priestes thare xls.
> Item to the reliques thare xiijs.

The Priory stood in what is now the upper graveyard. To this complex was annexed a nunnery, founded by the MacDuffs, the Maormohrs of Fife, at the foot of the Castle Hill in Cupar. A Maormohr or Maormor, was a nobleman of great power and influence, who governed a district. The title Earl is applied to one who has jurisdiction over a county and is of Saxon origin.

Later, both the St Monans and the Cupar properties were made over to the Convent of St Andrews, founded by William Wishart, Bishop of that city; the convent stood by the North Gate, the present-day West Port. Apart from the Auld Kirk, all the buildings were subsequently destroyed. Their destruction may have been the work of the mob, led by John Knox, at the time of the Reformation. Thundering from the pulpit of the Kirk of Crail, he preached: 'ding doon the nests and the craws will flee awa.' Many Roman Catholic monasteries, abbeys, priories and churches were desecrated in the East Neuk. The hand-cut ashlars, keystones and other materials would subsequently be used for building in the village but where to identify them today?

In 1471, the Customs of Cupar granted twenty merks (£2.67p.) for upkeep to '*fratribus, predicatorii et ecclesiae de Inneri*' i.e. 'to the brethren, preachers and ecclesiastics of Innery'.

4. *Interior of the Choir.*

This donation was followed, in 1471, by an annuity from John de Kinloch de Cruvie, who then owned the lands. In 1546, another annuity of seven merks (93p.) was given by the Mains family of Ardross to the Friars of St Monans.

The Provincial Chapter of Blackfriars, held in Edinburgh in 1519, granted a charter by which an annual amount of twenty merks, founded by Robert, Duke of Albany and uplifted from his lands of North Barns (now Kingsbarns), was reserved that two friars might say prayers at the tomb of St Monan forever; that charter was confirmed by James V. In 1563, yet another was granted by Mary, Queen of Scots and the Regent Murray, in which 20 merks from the same source would support 'two chaplains performing divine service at the kirk of St Monan of Inverroy'.

Until the chapel of St Monan became part of the parish of Kilconquhar, on 21st October 1646, the Synod annexed the village to the Parish of Abercrombie. The Parliamentary Ratification of the annexation, dated 26th June 1649, ordained that St Monans should be the place of meeting and that it should be called the kirk of Abercrombie 'in all time coming'. However, the name quickly reverted to St Monans. In 1804, the Reverend Robert Swann tried, unsuccessfully, to have the original title restored.

It was on 27th December 1646 that the Auld Kirk was first used as the Parish church, the one at Abercrombie having been closed. The Reverend Robert Wilkie, who had been in charge at Abercrombie since 1628, took over the new charge, being minister there until 1664. Much of the following description is taken, almost verbatim, from the pamphlet *St Monance Church*, the work of William P. Miller, OBE, for forty-one years the Session Clerk and, undoubtedly, the church's finest historian.

From 1646 until 1848, the choir alone was used for worship and the transepts were allowed to fall into disrepair. The interior of the building underwent changes. The pre-Reformation altars were removed, but fortunately, the trefoiled sedilia and the piscina on the south wall of the choir remain. The pulpit was on the south wall and there were galleries extending across the east end of the choir, and along the greater part of the north wall. To the west of the pulpit was the Newark gallery. General Sir David Leslie of Newark, being an elder of the kirk and a member of Presbytery, had this gallery built and enhanced with scriptural texts, although architects considered that it disfigured the proportions of the building. The north gallery was the Sailors' Loft. There can have been little enough headroom beneath the galleries and the area beneath the west gallery was not seated, the worshippers bringing their own creepies or stools. Close to the north wall, a single pew raised above the rest of the gallery was the Bailies' Loft.

The four windows on the south wall of the choir were originally the work of the Dominicans, but one of them, the second from the west, is a nineteenth-century reproduction. There are two small windows, each of two lights, in the south wall of the south transept, which may be the oldest feature of the building. Expert opinions differ as to their date, but agree that it cannot be later than the fourteenth century. The only original door is the small one on the north side of the choir.

The Town and the Kirk Session both appear as undertaking repairs upon the Church.

Extract from Session Minute, July 1692. 'It is agreed upon and apointed be the Session ys day that a door be struck out in ye east end of the Kirk, and ye necessaries thereto, in all heast prepared seeing yt ye Sacrament of the Lord's Supper is to be celebrat as soon thereafter as convenience will allow, and that tickets and others needful for that Sacrament be prepared.' In December, an eleborate bill of expenses of the smith for work done at the Kirk is given in the minute in detail, followed by the account of the wright as under:

David Couk, his account of timber work at ye Kirk of St Minians.

It. of old accompt,	£	14	0
It. for mending ye seats in ye kirk,		10	0
It. for making ye east door,	1	16	0
It. for making ye kirkyeard doors,	3	10	0
It. for a tree to ye west door head,		12	0
It. for horses hire,		6	0
It. for dails to my lord's glass window,		10	0
Summa est,	£ 7	18	0

In November 1729, the Session erected a porch to the church door. The mason was to make a pend over the porch, and thack it with stone. In March following, the minister and elders formally examined the porch, when 'The Session, considering the sufficiency of the work, did agree to allow him [the mason] 3 shilling more making in hail £3 10*s.* sterling.'

In February 1738, a new gate to the west entry of the churchyard cost £4. In October, 4*s.* was spent in 'mending ye window below ye Superiors' Loft'. In October 1743 'placing the Dial on ye kirk' before a celebration of the Lord's Supper, cost 4*s.*

> 'October, 1709. It. for cleansing the North Isle, biging the window and flagging ye Porch 02:00:00 (Scots).'
> 'It. for glassing three windows in the North Isle 04 :00:00'
> 'November, 1714 It. for a Barr to the Church window, and two crooks to Church Door 01:04:00 For a new hinge to the bell tongue 00:06:00'
> 'December, 1716. To George Scot, mason, for making a Sun Dayel for the Church 15:00:... for ale to the men who helped up with the Dayel 00:08:'
> 1717. It. for mending the keys and locks of the Church door 00:13:04'
> 'March, 1718. For a lock and key to the Lettron Ambrie 00:06:'
> 'December, 1720. it. for taking down Dial of the Church 00:04:00'

In the Town's Accounts, the repairs of the road to the church was a heavy item. (The road was exposed to the sea.)

For a series of years, a glazier had a contract with the town to mend the Kirk windows for 5*s.* a year.

January 15, 1735. To the Kirk glazier	1	6
To ale in James Key's with the glazier	12	0
To ale in Wm. Galloway's when locking ye papers in ye box	12	0

(Obviously glazing was thirsty work!)

February 9, 1775. Ane account of sclater work wrought upon the Kirk by William and Archibald Brown:

To one hundred sclates		9	0
To workmanship		16	6
To sclater pines		1	0
	1	6	6

Pressed for more substantial repairs to the church to satisfy the Presbytery, the feuars presented this certificate:

> We, William and Archibald Brown, Sclaters, and William Mackie, Wright, do hereby declare that the Reparation now given to the Kirk of St Monance is such as we serve the same for Twenty years, and if any articles in that time shall fail the same will be made good as other Kirks are. Witness our hands this 12th May 1776 and before signing we hereby certify that there is not a better oak roof in any Kirk within the Presbytery of St Andrews than the roof of St Monance Kirk is at present.

In the latter years of the eighteenth century, the building had fallen into a sadly dilapidated state and the transepts were roofless. In 1722, an effort was made to have much-needed repairs carried out, but disputes about who should bear the expense finished it. Commenting on its condition in 1789, Lord Kellie declared it to be 'as decayed and dirty as a kirk ought to be'. In February 1826, the minister, the Reverend Robert Swann, brought the state of repair of the church before the Presbytery. It had been further described as 'most uncomfortable as a place of worship: damp, cold, its walls covered in green mould, altogether an aspect of chilling desolation.' Again he writes: 'there was exhibited in a state of perfect preservation, a complete suit of church furniture, which, neither in pulpit, or in the galleries, nor in the ground pews, had experienced, for nearly 200 years, the least repair or even once been touched by the brush of the painter.' The coloured bands, which had originally enscribed the bases and capitals of the clustered columns, had disappeared completely.

After inspection, the local tradesmen formally condemned the building, but the heritors disagreed. They engaged the services of an architect, Mr William Burn of Edinburgh, who had overseen the renovation of the exterior of the Kirk of St Giles. Restoration was agreed on the understanding that the heritors would defray all expenses, which were in excess of £1,730. Thus, they released the feuars from their obligation under the conditions of the Charter of St Monans to uphold the fabric of the church. Again, from Willie Miller:

> William Burn planned to bring the whole church into use again and met with vigorous opposition. A long list of objec-

tions was tabulated. The fact that the congregation would be divided into three sections, in the choir and in the transepts, was held to be indecent for a Presbyterian Church, 'three congregations joining with one clergyman. Where the most may see, it is impossible they can all hear the same clergyman and they cannot see one another.' Burn must, nevertheless, be given the credit for having made the best possible use of the interior space. The floor level was lowered some four feet, probably to give easy access without interior or exterior steps. Doors were broken into the east wall of the choir. The galleries were removed and the church was given its present setting, the focal point of worship being shifted from east to west. Walls were plastered and plaster vaulting in the transepts reproduced the lovely stone-vaulted ceiling in the choir. To this restoration belong also the buttress pinnacles, which are a striking feature of the church's exterior.

Workmen digging under the floor to install the flue of a new heating stove found that, under the soft rock on which it was supposed the church was built, was a solid mass of very hard whinstone, which could only be penetrated by boring and blasting. The walls of the church are

> four feet and four inches in thickness and are evidently double shells of pebble-rock, hard as flint and well cemented in its successive layers, but, between the outer and inner coating of the hard stone, there was found a packing of very inferior sandstone, so soft that it could be pulverised by the gentle pressure of the hand, and so saturated with damp that it felt like moist salt.

On a visit to St Monans, Sir Walter Scott suggested that, instead of re-roofing the old church with vulgar blue Easedale slates, they should use the more appropriate grey sandstone flags of Forfarshire, which was done.

Unfortunately, however, the architect and contractor had not calculated for the additional weight involved. A short while after the church was opened, the south wall of the choir was pressed outward at the roof and a large stone fell out of the groining.

Great alarm was excited among the parishioners. The feuars and inhabitants held a public meeting. They employed architects who examined and reported that the church was unsafe as a place of worship. An architect appointed by the heritors declared that it was perfectly safe, but the church was deserted for a while, and services were held in the parish school.

During the reconstruction, particularly with the lowering of the floor, vast quantities of bones and ashes were dug out and applied as fertiliser to the lands of Newark. Unfortunately, there was little enrichment of the soil and there were poor yields for several years. The beadle of the day said that it was a curse for the violation of the sepulchre of the Saint, which had lain undisturbed for over five hundred years. A new bell, dated 1822 and presented by Lady Anstruther, was fixed to the parapet of the steeple, but in the open air. An etching of 1802 shows the pulpit with a canopy. This splendidly carved work is now on display in Balcaskie House. It may have been removed at the time of the 1828 renovations, the Anstruther family then being the heritors. This view is perhaps consistent with the moving of the pulpit from the south to the west wall. Painted panels, described as 'interesting', also disappeared at this time.

To indemnify the capital outlay for the renovations, the heritors had the agreement of the parishioners to levy a modest seat rent of one shilling per sitting (presumably a family pew) per annum.

The architect was not without his critics. To quote from Wilkie's *History of Fife*: 'even he could not quite destroy this little gem of the Middle Pointed Gothic art of its era.' Again, writing on Fife churches in the *Transactions of the Aberdeen Ecclesiological Society* in 1889, the Reverend T. Newbigging described the church as 'charming, though a trifle coarse'. Incidentally, he portrayed his visit thus: 'at St Monance, where you can get nothing to eat and which is the most odiferous place I was ever in.' However, it should be noted that the general tenor of his article was condescendingly critical of the rest of Fife. Perhaps not surprisingly, the reverend gentleman was banned by the landlady of his inn at Crail from entering the main dining room, which had a roaring fire. It may have been his description of her premises, with 'couples [rafters] unhappily whitewashed', which warranted his exclusion!

By 1837, the church again looked damp and comfortless. Although a new heating system using water had been installed, the ugly fire-clay pipes, which had formed the rough chimney of the previous stove, still disfigured the rood.

On 17th November 1844, Sir Ralph Anstruther, a heritor, wrote to the kirk session that 'it would be very desirable to have the church kept in a clean and comfortable state and that some person should be appointed to sweep it every week and wash it, perhaps twice in the year.' Ann Thompson was selected and paid sixpence (2½p) a week for her efforts. The congregation were reminded of their obligations by a notice on the church door, adjuring them to 'refrain from scattering down any nuisance on the floor.'

The *New Statistical Account* of 1845 states:

> The church is seated for 528; deduct free sittings for the poor, 36; preserved for heritors, their families, and their servants, farmers, their children, and servants, the elders' and minister's, and schoolmaster's seats, 200; there remain for letting 292; an ample supply for the parishioners, and considerably exceeding the number of applicants.
>
> The number of persons of all ages attending the Established Church, we cannot, in present circumstances, state with accuracy. But, without reference to our late alarms, we might say, towards 300. There should be many more, and we lament that there are not. Clerical means are used to augment the attendance, but we are apt to have offered as excuses, the difficulty of hearing, the want of decent clothing, the coldness of the church, especially in winter, – artificial heat, by means of stoves or otherwise, never having been introduced. [This appears at variance with the introduction of the new heating system in 1837, but the *Statistical Account*, although dated 1845, had been long in preparation.]
>
> The average number of communicants may be given at 210. It is low compared with the population. Many are absent at sea, when the sacrament is dispensed in summer, and when

we have it in February, when the men are at home, it falls in with the throng of the winter herring-fishing.

On 4th May 1857, it was reported that there was an echo in the church, although it had obviously been there since the restoration. The heritors agreed to an alteration 'as two thirds of the ministers who officiate are indistinctly heard and the present incumbent is obliged to strain his voice to a degree unnatural and most prejudicial to his comfort and health.' The Session suggested 'the propriety of lowering the pulpit two feet and absorbing the echo by a proper disposition of drapery.'

The remuneration of the clergy of the times was an admixture of goods, mostly farm produce, and money. Between 1617 and 1925, this stipend was payable by those people who had acquired the ownership of the teinds of the parish. A teind was originally a tenth part of the produce of land, which was payable to the church. By the time of the Reformation, teinds had become a separate heritable property from the lands from which they were payable. An Act of 1617 appointed commissioners to allocate a stipend from the teinds to each parish minister. When a parish was without a preacher, the stipend might be paid to a retired minister, a minister's widow in need, used to repair a kirk or manse or even build a local bridge.

In 1836, the charge was held by the Reverend Robert Swann. His stipend comprised:

Bear (barley)	84 bolls [5¼ tons]	1 firlot,	3 lippies.
Oats	45 bolls,	3 firlots, 2 pecks,	1 lippie.

What did a minister want with eight tons of grain? Well, there was a brewery in the village and no fewer than twelve spirit-and-ale houses! His money from the exchequer was £32 19*s.* (£32.95p.), and other monies £15 6*s.* 10*d.* (£15.34p.) a total of £48 5*s.* 10*d.* (£48.29p.). The session expenditure was £191 5*s.* (£191.25p.) and the income from collections £31 1*s.* 9½*d.* (£31.09p.), the deficit being supplied by the heritors by voluntary assessment.

In the 1950s, a sister of the Reverend Doctor Turnbull willed a considerable sum of money for the 'restoration of the church'. This was interpreted as meaning 'renovation' but the Church of

Scotland headquarters ruled on a complete make-over. In 1955, under the architectural direction of Mr Ian G. Lindsay, OBE, RSA, a restoration was planned,

> whose aim was to have due regard to the orientation and architectural conception of the church and to be at the same time functionally appropriate for modern Presbyterian worship. The main features of this restoration are (1) the raising of the floor level to the original height; (2) the building up of the dilapidated doors in the east end of the choir, and opening of the sedilia and piscina to view at their proper level; and (3) the removal of wall plaster. A flat timber ceiling replaces the plaster one beneath the tower, and rounded timber ceilings in the transepts take the place of the vaulted plaster ones. The 1828 west windows behind the pulpit have been removed and a much smaller window, high in the west wall replaces them. Walls have been lime-washed.

The church was closed for worship for about four years and was re-dedicated in 1961.

The following features, some of which have been already mentioned, should be noted:

(1) Sedilia and piscina on south wall in east end of choir.

(2) Aumbries on north wall in east end of choir.

(3) Twelve Consecration Crosses, six in north wall and six in south wall of choir.

(4) Piscina in north transept.

(5) Piscina and aumbry in south transept.

(6) Piscina in sacristy (vestry).

(7) Vaulted stone roof of choir, with heraldic shields.

(8) Full rigged ship of 1800, the *Mars.*

(9) Model of the steam drifter, *Pursuit.*

(10) Plaque showing the Arms of St Monans and bearing the date 1792. This probably hung in front of a gallery prior to the 1828 restoration.

(11) The turnpike stair, close to the pulpit, which ascends to the bartizan of the steeple.

(12) The marble mural monument in the north transept to Lieutenant 'Young Harry' Anstruther, aged eighteen, who fell in the Crimean War at the Battle of Alma (1854), while carrying the colours of his regiment. An unknown poet penned the words:

> His bosom with one death shot riven
> The warrior boy lay low;
> His face was turned unto Heaven,
> His feet unto the foe.

Sedilia are seats, usually three in number, often located in niches for the officiating clergy, designating Father, Son and Holy Ghost.

Aumbries are recesses for church vessels.

A piscina is a basin and drain into which was emptied the water used in washing the holy vessels.

A bartizan is a parapet or battlement.

The frigate of one hundred and thirty guns was presented in 1805 by Captain William Marr, a native son of the village. It was paid for by prize money from a captured French vessel and was a model of his own ship. That same year, Captain Marr fought at the Battle of Trafalgar, under one of Nelson's admirals, Sir James Black of Anstruther. However, the warship *Mars* of that encounter had only seventy guns. The records of the kirk session for 5th February 1925 state: 'Old ship: The *Mars*, suspended in front of the Sailors' Loft for generations, was bought by Mr J.R. Lorimer, Fellow of the Royal Society of Architects, of Kellie Castle, from the widow of Mr W.F. Vallance, R.S.A., Edinburgh, presented to the church and moved to the South Transept.' Again, it may have been stolen during the renovation. It was ceremoniously unveiled, on 12th March 1925, by Mr Thomas Miller, the boatbuilder, who restored it, and Miss Lucy Alison, a washer-woman at the public wash-house at Burnside. Willie Miller tells that when the sheet covering the ship was removed, it floated gently down and totally enveloped Lucy, resplendent in her mutch! Tradition has it that the minister of the day, the Reverend Dr John Turnbull, collected the vessel from Edinburgh. Returning from the railway station to his manse at Abercrombie in the dark, he discovered that a small flag or pennant had fallen off and been lost. Diligently, he re-traced his

5. The Mars

steps in daylight, persevering in his search until the flag was found. For Dr Turnbull to have travelled to and from Edinburgh by train was very much a departure from his normal practice. He usually walked, particularly to the General Assemblies of the Church of Scotland. In more recent years, the ship has been again restored by an elder of the kirk, Mr Robert Ovenstone. The decks were painted red so that the blood of the injured and the dead would be less distressing to the seamen and marines still fighting.

The *Pursuit* was a wooden drifter built for the Wood family of West End, who lived near Robertson's boatyard, the predecessor of Walter Reekie's, on the West Pier. She was requisitioned by the Royal Navy during the Great War (1914–18), but was sunk in the Adriatic. The model was made in Balmullo and was originally on loan to the Scottish Fisheries Museum. It was bought and presented to the Auld Kirk by Mr and Mrs Hamilton of West Shore and was consecrated and hung in the north aisle, *circa* 1991.

The kirk session records of St Andrew's Day 1935 note that the plaque was presented by a Mrs Henderson of London, in whose house it had hung for many years. She had bought it in a shop in Pittenweem, owned by a Mr Lindsay.

6. The arrival of the Sea Queen.

Despite the almost total disappearance of fishing from the village, the centuries-old links with the sea are commemorated with the Festival of the Sea Queen, held during Civic Week in the summer. The date is decided by the time of high tide on the Saturday afternoon. Elected from the village, the Queen, with her entourage, sails from Anstruther harbour in the *Reaper*, a Fifie fishing boat of a bygone era, which has been restored for the Scottish Fisheries Museum. Arriving at the Middle Pier, St Monans, she is greeted by the Chairman and members of the Community Council, and then walks in procession to the Town Hall for her crowning.

The Kirkin' o' the Sea Queen takes place on the day following her Coronation. She walks, with her attendants, members of the Community Council, and people of St Monans, from the Town Hall to the Auld Kirk by the sea. The procession is led by a page boy, carrying a banner bearing the Coat of Arms of St Monans.

On the old bridge over the Inverie Burn, the Sea Queen is met by the parish minister, who invites her to throw a handful of grain into the sea. This action of offering some of the harvest of the land to the sea, on whose bounty the town had depended throughout its history, is both a thanksgiving and a recognition of the motto of St Monans, '*Mare Vivimus*' (We live by the sea). The Sea Queen and the minister then eat an oatcake sprinkled with salt, the produce of land and sea, symbolising the village's dependence on both. She then proceeds into the kirk to attend the service of worship, during which she offers a prayer for God's continuing blessing on the community.

Like many parish churches, St Monans has had its own share of beadles, whose longevity in office often outstripped the remarkable tenures of the ministers. In the 1920s, 30s and 40s, there was the every-present Alex Ferguson, erstwhile postman, whose property at Burnside abutted the Hermit's Cave.

The pawky nature of one of his predecessors was detailed by the *East Fife Record* of 24th April 1868.

> In connection with the church, the name of Peter Drummond, the former venerable beadle has been long associated. He died in the year 1849 at the age of 90. His aged and somewhat

7. *Sea Queen 1992, Lorraine Hughes with her attendants and the crew of the* Reaper.

picturesque habiliments, were well known, not only to the inhabitants of the district, but to the summer residents at Elie, who never failed, in the course of the season, to pay a visit to 'St Minnan's Kirk'. Nobility, gentry and artizans – the aged in their quiet strolls along the beach – artists in search of romantic scenery – young ladies, with their sketch books in quest of old houses and fantastic rocks as subjects for their pencils, might be met at times in or near the church, and, to all such visitors, old Peter was well known, while his familiar and patronising air were considered as a pleasant treat.

At his departure from the locality, a few years before his death, it was felt that the church had lost one of its most familiar associations.

Numerous anecdotes have long been current in the district regarding him; and he seems to have been, from his earlier day, noted for his intelligence and his disposition to waggery. When a youth, he acted as the farm servant to the manse at Abercrombie, where his jokes and tricks were very annoying to his master, presumably the Reverend Archibald Gillies, who was of an irritable temper and dignified deportment.

One day, the minister remarked to Peter that he was a lazy, slothful fellow, giving but a short day's work, as he left off at sunset and spent his evenings in idleness, while his neighbours set him a difficult example, as they might be heard in their barns, flailing their corn by candle-light.

'Aweel, aweel,' answered Peter, 'if ye want yer corn flailed by can'le-licht, I'll dae yer wull.' Accordingly, next day, about noon, as the minister passed the barn in search of Peter, he heard the sound of the flail in full operation within, and, opening the door found, to his amazement, that his servant was flailing his corn – by candle-light! 'What's the meaning of this folly and waste,' cried his annoyed master, 'burning my candles in the full light of day?' 'Div ye no mind,' answered Peter with affected surprise, 'that ye tell't me last nicht that ye preferred yer corn being flailed by can'le-licht?' 'Oh, Peter,' replied the minister, 'you think you have caught me in my own trap, but I'll take care that you shall have no more candle-light after this.'

A few days afterwards, the minister, intending to repair to St Andrews, came out of his manse, equipped for his journey and immediately ordered Peter to saddle his pony. 'Aweel,' said Peter, 'I am wulln't to dae't but I am maist afeard I'll no hae licht.' 'Go immediately,' said his master, 'and don't keep me waiting here.' Peter vanished into the stable, and after keeping the minister waiting a considerable time, and in answer to his expostulations, muttering audibly, 'I hae nae licht. I canna see what I'm daein; muckle need o a can'le-licht here,' he at last appeared with the cow, saddled and bridled, leading her daintily out of the stable. 'Oh Peter,' said his indignant master, 'what do you mean by this folly?' 'Deed, sir,' answered Peter, 'I appeal tae yer judgement; hoo can a man in a dark stable tell a coo frae a powny? I think ye man alloo me a can'le again.'

His oddities of thought which he had cherished through life and the waggeries he had practised had become so ingrained into his mind, that, at last, he deemed to believe as truths the old traditions with which he used to entertain visitors to the church.

He never failed to tell his visitors that the church was built by King David. 'What King David?' said a pompous gentleman once, looking around to his company with such a quizzical grin as to say, 'We'll take our fun out of the old man.' 'What King David do you mean? The King David that wrote the psalms?' 'The verra same,' answered Peter, looking his interpreter full in the face, with a broad stare and a certain twinkle in his eye, which indicated his suspicion of the intended jest, 'the verra same; the verra man; and, as ye seem to ken history fu' weel, I'll tell ye something else ye would like to hear. There is na doot that as ye cam doon the burn side, ye would see that the auld steeple has nae wathercock. Weel, man, ye may mark it doon in yer book as a fact that the pechts [pixies] cairrit it aff ae nicht tae Pittenweem and clippit it on the steeple o' the kirk there.'

In the author's life-time, the most memorable of beadles was Jimmy Patterson. A road-man in everyday life, whose gleaming scythe kept the verges between St Monans, Elie and the surrounding district as immaculate as his thriving and colourful cottage garden by the burn, just across from the kirk, Jimmy appeared to be hewn out of granite. Gravedigger and bell-ringer, every Sunday, without fail, saw him perform his pastoral duties with great solemnity, his ever-bronzed features in stark contrast to his spotless, white collar and navy-blue suit. Often after a day's work and later, in his retirement years, he worked ceaselessly to maintain the graveyards and the entire burn side from the sea to the Elie road in splendid order. He also took upon himself the onerous task of the refurbishment and upkeep of the coastal path towards Elie, gleaning materials from flotsam and jetsam. A curiosity of things natural made him an avid collector of interesting stones and rocks, such as volcanic obsidian, which he discovered during his regular clearances of the bottom of the burn. Jimmy certainly ranks high among the beadles who have served the kirk with such dedication through the centuries.

Today's church is thriving and vigorous and will, no doubt, add many more centuries of service to the community to its illustrious past.

Appendix 1

Names of Clergy who have served in the Churches of Abercrombie and St Monans

St Monans Church under the Blackfriars

1364 Sir Lawrence de Fernwall, Sir Thomas Murray and Sir Stephen de Passagio.

1446 Magister Thomas Marshall and Sir Andrew Preston.

1456 Patrick de Cockburn and David Admulty.

1464 John Clerk and John Whyte.

1465 Patrick Tait and John Clerk.

1468 Alexander Barker and Archibald of Wemys.

1473 Stipend paid to Predicant Friars. No names given.

1479 Thomas Dunning, Prior.

1483 William Davidson, Prior.

1488 Andrew Ramsay, Prior.

1498 William Davidson, Prior.

1501 Patrick Sharp, Prior.

1503 John Caldwell, Prior.

1507 John Murray, Prior.

1508 Alexander Anderson, Prior.

1509 Andrew Anderson, Prior.

1510 William Burns, Prior.

1516 Hugh Ramsay, Prior.

1518 Thomas Simpson, Prior.

1521 Stipend paid to Predicant Friars, St Andrews.

1542 Patrick Hall, Prior.

Abercrombie Church

1563 Parish supplied by John Ferguson, reader.

1576–78 Parish supplied by Thomas Young, reader.

1579–86 Parish supplied by Alexander Borthwick, reader.

1588 Rev. Robert Durie.

1593 Rev. Alexander Forsyth.

1605 Rev. Daniel Wilkie, AM

1628 Rev. Robert Wilkie.

St Monans Parish Church

1646 Rev. Robert Wilkie.

1664 Rev. James Rattray, AM.

1682 Rev. Andrew Burnet.

1689 Rev. Walter Wilson, AM.

1704 Rev. John Craigie AM.

1734 Rev. John Cook.

1752 Rev. William Trail, AM.

1757 Rev. John Chieslie.

1769 Rev. Archibald Gillies.

1804 Rev. Robert Swann.

1852 Rev. David Lindsay Foggo.

1882 Rev. John Turnbull, DD.

1934 Rev. Walter J. Gordon, BD.

1940 Rev. Thomas Shearer, MA, BD, BLitt.

1944 Rev. J. Stewart Rough, MA.

1972 Rev. Gordon W. Craig, MBE, MA, BD.

1975 Rev. Richard M. Findlay, BD.

1983 Rev. David Reid, L. Th, FSA Scot.

1993 Rev. Gilbert C. Nisbet, CA, BD.

Appendix 2

The Bull of Sixtus IV Erecting St Monans into a Priory (translation from the Latin)

ORDERED THAT TWO HOSPICES in the kingdom of Scotland be distinguished by the name of Convent.

Sixtus, Bishop, Servant of the Servants of GOD, to his beloved son, the Arch-deacon of St Andrews, greeting and Apostolic blessing.

To the rich fruits, which the Sacred Order of Preaching Friars, planted in the field of the LORD, hath hitherto produced and ceaseth not to produce for the exaltation of the Catholic faith, We, extending the keen glance of our considerations, willingly apply [our] efficacious hands to those things by means of which the Order itself, to the increase of Divine worship and the devotion of a faithful people, may be continually extended, especially when the prayers of Catholic Kings demanded it, and we perceive that the salvation of souls is thereby advanced.

Since indeed the petition presented to Us lately on the part of our beloved son, the Vicar General of said Order, our deputy in the kingdom of Scotland, set forth that in the foresaid kingdom – to wit in the city of St Andrews one, in the church of the Blessed Mary; and in the diocese another, in the former Chapel Royal dedicated to Saint Marianus [*sic*] at Inverry – places [whether] 'oratory' or 'hospice,' [so] named according to their ritual, are known to have been canonically granted to the Brethren of the said Order at one time, and to have been inhabited from that time by them, and if for the future they were, and were called not 'oratories' or 'hospices' but conventual houses of the same Order, assuredly that would conduce to the singular pleasure and spiritual consolation of the faithful of those parts.

Wherefore on behalf of our very dear son in CHRIST, James [III] the illustrious King of the Scots, as well as of the foresaid Vicar, humble supplication has been made to Us that We should deign to grant to the foresaid Brethren and otherwise in the foresaid [places] opportunely to provide of our Apostolic benevolence that the foresaid places should henceforth be and be called not oratories or hospices but conventual houses and that the Brethren themselves should be empowered to construct and build houses in the same place with churches, cloisters, cemeteries, dormitories, refectories, bell towers, bells, gardens, and garden adjuncts and other necessary offices for the same Brethren's perpetual use and habitation.

We therefore, who wish with sincere desires Religion and Divine worship in all places soever to flourish and increase, especially in our own times, being moved by such supplications, do entrust it to thy discretion by [our] Apostolic writings – in order that if it is so, thou mayest grant by our authority to the same Brethren – that the foresaid places henceforth should be and be named not oratories or hospices, but conventual houses of the said Order, and that the Brethren themselves should be authorised to construct and build (without prejudice however to any one) in the same place houses with churches, cloisters, cemeteries, dormitories, refectories, with bell towers, bells, gardens, garden adjuncts and other necessary offices for the perpetual use and habitation of the same Brethren;

For We – if it happens that a concession of this sort is made by thee in virtue of these presents as it foresaid – do by our Apostolic authority by the tenor of these presents as is foresaid – grant indulgence to the Brethren remaining dwelling in the same houses for the time that they may be empowered to see all and several the privileges, exemptions, immunities and indulgences to the said Order; and the concessions to the Brethren of it in whatsoever rank; and to rejoice freely and lawfully; notwithstanding [any] appointments and ordinances Apostolic or other whatsoever.

Given at Rome and S. Peter's in the year of the Incarnation of Our LORD, 1476, on the 15th day before the Kalends of April, [18th March] in the 6th year of our Pontificate. 1476 is the custom of the Bulls for 1477.

From the *Apostolic Archives* Bk. CX. fol. 165.

Appendix 3

The Architecture of the Kirk

THE FOLLOWING DESCRIPTION is largely taken from a paper by Hippolyte J. Blanc, an architect of Edinburgh, read at a meeting of the Edinburgh Architectural Association in St Monans church in July 1888. Some features will have been altered by the restoration of 1955 as given in Willie Miller's description.

The fabric of St Monan's Church, though incomplete, suggests a cruciform outline, the western limb, or nave, of which is believed never to have been built; though a projecting piece of the north wall foundation, which still exists, shews that something was intended. Among other instances where the nave has not been completed may be mentioned, Seton Church (1493), Roslin (1446), and the late Church of The Holy Trinity, Edinburgh (1461).

The Church comprises Choir, North Transept, South Transept, and Tower. The north and south walls of the tower are sustained by sub-arches in the same manner of construction as may be seen at Greyfriars Church, Stirling (1424), and at St Cuthbert's, Edinburgh (1789). At Stirling, the tower stands out from the west end of the nave (a very usual position in fifteenth century churches), and shows the intake from the oblong form to the square; at St Monans, however, the intake is concealed within the roofs of the transepts.

The choir is well lighted by large windows. On the south wall there are three windows of four lights each, and one (the westmost) of three lights, while on the north side the two extreme bays have windows of three lights each, the two bays between being obscured by a projecting vestry. In each case, the windows fill nearly the whole space of each bay. They have deeply bevelled jambs both on the interior and exterior, the outer rybats being simply splayed and grooved, while the inner have shallow roll and hollow mouldings.

The tracery is interesting and very characteristic of the period. It is composed of cusped pear-shaped loops, a form frequently found in fifteenth century churches in Scotland. The east end has two windows each of two lights, with tracery similar to that in the side windows, and, in a central position above, there is a small window of cusped tracery enclosed within a deeply bevelled segmental arch. The inner roof is of stone, groined with main ribs rising from attached wall shafts. The shafts are semi-octagonal in plan, the face and side angles of which, instead of being plain are slightly hollowed. The shafts rise from a horizontal string moulding at the level of the bottom of the splay of the window sill. They have no bases, and, as the moulding is of plaster, it is possible the shafts may have been continued to a stone tabling near the ground. As the whole walls have been plastered on boarding, any architectural detail which may exist cannot be seen.

The rib mouldings spring from a moulded capital unenriched, the ribs themselves being composed of two shallow cavities. The groining is complete and interesting, the intersections of the ribs being ornamental with bosses, each bearing an emblem or crest. In the transepts, there are no features worthy of notice, excepting two windows in the south gable. They are each composed of small twin lights, with lancet heads deeply recessed within a semicircular arch, very widely bevelled. Of details, the door leading from the choir to what has doubtless been a sacristy on the north side, shows a rare treatment in the moulded termination of the lancet arch. These mouldings, which are undercut and filletted, fade away upon the deeply splayed jambs of the door. The original floor-line of the church, which was about two feet above the present, is traced from the jambs of this door.

A similar treatment of moulded termination occurs at Pluscarden, but, as an original treatment, Rickman informs us there are no examples in England, though he refers to instances of analogous treatment in flamboyant work in France.

The triplet sedilia on the south side are interesting, though the stone bench seems a restriction, while further east on the same side is a cusped ogee-headed rectangular niche. This may have been a credence, as there is nothing to support Muir's conjecture that a piscina existed there, the rybat mouldings returning complete along the sill. The two doors at the east gable (now the entrance) and that in the east wall of the south transept are modern and uninteresting.

The bosses at the intersection of the ribs of the roof are worthy of examination and study. They exhibit twelve varieties of design, chief among which are representations of the Lion *passant* within a double tressure on a shield, Fleur de lis, Heart, Rose, Three Stars and a Heart. Originally, from one of these bosses (which are repeated over the roof) a pulley was fastened, from which was hung the model of a ship. This pulley may in previous times have served to suspend the sanctuary lamp.

The transept ceilings are treated in a similar manner to the choir, but in a plaster imitation.

The main pier shafts at the outer section of choir and transept are of stone, those on the east side only being plaster imitation. They are composed of two three-quarter shafts sunk in rectangular nooks on each side, with a half round shaft on the face. Each shaft supports two orders of shallow cavetto arch mouldings, and has an annulated sloping base, resting on a semi-octagonal sloping plinth.

Looking to the exterior, the divisions of the interior are marked by bold buttresses, which rise from a broadly splayed base, which continues round the building. At the level of the window sills, a horizontal moulding is continued round the entire building at the level of which the buttresses have a broad intake course. The buttresses are continued through the eaves, above which they are terminated with square cone-shaped pinnacles. Each angle of the building is also buttressed, each buttress having four intake courses, and the terminations are gabletted.

On each of the gables, a central buttress divides the surface to the height of the base line of a triangle formed with the angles of the gables. The base line is defined with a moulded cornice in continuation of the eaves course, decorated with carved faces, mask heads, and ornamental filling in the hollow moulding. The gables are set considerably within the outer face of wall beneath, leaving a comparatively broad platform, which may have been originally protected with a parapet carried along between the buttresses. In each gable, a door exists giving egress from the roof within.

The north elevation is uninteresting, and rendered more so by the unsympathetic modern addition of a vestry.

The west front shows the stepped ascent of the base intercepted by the intended nave projection. That front has been much altered by the operations of 1828, by the opening up of windows and introduction of architectural features not of ancient feeling.

The tower exhibits evidences of having been changed in the detail of the parapet. The parapet cope is 53 feet from the ground at the north-west corner.

The spire, of octagon form, springs very low down in the tower. The faces of the spire are ornamental with gabled lunettes, the jambs of which have a filletted roll moulding.

The choir measures 50 feet 8 inches in length and 22 feet 9 inches wide. The south transept is 17 feet 9 inches long and 18 feet wide. The north transept is 17 feet 6 inches long and 18 feet wide. The tower at the intersection is 21 feet 3 inches east and west by 16 feet north and south inside. The total length inside is 71 feet 8 inches from east to west, and 66 feet 6 inches across the transept from north to south.

In Bishop Pococke's *Tour through Scotland*, 1760 (Scot. Hist. Soc., pp. 274–5), St Monans Church is described as follows: 'It is a very solid ancient building with an old plain cornice, the cavetto of which is adorned with heads of beasts. The windows of the Transept are like those of a Castle splaying outward and turned with true arches. The south side seems to have been the model for the Chapel of Derisy (Dairsie) with three windows and ornamental buttresses, but where the door is in the next but one to the transept there is only a narrow window to the east of it; there are two windows at the east end divided by a buttress. To the north there was a building joined on to it, now destroyed, which took up almost the whole side of the Cross. It is built of freestone, which in some parts is beautifully honey-combed by the weather.'

McGibbon and Ross, in their description of St Monans Church, say: 'The crossing has large clustered piers supporting the arches which carry the tower and spire. The western end is built up with a solid wall without any indications of an arch to the nave. It contains a tall traceried window of two lights, with a transom in the centre of the height. A turret stair at the north west angle leads to the top of the tower. The evidence of the *Exchequer Rolls* is conclusive as to a church having been erected here, at considerable outlay, in the Fourteenth century; but to judge from the architecture alone, it seems scarcely possible to believe that the church we now see is the one erected in the time of David II. All the features of the structure point to a date later by about a century ... The style of church erected in the Fifteenth century was generally a cross church, without aisles. St Monans is designed on that plan, and, like many of the other cross churches, remains incomplete, the nave not having been erected. In almost all its details it corresponds with the Scottish structures of the Fifteenth century. The windows have all splays running round the jambs and arches, without caps; and the tracery is of an undoubtedly late form. The curious small upper window in the east end could scarcely be of Fourteenth century date.

'The vaulting is groined, and has main and subsidiary ribs or tiercerons. This is not usual in the collegiate churches of the Fifteenth century, in which the pointed barrel vault is commonly used; but there is one prominent example in the Trinity College Kirk of Edinburgh, built about 1460, in which groined and ribbed vaulting was fully carried out. The ribs at St Monans are arranged in a rather singular manner. There is a well marked ridge rib, and there are also tranverse ridge ribs; but the latter stop at the point where the tiercerons meet them; and from that point the transverse ridge ribs slope down to the apices of the windows, where they are received by a small corbel.

'The tiercerons are also irregularly placed; they do not spring, like the other ribs, from the cap of the vaulting shaft, but die away into the wall some way up the wall rib. These peculiarities have the appearance of late and imperfect workmanship. It will be observed that the single wall shafts, from the capital of which the vaulting ribs spring, have no bases. The sedilia in the south wall of the choir may be regarded as Decorated work. It is evident that a parapet has been intended at the gable at the south transept, where there is a door for access to the parapet walk. The peculiar character of this transept is remarkable. The two small round-headed windows, with their deep recess, and the great expanse of dead wall above them, most certainly can be considered as of late design ... Although from what is above said we cannot regard this structure as so old as 1360, still we consider it worthy of being included among the Scottish examples of decorated work.

'The two south windows in the south transept look like late Norman stripped of its mouldings to form large outside splays, their single openings being filled with stone work to make windows of two lights of Early English character. The buttresses may be of Fourteenth century date or later. But all other details belong to the end of the Fifteenth or beginning of the Sixteenth century, except the spire which cannot be earlier than the Seventeenth century.

'It seems that the conversion of the late Norman into Early English was the work of Dishington, who likely made all the windows the same. And the buttresses may have been built by him if he proposed groining the roofs. But the present groining and all other details except the spire belong, probably to the beginning of the Sixteenth century.

'Shrines were originally placed in crypts, but in the Thirteenth century they were brought to the floors of the churches, and as pilgrims came to them, especially on the Saint's Day, in large numbers, bringing gifts, they were sources of revenue. It is therefore hardly credible that in the Thirteenth century the famous shrine of St Monan could have stood anywhere but in a suitable church.'

Chapter 7

Early Wars and Invasions

BECAUSE OF ITS SMALL POPULATION, St Monans could never be regarded as playing a major part in Scottish history, yet a brief chronological review reveals interesting events and contributions, specific to the community.

After the Union in AD 843 of the Kingdoms of the Picts and the Scots, the Danes invaded the East Neuk of Fife. In AD 874, St Monans men took part in a pitched battle at Crail, but the Scots, over-confident of victory, were defeated. King Constantine, son of Kenneth McAlpine, was captured and beheaded in what is known as the Devil's Cave.

Some historians believe that MacDuff, Thane of Fife, although often credited with slaying MacBeth in 1057, was a mythical person. However, tradition has it that the men of Fife supported him as their Maormor in assisting Malcolm, son of King Duncan, and the Earl of Northumberland in the defeat of MacBeth at 'high Dunsinane', as William Shakespeare immortalised the battlefield in 'the Scottish play'.

In July 1490, the shores of the Firth of Forth, or the Scottish Firth as it was then known, were crowded with spectators, daylong, to witness the capture of three English men-of-war, sent by Henry VII to seize the ships of Admiral Sir Andrew Wood. The Largo man owned two vessels of some three hundred tons each, the *Mayflower* and the *Yellow Caravel.* Crewed by local men, they plied trade to the Dutch and Hanseatic ports, which had close commercial ties with Scotland The out-going cargo was usually wools and hides, the return trips bringing such vital agricultural equipment as carts and wheelbarrows!

In 1481, Sir Andrew had repulsed a squadron of English ships which had appeared in the Forth and, in the same year, successfully defended Dumbarton when it was besieged by a fleet of Edward IV.

Although, in 1489, there was a truce with the English, their pirate ships infested the coast of Scotland. King James IV asked the old sea-dog to rid the country of this annoyance, which he did, taking the marauders' vessels into Leith as prizes.

Here now was the Tudor, Henry VII, seeking retribution and offering one thousand pounds per year for life to the man who would bring Wood to London, dead or alive. However, none of the English captains, who were under the command of Admiral Stephen Bull, a London merchant, reckoned on the cunning of their Scottish opponent. Using sun, tide and seamanship, he captured all three and sailed with them into Dundee.

On 9th September 1513, many men of Fife died with their king, James IV, in the Battle of Flodden Field against the English under the Earl of Surrey. As the old song by Jane Eliot relates, 'The Flowers o' the Forest are a' wede away.'

In 1544, the English 'landed divers of their boats at a town, named St Mynills on the north side of the Firth, which they brent [burned] and brought from there divers great boats.' The kirk was put to the torch, as was the whole village and neighbouring Pittenweem. The commandeered craft were used as part of an invasion fleet to land on the Lothian shore, when Portobello, Leith and Newhaven were destroyed.

Another defeat by the English, at the Battle of Pinkie in 1547, saw ten thousand Scots die. The following year, Kinghorn was razed to the ground and troops garrisoned on Inchkeith. Expanding their campaign, twelve hundred soldiers, led by Lord Clinton, landed on the beach to the east of St Monans. On the Mair, the present site of the Bowling Club, they were engaged in battle and defeated.

The Scottish army included many local volunteers and the cream of Fife's nobility. In command were the Laird of Wemyss and the Prior of St Andrews. The latter, Lord James Stewart, half brother to Mary Queen of Scots and later to be the 'Good Regent', Lord Moray, was scarcely seventeen years of age. It was customary and expected that churchmen would not only bear arms but also lead their countrymen in battle. At the end of this encounter, no fewer than six hundred English had perished and a hundred more taken prisoner.

There are various versions of this fight, particularly with regard to the statistics of the numbers of men-at-arms involved and those slain or taken. Pitscottie's account is that the enemy landed at St Ninian's, with the intention of marching eastwards on Pittenweem, fortifying it with men and victuals and then proceeding to despoil the surrounding countryside. However, being confronted with the forces of Fife, they 'arraigned for battle on St Ninian's Mair', setting up artillery pieces, which they had landed from their ships. The count was six hundred and twelve dead, having been slain or drowned trying to regain their vessels, and one hundred prisoners.

The numbers given by David Calderwood were at 'Sanct Minnans were three hundred slain, many drowned.' According to Sir James Balfour, five thousand landed and seven hundred perished.

Perhaps the most interesting account is that of Bishop Leslie, who wrote that one thousand landed but only three hundred got back on board. He stated that 'the village of Sanct Minanis could only raise troops locally ... not abone the nowmer of sax scoir.' At break of day, the dreaded English archers were among them. However, they dug trenches, which they filled with ferns, straw and rubbish and then set it alight, 'makin gret reik' – a smokescreen! The Fife artillery consisted of three small cannons, which assisted Lord Wemyss and his troops to inflict great slaughter. Meantime, a company from the village, consisting mainly of women and children, screened behind a hill, made 'sic ane hidderous noise and cry' that, suspecting the arrival of fresh reinforcements, the foe fled. Almost two hundred and fifty years later, the women of Fishguard in Pembrokeshire, clad in their traditional Welsh red cloaks and tall black hats and led by the local cobbler, the awesome Jemima Nicholson, were to accomplish a similar defeat as had the mothers and bairns of St Monans. Fourteen hundred French militia had landed on 22nd February 1797 at Carreg Wastad. The women frightened them into surrender, thus ending the last invasion of mainland Britain. The event is commemorated in Fishguard on a Bayeux-style tapestry and celebrated on suitable occasions by a pageant. Perhaps St Monans should stage a similar event.

History does not seem to record any trace of skeleton, armour or weaponry being retrieved consequent to the battle or recovered at a later date. It was, however, remembered by the naming of an area of the village as the 'Crook i' the Lot'. The title has fallen into disuse, but the land was part of the estate of Barronhall, near today's Elm Grove and Hope Place.

This curious title was derived from yet another traditional version of the invasion. One Tibbie Dawie of the Uppertoun was reputed to possess the double gifts of divination and witchcraft. Living on the benevolence of her neighbours, by speying fortunes and foretelling events, she had narrowly escaped being burned as a witch by warning the local minister not to undertake a sailing, with a pleasure party, to the Isle of May. The boat had been swamped and all the occupants drowned. The cleric was most grateful to Tibbie and, like many in the area, believed in her powers.

At the end of the harvest in 1548, the Lord of the Manor, enjoying a walk around his property, met the carlin. 'Aweel, Tibbie, what's this yir sae eident [industrious] wi' noo?' 'A trow [in truth] Sir, I'm jist gatherin a wheen sticks tae win my bield [reach my home], ere they be steepit [soaked] wi English bluid [blood], for, ere they whins be i' the bloom again, ye'll live tae see a fell stour [deal of dust] among them. An', I'm unco wae [very sad] for a bonnie lass o' high breedin', for there's a sad crook i' her lot [trial in her destiny], which she winna see till her cuits [ankles] be jobbit [pricked] by they verra whins that stands in the neuk there.'

Not knowing if he should believe the prophecy, the Lord erred on the side of prudence and promptly provided for any emergency. After the lapse of a few weeks, Tibbie's forecast came true. With secretive whispers, she announced to the Baron that the enemy had landed and were encamped on the Mair. The war-horn was sounded from the observatory and all the vassals assembled in front of the castle. A scouting detachment of Scots lay quartered at Ardross, while the men of the Nethertoun, armed with boathooks and leisters (fish spears) and those of the Uppertoun with pitch-forks, axes and all manner of crude weaponry, marched into battle. By some mysterious enchantment, Tibbie confounded the enemies' eyes, so that the small detachment of Scots loomed up like a Roman cohort, creating terror and confusion.

The strife over, a serf, who had taken no part in it because he had been asleep, sauntered around the battlefield, slaying the wounded and even further mutilating the slain. He came upon a fine young man in officer's uniform, whose sweetheart, with her baby beside her, was binding his wounds. Callously, the scoundrel killed the husband with his sword, whereon the poor wife shrieked, 'This must be the crook i' my lot, of which the astrologer spoke before my mother conceived me.' Ruthlessly, the vassal murdered her too and was about to dispatch the child, when he was stopped by the Baron himself. Appalled by such wanton slaughter, he struck off the offender's head.

Legend has it that the mother was the only daughter of a wealthy Esquire of the English Borders, who made intercession with the Baron for the restoration of his grandchild. His request was rejected; the orphan was brought up in the castle, married the Baron's eldest son, and, on the Baron's death, became Lady Newark.

In 1563, Mary Queen of Scots stayed at Newark Castle. The steeple of the Auld Kirk gave welcome refuge in 1589 to a party of soldiers, commanded by Francis Stewart Hepburn, Fifth Earl of Bothwell. Under the pretext of obeying orders from the Court, they oppressed the towns and villages along the coast, with demands for victuals and quarters. James Melville of Anstruther, the famous Reformer and later Moderator of the General Assembly of the Church of Scotland, was, at that time, minister of Kilrenny kirk. Immediately, he set out to the Court at the Palace of Holyrood, Edinburgh, to instigate measures to prevent bloodshed. The men of Pittenweem, Anstruther and Crail were resolved to resist and to fight the intruders. It was when hostilities broke out that the Earl and his men were forced to seek sanctuary in the steeple, 'Otherwise,' said Melville, 'they had gotten sic wages as would entertain them all thir days.' Fortunately, he was successful in obtaining letters from the King, forbidding Bothwell to proceed. Three years later, that noble lord was accused of consulting witches and was exiled.

In 1592, an Act of Parliament forbidding the killing of geese on the Bass Rock was published at the 'market cross of Sanct Monanis'. The Royal Society for the Protection of Birds is really a Johnny-come-lately organisation!

With the passage of time, and the loss, or lack, of documentary evidence, the exact locations of many of the old landmarks have been forgotten. Already mentioned have been the Crook i' the Lot, the Doocot Hill, Queen Mary's tree and Barron Hall, although a house at the beginning of George Terrace is so named. There seems to be no history or explanation of 'the Slap o' the Mair', the general area at the north end of the caravan park, adjacent to the main St Monans–Pittenweem Road. The old Scottish word 'slap' can mean an opening in a wall or hedge or a narrow passage or lane between houses. Without the knowledge of when the location was first introduced, it may be surmised that it has one of those simple explanations.

Chapter 8

The Fife Expedition to the Hebrides

IN 1598, JAMES VI OF SCOTLAND decided to colonise the Hebrides and to bring the West Highlands into submission. It had long been a lawless area; death by the sword or hanging at the hands of the MacLeods and MacDonalds, was the fate of intruders. During the reign of Robert the Bruce, Angus Og, Lord of the Isles, even had his own navy. Great war galleys of twenty, forty or even sixty oars, carried up to two hundred and fifty armed clansmen. They, in turn, were supported by smaller craft, galleases and carricks.

A council was convened to advise the king how best to proceed; among its members were Lord Lindsay of Balcarres, Sir William Stewart, the Commendator of Pittenweem and Sir James Anstruther. As the clan chiefs had not paid feu duties for many years, the council recommended the passing of Acts requiring them to appear in person in Edinburgh at Whitsuntide, 1598, to produce the title deeds of their lands. The penalty for failure would be the forfeiture of all properties to the Crown. As expected, none appeared, so the Isles of Harris and Lewis and the territories of Dunvegan and Glenelg in Skye were declared annexed by the king.

The real objective was not to punish lawbreakers but to raise money. The King had long been impecunious and many of the Fife lairds were no better off. Accordingly, in June 1598, an Agreement was drawn up between the King and a group of gentlemen, the so-called Fife Adventurers. Their objective was 'to plant civilization in the most barbarous Isle of Lewis and to develop its rich resources in corn and fish.' Burghs were to be built in Kintyre, today's Campbeltown, in Lochaber, now Fort William, and Stornoway on Lewis. It might have been expected that an invasion force would have been raised, which would be strategically situated in the West and whose men would have been more akin in temperament, tradition and outlook to the Hebrideans. However, the men of Fife, with many from the St Monans community among them, were considered to be the most industrious in farming and the most skilled fishermen in Scotland.

Although promising to 'advance the glory of God, the honour of our native country and His Majesty's Service, to augment the yearly revenue of the Crown, to plant kirkes at all personal expense', besides risking their own lives, they were mercenaries, legalised land grabbers, chartered buccaneers and, more direly, killers and murderers. The King made it clear that they were to suppress all opposition and to destroy the Islesmen's fleet, Lewis, in particular, being a prime target. Labelling its inhabitants as ungodly and inhumane, he exhorted extermination, so that, in future, only Lowlanders would own and inhabit the new colony. 'Muskets, not missionaries; swords, not schoolmasters,' were the weapons of civilisation chosen by James.

All provisioning and shipping would be supplied by the King for two months. The colonists would pay no feu duties until the year 1600, when there would be an annual rent of barley for Lewis, Rona and the Shiant Isles. It seemed a particularly propitious time to mount an invasion, as Lewis was then torn by bitter internecine feuding between the clans of MacLeod and Mackenzie. Rashly, the King, who did not normally venture his sacred person into danger, declared that he would lead the expedition. He actually reached Dumbarton Abbey before his courage failed and he turned command over to his lieutenant, the Duke of Lennox.

The Adventurers set sail from Leith in late October and reached Lewis in four days. The Fife seamen should have known from experience not to attempt passage up Scotland's stormy east coast so late in the year. Not every boat made landfall. The ship of James Learmont the Younger, of Balcomie in the East Neuk, was attacked by the fierce Highlanders of Murdoch MacLeod. Putting to sea in small half-decked rowboats called birlings, they massacred Learmont's crew, sparing only the young laird, who was imprisoned on Lewis. When at last, he was ransomed and released, he died of the deprivations he had suffered. Even when the Fifers landed, they encountered fierce gales and driving, bone-chilling sleet.

Some six hundred hired soldiers, seamen and merchants were to set up the new colony. Although an embryonic settlement was established, the colonists made no attempt to wipe out the 'untutored savages'. Lack of food, the dreadful climate, illness and inadequate shelter, had them attempting to petition the king for more support. On the way to Edinburgh, their emissaries were seized and held to ransom. Neil, brother of Murdoch, raided the colony with two hundred 'barbrous, bludie and wicket Hielandmen', killed twenty two of the settlers, looted and burned much property, and carried off cattle and horses. So incensed was the king that he gave the Adventurers a free hand to perpetrate slaughter, mutilation, fire-raising and 'other conveniences' to subdue the island. Neil MacLeod was captured, but handed over his brother Murdoch and twelve men in return for a reward from the government. The twelve were beheaded and the heads sent in a 'poke' to Edinburgh where, stuck on pikes, they were displayed at the city gates. Murdoch was later executed at St Andrews.

By December 1599, the king had accused the natives of all manner of treasonable practices, including witchcraft and the ravishing of women. The yearly duty of the Fifers was reduced to one thousand each of pounds sterling, codling, ling and skate. Fraternisation with the islanders was strictly forbidden. This first attempt at colonisation ended ignominiously with an attempt to recapture Neil MacLeod going badly awry, nearly sixty colonists being killed. The king's coffers were now emptier than ever and he even contemplated minting false money to hire troops.

The year 1603 saw the organisation of the second expedition under the Marquis of Huntly. The king summoned all men between the ages of sixteen and sixty in the Orkneys, Shetlands and the North to rally to his colours under penalty of death. The disheartened gentlemen of Fife tried to withdraw but each member of the Syndicate had to hire, furnish and feed thirty soldiers. The penalty was a fine of one thousand pounds and the forfeiture of any share accruing from the venture.

However the death of Queen Elizabeth the First on the 24th day of March, and the accession of Jamie Saxt to the throne of England brought a temporary halt to plans. Trade and commerce had declined drastically and villages and harbours were in a ruinous state. By the time the expedition had gathered momentum again in 1605, the Fifers believed that, this time, their efforts would be successful. They were supported by a proclamation of the Privy Council, in 1606, forbidding all Islesmen, under pain of death, to aid the men of Lewis against the Adventurers. Death was also to be the penalty for any islander having a weapon, save one knife and that 'without the point to cutt their mait'.

However, Neil MacLeod's brigands continued to harass the settlement, money was short, the poorly-paid soldiers were deserting and the threats against the other islands for abetting MacLeod were of no avail. Then, craftily, Neil changed his tactics, announcing that he had been wrong to hinder the colonists and indeed offered to help them. Naively, they believed his story and gave him a position of trust. They paid dearly as, with three hundred men, he fired the sleeping camp of Stornoway and slaughtered the fleeing victims. The king, furious at such treachery, ordered the Catholic Marquis of Huntly to subdue all of Lewis and to arrange 'the extirpation of the whole population within a year', but every attempt to accomplish such a vile objective failed. Neil and his men struck again, capturing Stornoway Castle and destroying more houses. The colony was disbanded and the survivors took passage for home.

A third and last attempt to subdue the Hebrides was made in 1608. A strong force, led by Lord Stewart of Ochiltree, now a Lieutenant of the Isles, brought several of the chiefs to heel and they were imprisoned in Blackness, Stirling and Dumbarton. The king appeared to be achieving his aim of ridding Lewis of Celts and replacing them with Lowland Scots. At this time, he was also busy expelling the natives of Ulster in favour of settlements of English and Scottish colonists. He now tried pacification by freeing the chiefs and, in 1609, the Bishop of the Isles met nearly all of them on the island of Iona. They submitted to him as Commissioner for the Crown and signed a paper called the 'Band of Icolmkill', Icolmkill being another name for Iona. This band or bond set out nine statutes for the better government of the Western Isles and is a landmark in Hebridean history.

Lewis, however, did not accept any offer of peace. When lack of stores in the colony necessitated a journey to Fife, Neil MacLeod attacked the small garrison which remained, slew many and imprisoned the rest. These he subsequently sent home in disgrace and the third expedition, as the other two, ended in complete failure. James, however, was not finished with Lewis. Mackenzie, Lord Kintail, led seven hundred men to the island, and the Lewismen surrendered, but not Neil MacLeod.

Every attempt to capture him failed. Although his support dwindled, with forty men he withstood siege successfully for many months on the islet of Birsay in Loch Roag. Eventually, he tried to reach England to seek pardon from the king, but his companion, a fellow clansman, betrayed him. After fifteen years of defending his homeland against the Fife Adventurers, he was hanged, drawn and quartered and his head placed above the Netherbow Port in Edinburgh.

Despite their failures, the men of Fife had contributed in no small degree to the development of the Western Isles.

Chapter 9

The Charter of St Monans and the Auld Superior

THE TWENTY-EIGHTH OF OCTOBER 1622 was a red letter day for the villagers of St Monans. Sir William Sandilands, the 'Auld Superior' of Newark Castle, and his son and heir, Sir James Sandilands, Knight Friar of St Monans, granted a charter to the feuars.

For the sum of 'Ten Pounds usual money of this realm' he rented to them annually 'the mair and sward', pointing out that they had never been charged before. There would be 'free ish and entry' (legal terms) to 'gaits, wynds, vennills, common lones and passages', profits from customs dues and anchorages and seemingly almost unlimited privileges. However, the velvet glove held the customary mailed fist.

The rent on feu duty, that peculiarly Scottish licence to tax to eternity, was set in five pound portions at Whit, May 15th, and Martinmas, November 11th, still Scottish Quarterdays. The Auld Superior also demanded to be paid, '200 herring per drave boat from the Isles in winter; for ilk boat passing to the Lentrone [Spring] lines within the Scottish Firth – ane Killing [cod] and ane Bannock fluck [turbot] yearly.'; 'Also for Bark and Boat passing to the fishings to Peterhead, Orkney or Zetland yearly, one dozen sufficient Killing.' A trip to the Isles in winter demanded 'a half Barrel of sufficient well-made herring'.

There were many obligations to be observed: 'the Community of St Monance, their heirs and successors shall be holden and restricted to repair, beit [adorn] and uphold the kirk and kirkyard Dykes of St Monance in Timber, Slait, Lime and Glass sufficiently as Effeirs in all times coming …' So strictly did the feuars obey the letter of the law that, for a whole summer, the principal door of the kirk stood open during divine service for want of a latch. It was made of iron, which they were not bound to supply! However, with the approach of winter, the kirk session met and agreed its purchase!

All mineral rights were preserved, so that no tenant farmer need try to augment his income by mining coal or ironstone. Everyone's 'hail malt corns', either grown locally or brought in, were 'bun-sucken', the old Scots or Lallans word meaning that it had to be 'milned and grinded at our milne' and '. . . ye maun pey the mullure.' Cottars and ploughmen were exempted from these charges as the flour was part of their pay. Nor were they liable for duties on goods sold in the town.

The Baron also owned the windmill and the salt factory, St Philip's Works, described by Sibbald as 'the neatest and best contrived salt works on the coast'.

The first Town Council was 'selected', not 'elected', by 'special advice and consent' of Sir William and Sir James – an early quango! All courts were held, usually three times a year, at Newark and there was no appeal against sentences. 'If any of our feuars sall speak disrespectfully uproariously to any of our bailies, he sall for ilk siklike offence be amerced [fined] in the sum of four pounds Scots.' Again, 'Sall ony fewar or inhabitant purchase bread frae ony baxter [baker] out o' the toun, provided he can be as cheap saired [served] in the toun, he sall be fined three pounds Scots for ilk like offence, that trade may prosper in our ain toun.' Sanctions!

All petitioners and evil-doers were 'warned thereto that they no more of them decline our judgement' – a puppet government! The bailies and council, fifteen in total, were adjured to 'erect honest and sufficient houses'. No council transactions except the annual elections were minuted in the eighteenth and nineteenth centuries.

However, the Charter predicted prosperity for the town once the inhabitants had 'executed the bigging and repairing of the said Haven and Bulwark therein.' Further, they were to attend to the 'up bigging and erection of ane Tolbooth and Commonhouse in our said Toun for the better administration of justice in time coming.' The Tolbooth was built under the supervision of the

Superior in 1630, being paid for by Town funds and voluntary subscription. The site was a piece of unfeued ground, granted by the baron. Having ineffectively relinquished ownership of the lands, the Sandilands still kept a stranglehold on the village economy. Despite the Superior's generosity, the Valuation of Fifeshire 1695 shows that St Monans Parish was owned by the Earl of Crawford and Balcarres – £105; Sir Robert Anstruther – £1,486; and Sir Alexander Anstruther – £1,102 13*s.* 4*d.* (£1,102.66p.)

The charter delineates the boundaries of the lands bestowed on the villagers. Landmarks such as the 'Braehead' and the 'old Wind Milne' are still part of the scene but what of the yards of Thomas Brown, Robert Boyd and David Stevenson, of the house occupied by Grisell, or Grizzell Millar, relict (widow) of William Bollo Smith; the abode of Annable Martine (a reminder of Scotland's Auld Alliance with France) and 'the tenements of James Binning and Andrew Dischington'? Strangely, there was no attempt to tax brewing or the selling of 'vivers' (food) by the Superior's tenants or cottars, as long as their vendors obeyed the rules and ordinances of the burgh. Grizzell Millar was the landlady of the first recorded and principal ale-house in St Monans, where the Lord of the Manor regaled himself, whenever his presence was required in the town.

The account of the Seamen's Box was to be made yearly in the presence of the Superior. He and his predecessors had always ruled the village; the Charter, whilst appearing charitable, put their supremacy on a legal and commercial footing.

The full text is printed in Chapter 24. Legal documents, by their very nature, are complex and repetitive but this seventeenth century charter, apart from the many spelling variations, is a gem of abstruse verbiage! The wonder would be if any villager, baillie, dominie or otherwise, comprehended its full significance. Certainly, the Auld Superior wanted to improve the village and keep kirk and harbour in a good state of repair but he took great care to ensure that to the population would go the responsibility of providing the funds.

Chapter 10

The Covenanters and Sir David Leslie

THREE YEARS AFTER THE SIGNING of the St Monans Charter, James the Sixth of Scotland and First of England died and was succeeded by his son, Charles I. However, the new king did not come to Scotland to receive his crown until 1633. Despite elaborate preparations for his Coronation, including the cleansing of Edinburgh's filthy streets, driving all beggars from the town and removing the heads of executed criminals from prominent places, he did not prove to be popular. When crowned in the Chapel of Holyrood, he angered his subjects by being anointed with oil, a custom of the Church of Rome, disliked by Scottish Protestants. Again, at the religious service which followed in the Church of St Giles, two clergymen used the English form of worship. Additionally, they were clothed in white robes, which the Scots, whose ministers always wore black, deemed to be Roman Catholic. He made Edinburgh a city, ordered it to be recognised as the capital of Scotland and appointed a bishop to have St Giles as his cathedral. It was his avowed intention to make his Church in Scotland as much like the Church of England as possible.

He let it be known that a Service Book would be issued in Scotland to replace the Book of Common Order, known as Knox's Liturgy. It was ordered to be read in St Giles on Sunday 23rd July 1637. It was on this occasion that the famous incident took place during which a worshipper flung the stool on which she had been sitting at the Dean's head, calling out, 'Dost thou say mass at my lug?' The perpetrator, now renowned in Scottish history, was Jenny Geddes, a green-wife or herbwoman, who kept a stall on the Royal Mile, near the Tron Kirk. So great was the opposition

8. General Sir David Leslie, Lord Newark
(by permission of Scottish National Portrait Gallery).

to Charles' edicts that, on 1st March, 1638, nobles and gentlemen signed the National Covenant in Greyfriars churchyard, Edinburgh. Copies were sent throughout the land and people flocked to endorse it. Thus were created the Covenanters, who demanded a free Parliament and free General Assembly. The Bishops' Wars which followed were concluded by the Treaty of Westminster in 1641, with Charles meeting the demands of the Covenanters to approve the National Covenant and to abolish Episcopacy. However, they were well aware that if he should ever regain power in Scotland, he would never allow Presbyterianism to become the nation's religion.

In England, he quarrelled with his Parliament and in 1642, the Civil War broke out between the Royalists and the supporters of the Palace of Westminster. Both sides were anxious to have the backing of the Scots. The Covenanters, although divided amongst themselves, signed the Solemn League and Covenant with the Parliamentarians in 1643.

Having made this treaty, the Scots now raised an army to help in the war against Charles. Under General David Leslie, it marched into England where it remained for three years, helping to win the Battle of Marston Moor and in other ways assisting Parliament to defeat Charles completely. Leslie, the fifth son of Patrick Leslie of Pitcairlie, near Auchtermuchty, Lord Lindores, had distinguished himself as a Colonel-of-Horse in the service of Gustavus Adolphus. During the Thirty Years War (1618–48), over 20,000 Scots mercenaries fought for the Swedish King. Leslie returned to Scotland with the rank of Major-General.

During the absence of the Scottish Army in England, the Marquis of Montrose, initially a staunch Covenanter, determined to try to conquer Scotland for Charles. Supported by a wild bunch of Irish mercenaries, he had the King's order to summon the Highlanders. This he did by the age-old custom of sending out the 'Fiery Cross'. Made of two sticks, the ends of which were burned in the fire and then dipped in goat's blood, it was carried by relays of runners, over mountain and glen, until the whole country knew that the chiefs were about to go to war. Failure to obey meant banishment from the clan, the greatest punishment a Highlander could suffer.

Montrose led a bloody campaign, murdering, looting and burning his way across Scotland, but his greatest victory at Kilsyth in Stirlingshire on 15th August 1645 was the last he was to gain. General Leslie and his army were recalled from England, joined battle with Montrose's troops at Philiphaugh, on the banks of the river Ettrick near Kelso, on 13th September 1645, and routed them completely.

The burghs of the East Neuk of Fife were Covenanter strongholds but there was considerable reluctance to join the army. This hesitancy was well justified as many small landowners and ploughmen had been killed at Kilsyth, when over three thousand men of Fife fought for the Covenanter cause.

The Laird of Kilbrackmont, whose lands lay to the north of Rires, together with the minister of Kinneuchar, a Dr Munro, had been sent to St Monans and Earlsferry to hound men to the colours. There were dire threats as to the penalty for disobedience.

To his eternal infamy, Leslie consented to the massacre of prisoners as demanded by the 'grim Geneva ministers', some two hundred of them, who, to quote Wilkie, 'hovered like carrion crows in the wake of the Covenanting army'. One of these clergy, taking his text from the first book of Samuel, Chapter 15, commanded Leslie's soldiery, 'Now go and smite Amalek and utterly destroy all that they have and spare them not; but slay both man and woman, infant and suckling, ox and sheep, camel and ass.' Most of the prisoners were butchered in the courtyard of Newark Castle, on the river Yarrow near Selkirk. By strange coincidence, this was the name of the castle which would become Leslie's place of residence in St Monans.

In addition to the fighting men who died, none of some three hundred women and children, horse-boys and camp scullions was spared. They were buried in a mass grave in what became known as the Slain Men's Lea. Many of the soldiers were Irish mercenaries, who were accompanied by their families. Their murders were justified, in the eyes of Leslie and the Presbyterian ministers, by considering that their savage mode of battle placed them outside the pales of the laws of war.

The merciless injunctions of the preachers were completed, when eighty women and children, fleeing from these barbaric Scots, were overtaken at Linlithgow. Flung from the bridge into the swirling waters of the river Avon, fifty feet below, they were then thrust back from the banks with pikes until all were killed or drowned. In consequence of his victory, Leslie was rewarded by the Scottish Estates with a gold chain and a large sum of money. He may have become the most important man in Scotland, but the Royalists named him the Executioner.

With so many people of the agricultural communities either committed to war or dead, the land lay untended and uncultivated. In those days, when no grain was imported, loss of the harvest spelled scarcity. War, famine and pestilence form a natural progression and so it was then. The plague was raging so furiously in St Andrews that in May 1647, the Presbytery had to meet in Anster Easter. Furthermore, it was convened only once a fortnight to minimise the spread of infection.

Chapter 11

Newark Castle

IN 1649, GENERAL SIR DAVID LESLIE bought the baronies of St Monance and Abercrombie, Newark Castle and other properties in Fife for upwards of 67,000 merks (£4,000). This price was verified from the details of a lawsuit between Sir David and the previous owner, Sir James Sandilands.

Little is known of the origins of Newark Castle except for the derivation of the name which was, simply, the New Wark. The building of the present castle is usually credited to the Sandilands family and may date from the fifteenth century. Extensions, towards the end of the sixteenth century, saw enlargements on the landward side and the creation of a courtyard to the west. There is every likelihood that it was the site of an earlier building, owned by the Kinloch family, who occupied it for several generations, as mentioned in Chapter 6. It is believed that King Alexander III (1249–86) lived there during his early years. At the beginning of the twentieth century, it was proposed that the world-famous Burrell Art Collection, now in Glasgow, should be housed in Newark Castle. Sir Robert Lorimer (1864-1929) drew up plans for a total restoration, but the project was never realised. Sir Robert, Scotland's leading architect, designed the Chapel of the Order of the Thistle in St Giles Cathedral, the National War Memorial in Edinburgh Castle, many country houses, churches and memorials.

The building, one hundred and twenty-eight feet in overall length, consisted of five floors, each with a huge central fireplace. At the north east corner was a round tower, twenty-five feet in diameter. On acquiring the castle, Leslie had it refurbished as a house with a fine Dutch gable. At the time of Miller's account in 1895, there still existed a circular staircase. Also now disappeared was a smoke chamber for the curing of meat and fish. According

9. *Newark Castle from the west.*

to Sibbald, the Barony of St Monance was acquired by James Sandilands of Cruvie, a descendant of Lord Torpichen.

Dying in 1585, he was succeeded by his son, Sir William, the benefactor of the St Monans Charter. In 1644, the estate passed to his son, Sir James, who, in the following year, obtained the Charter of the Lordship of St Monance, together with the tower and fortalice. On 12th December 1647, he was made Lord Abercrombie by King Charles I, but proved to be 'ane ryotous youth, wha spent ane olde estate in the space of four or five yeares.' This inheritance had been in addition to the tocher or dowry of ten thousand merks Scots (£569) brought by his bride, Agnes, daughter of David, first Lord Carnegie. He also had to find large settlements for his four daughters to ensure that they would marry well; there was no male heir.

In 1649, he and his lady caused a great uproar in Fife. That August, the Presbytery of St Andrews arraigned them both on a charge of assaulting a beadle and an elder. The wife was summoned to appear before the Kirk Session of Falkland, her husband himself having rashly raised charges of scandal against her.

On 30th January 1649, Charles I was executed in Whitehall. When the news reached Edinburgh, his son was proclaimed King at the Mercat Cross but Oliver Cromwell, the Lord Protector, was the true ruler of the country, and in July of the next year, his Ironsides marched into Scotland. David Leslie was then supreme commander of the Scottish forces, and, following the old tactic of Robert the Bruce, he ordered what came to be known in warfare as the 'scorched earth policy'. All counties through which the 'auld enemy' had to pass were left burned and deserted of any form of sustenance for either man or horse. Leslie also cut off supply lines and out-generalled Cromwell's every move, eventually trapping his troops on a little peninsula of land near Dunbar on 3rd September 1650.

Unfortunately, the Kirk militants, now four hundred strong, urged the Scots to descend against the 'Philistines at Gilgal' and 'to cut off the ungodly even to the last of the sons of Belial'. The loss of advantage of Leslie's high commanding position was fatal. Cromwell could not believe that this great general would commit such a cardinal error. 'The Lord has delivered them into our hands,' he cried. The watchword of the Scots was 'The Covenant', the English war-cry, 'The Lord of Hosts'. Leslie's troops suffered dreadful losses and such prisoners as were taken were banished to the cotton plantations of America. Significantly, few of the clergy, who had effectively lost the battle, suffered in any way.

Leslie retreated to Stirling and Charles II was crowned at Scone Palace on New Year's Day, 1651. The war then rolled right up to the shores of Fife. Battle was joined at Inverkeithing but Cromwell's forces prevailed. Leslie had blundered yet again. He next moved his army over the Border to try to rally the English Cavaliers, but the end came with the Battle of Worcester, exactly a year to the day since Cromwell's victory at Dunbar.

Leslie went into hiding in Yorkshire but then fell into Cromwell's hands. He was fined four thousand pounds and, with the Earl of Crawford and Balcarres, was imprisoned in the Tower of London.

With the Restoration of the Monarchy in 1660, General Leslie was released and returned home to St Monans. To commemorate the event, he built the 'doocot' or dovecote on prominent high land between the Castle and the Auld Kirk. Once used as accommodation in the 1920s and 30s by salmon fishers for their nets and gear, it has now been restored by the East Neuk of Fife Preservation Society.

In the Middle Ages, such a pigeon loft was only permitted to people who owned a certain area of land and was therefore a valuable privilege. The owner usually erected his doocot on the edge of his property so that his birds could 'board' on his neighbour's grain, giving him a certain satisfaction in eating his pigeon pie, a regular item on the daily bill of fare. These doocots normally held some two hundred birds.

On 31st August 1661, Charles II created Leslie, Lord Newark, which title carried a pension of £500 per annum. This royal gesture provoked some ill-natured remarks from a courtier. 'New Wark,' cried bluff Sir David Erskine of Cambo, the Lord Lyon, King-of-Arms, 'it would agree better gif Your Majesty were tae hang him for his auld wark.' Smiling, the Merry Monarch replied, 'We cannot afford to do that – not yet at least!' Indeed, Leslie had fought against Charles I and for his son, Charles II.

In Leslie's day, the castle had 'a flaunting roof of red to the turret and part of the wing'. After it fell into disrepair, farm servants inhabited such rooms as were weatherproof. Eventually, it was used to store agricultural implements. The remains of the massive fireplace, measuring twelve feet by six feet and the huge chimney are still visible.

The Auld Kirk's most famous elder, Leslie worshipped regularly from his seat in the Newark Gallery. He died of apoplexy in 1682, aged eighty-one, and was buried in a vault in the church. His remains were dug up during the restoration of 1828 and Dr Turnbull relates: 'A velvet skull-cap and bits of gold lace were found in what was supposed to be General Leslie's tomb. His bones and those of many others were tipped over the wall, towards the sea, where the farmers lifted and carried off soil for manure and where the sea, when high tide came, wrapped its mantle over the remainder and hid it from the vulgar gaze.'

In 1746, Newark Castle was to provide refuge for a young Jacobite, one of the sons of Lord Lindsay, Earl of Crawford and Balcarres. The Duke of Cumberland had crushed the Forty-Five Rebellion at Culloden Moor and driven Prince Charles Edward Stuart, 'Bonnie Prince Charlie', into exile in France. Fleeing from the Butcher's troops, the fugitive was hidden by the daughter of Lord Newark, unbeknown to but a few trusty servants. Surreptitiously feeding the young Laird, she was regularly reprimanded and scolded by her family, at meal-times, for having a seemingly gargantuan appetite. In truth, she was secreting food in the ample folds of her kirtle, or outer petticoat. The window of the room where the lad was hidden used to be pointed out to visitors, but subsequent deterioration of the masonry destroyed it.

Wilkie states that:

> ... nothing is known as to the sequel to the romance ... If the refugee were Alexander, who became the fourth Earl of Balcarres, he married Elizabeth Scott of Scotstarvit, near Cupar, three years later; and if he were James, the fifth Earl, who became Chief of the Lindsays, he remained single until the age of 58 ... Christian Anstruther, the eldest daughter of the Newark family, died unmarried, at a great age. Maybe, there was a tale she never told!

Subsequent to Leslie's death, historical accounts of the castle became interwoven with legends, engendered, as is most folk-lore, to explain and colour the actual events, as the following account exemplifies.

Remote though St Monans was in the days of poor roads and difficult travel, its insularity was disturbed from time to time by the arrival of mysterious strangers. Jack tells the story of one such, a young woman of the wandering folk, Pauperima by name, who, on a wild night at the beginning of the eighteenth century, appeared carrying an infant, strapped in a plaid on her back. Given shelter and sustenance, she then worked teasing oakum, used in caulking the seams of boats' planking to render them waterproof, and spinning hemp for ropes. Her son grew to manhood and soon was suspected of being a warlock. Legend had it that he was carried off for a fortnight to visit his father, the Devil. On his return, he became head of the local coven. Terror reigned in the village; communion wine was stolen from the kirk and used in heathenish rites, held on the braes between St Monans and Pittenweem. Jack states that, in his day, on the grass where these ceremonies were allegedly held, there was a permanent circle, green in winter, brown in summer, which no naturalist could explain.

Foolishly, Lord Newark employed this young scoundrel in a

herring curing venture. Unsupervised, he filled the barrels with sand and topped them with a scattered handful of fish. Manipulating the accounts, he pocketed much of the profits. His Lordship was arrested for fraud and died in the Tower of London, reputedly from a broken heart. Pauperima's son escaped but his wife refused to divulge his whereabouts. She was imprisoned and sentenced to make three circuits around the Mercat Cross of Edinburgh in a state of nudity.

However, it may well be that this particular piece of folkore had been confused by Jack with an authenticated incident of a later date. The title of Baron Newark had become extinct with the death of the second David Leslie. A man of expensive tastes, and further crippled by having to bestow large dowries for the marriages of three daughters, he left little money.

His eldest daughter, Jean, Baroness Newark, was married in 1694 to Sir Alexander Anstruther. He assumed control of 'the Estate of Newark, consisting of the half-lands of St Monance, called Inverye, including Easter St Monance, together with the other half-lands, called Wester St Monance and the Barony of Abercrombie.'

After the Act of Union with England was ratified by the Scottish Parliament in 1707, funds were devoted to the promotion of trade and industry in Scotland. The dispensation of money for bounties for curing herring in St Monans was entrusted to Sir Alexander who, unwisely, delegated the task to some untrustworthy minions. They perpetrated the confidence trick using sand, as described by Jack. A quantity of counterfeit copper money, which had been smuggled in from Holland, was also put into circulation at the time of these transactions. The deception having been discovered, in 1725, Sir Alexander had to sell his estate at public auction. It was bought by his nephew, Sir John Anstruther, to whom he also resigned the Office of Conjunct Clerk of the Bills. Sir John paid his uncle £11,000, 'advanced to procure his pardon for certain alleged offences for which he had lately been committed.' These crimes included smuggling in which he had been heavily involved.

The rocks on which the Castle is built were honeycombed with caves. Traces can still be seen from the Elie side, although they were built up and sealed off for public safety. There were often skirmishes between the smugglers and the Customs and Excise officers on the beach below. There is still, in St Monans, the legend of the Green Lady, whose ghost may be heard, or even met, swishing along the corridors of the Castle in her silken gown. Sir David Leslie's wife, Anna, is buried in the Palace of Holyrood in Edinburgh, but his daughter, known as Green Jean, is buried in the Auld Kirk graveyard. Rudyard Kipling in his 'Smuggler's Song' quotes 'brandy for the parson, baccy for the clerk'. It was long rumoured that the clergy of the Auld Kirk had their share of the spirits, tea and silks being landed illegally on the foreshore from the Continent. Vaults below the kirk provided shelter for the contraband goods. Mysterious lights were seen at night, with white-clad figures flitting among the tombstones. The superstitions of the simple fisher folk did the rest as the 'ghosts' of castle and kirk provided the smugglers with perfect cover for their nefarious activities. The last of the Anstruther family to own Newark was the prodigal, Sir Wyndham Carmichael Anstruther, who had to sell the whole of the Elie estate to the Baird family with whom it remains.

The castle has twice been destroyed by fire. Thomas of Ercildoune, the Rhymer of Sir Walter Scott's poem, who was known as the Merlin of Scotland, in allusion to the wizard of the great Welsh saga, the Mabinogion, prophesied that the castle would 'blink three times on the Bass'. The latter, a world-famous sea-bird sanctuary, is the prominent rock near North Berwick, lying across the Firth of Forth from Newark. Although a ruin for many years, there was a fire at the castle in 1996, so perhaps the prophecy has been fulfilled.

Chapter 12

Fishing

The Hollander Tigers

FISH HAVE PLAYED AN IMPORTANT PART in the religious, economic and political history of Scotland since antiquity. The salmon with the ring in its mouth, on the Coat of Arms of the City of Glasgow, dates from Saint Mungo in the sixth century. Throughout the Middle Ages, abbeys and other religious houses were granted rights by the Crown to take the red fish – East Neuk fishers never say salmon! The 'royal' fish, like the sturgeon today, was the unique property of the monarch. The kirk, laird and state too, all contrived to take their pickings from the bounty of the sea and the labours of its mariners. The payments in kind to the Laird of Newark by the St Monans fishers have already been detailed in the story of the village Charter.

Commercially, the herring were as important as North Sea oil is today. The German Hanseatic League and the Dutch, Flemish and Brabantine communities founded their fortunes on fish; the city of Amsterdam was built on herring bones.

The constant encroachment of these foreign vessels into British waters forced a succession of rulers to attempt to encourage more interest in this lucrative trade. There were three naval wars with the Dutch, as a direct consequence of fishing squabbles. In 1493, James IV ordered 'all coastal burghs to build vessels of twenty tons and put idle men to crew'.

By the middle of the sixteenth century, it was a common sight to see as many as two thousand Dutch 'busses' assembled in the Shetlands; they also fished the Fife and Aberdeen coasts. The role of the Fife Adventurers in 1599 to stimulate the fishing industry of the Isle of Lewis has already been related. In England, to benefit her fishermen, Elizabeth I, in 1580, banned the import of foreign cured fish and later, on the pretext of religious precedent, revived compulsory non flesh-eating days, no fewer than one hundred and fifty-two of them!

By 1601, Holland had twenty thousand sailing ships, more than the combined totals of Scotland, England, France, Spain, Portugal, Italy, Denmark, Poland, Sweden and Russia! Her herring fleet with their half-mile-long drift nets, of best hemp or coarse Persian silk, dominated British waters. The Hollanders (the so-called Tigers) called Fife 'The Treasure House of Scotland'.

Poor Catches

The fickleness of Nature in refusing to guarantee a regular supply of fish has been an ever present threat to communities, totally dependent on such an economy. The Firth of Forth is no exception as the following abstracts relate.

Gourlay, in his *Fisher Life*, quotes Clerk Spalding, writing in 1642:

> There was a scarcity of white fish along the East Coast and to the hurt and hungering of the poor and beggaring of the fishermen. It was reported that, when the fishers had laid their lines and taken fish abundantly, there came ane beast, called the sea dog, to the lines and destroyed the hail bodies and left nothing on the lines but the heads. A judgement surely from God Almighty for the like scarcity of fish to continue so long as has scarcely been seen here in Scotland, whilk bred great dearth of meal and malt at aught, nine or ten pounds the boll and all other meats also very dear.

Again, from the diary of John Lamont of Largo in 1657 and 1658:

> Thir two yeares ther was few or no herring gotten in Fyfe syde and not many in Dunbar so that divers persons began to feare ther sould be no drewe [drave] hereafter, which was a great prejudice to the poor fishermen and als to the whole places nereabout (for the like had not beine, as some may thinke, for a space of a hundred yeares before).

10. Mussel shelling – late 19th century. Ann Grainger, Margaret Morris and Sandy Ireland (rear man and child unknown).

In 1662 and 1663 'there was no herring gotten in like manner'. The boats that followed the white fishing usually had a crew of eight, each with lines of twelve taes or ties. A tie measured 144 yards and held 120 hooks. The lines of one boat could stretch for eight miles and the fleet often shot over three hundred miles. The great lines or gartlins favoured nine taes and, at a cost of four pounds each, represented a significant investment. There was seldom enough local bait and mussels were shipped in from the Clyde. Each boat took four bags, weighing at least a quarter of a ton, on each trip to the fishing grounds, normally twice a week.

The fish were laid out in scores on the pier, the auctioneer claiming a fee of one shilling in the pound sterling.

In the eighteenth century, great pods of whales and herds of dolphins were regularly seen in the Firth of Forth. Seemingly, by tradition, they were hunted and shot by the fishermen of Kinghorn.

Both Charles I and Charles II founded Royal Fishing Companies, with financial support and the right to raise money by lottery and to collect in churches. Bounty systems were introduced, much criticised by Kirkcaldy's favourite son, the economist Adam Smith, in his *Wealth of Nations*. As ever, heavy-handed regulations penalised the Scots. English boats, fishing Shetland, could shoot their nets on Midsummer's Day; the smaller craft from Fife and the Clyde were prohibited from sailing until 12th September, thus being denied the prime catches and the best prices.

Ancient Practices

Before the granting of the Charter, five or six creers, with crews of ten men, sailed regularly to the herring fishing in the Orkney Islands. Barrels and salt were carried and the catches cured in the boats. The fishers lived aboard and had enough victuals to last for the entire season.

Closer to home, smaller boats sailed for haddock and to the Lentrone great lines for cod to replace meat at Lent, St Monans still being an almost wholly Roman Catholic community.

Division of catch and profits was on the basis of one share for each man and one for the boat. A 'fry' for consumption by the families was divided on the same principle. Selected fish were laid out on the deck, a crew member would turn his back and the skipper, pointing to the fish at random, would ask, 'Wha taks this ane?'

The division of money, called 'counting the sculls', a reference to the wicker baskets which held the lines, could occupy a whole winter's night. The crew met the skipper, who would place the takings for the week in a wooden cup or platter. He then proceeded to dole out the shares, hopeful that the last recipient was not short, or that there were no coins left in the kitty! So acrimonious did this sharing of the deals become that, occasionally, the minister, never welcome at any other time at the harbour, had to be called in to see fair play! There was, however, a great advantage to this ancient custom. Every man knew that it was in his own interests to work hard, so that his application and industry would be rewarded. The democracy of the division avoided all wage disputes and any need for a trade union.

There was undoubtedly great rivalry between the fishers in the different villages of the East Neuk. The *East of Fife Record* of 1871 highlights the length to which such opposition could be taken. A Crail correspondent wrote to the Editor, answering an allegation, printed the previous week:

> ... that the crews of two St Monance boats had cut the lines and taken the fish belonging to a Crail boat. The skipper of one of the former totally denies the charge. Their lines, he says, were in the water before the Crail boat came out, and both his and the other St Monance crew advised the former to take up a position further south so as to prevent any danger of the lines being crossed, but this he refused to do, and shot his lines right across the front of their boats. The tide, as occasionally happens, might have cut the lines in consequence of their hanging to the bladders; but when they came across the Crail fishermen's lines, they drew their skulls through them and left them in the water as they were before. Very few fish were seen but not one was touched, and our informant states that for the past twelve or fifteen years, none of the St Monance fishermen ever thought of taking a fish from a line belonging to others of the same calling. Formerly, he said, it was quite common to do so; but on one occasion a man, reflecting that it took 14 fish before he was entitled to one, thought it was not worth while stealing his neighbour's fish for such a small share, and as more commendable ideas in

regard to 'meum' and 'teum' began to prevail, the custom had gradually been discontinued.

In later years, there would be confrontations, both verbal and physical, as the traditional drift-net fishers were at odds with the ring-net men.

The May Island Lighthouse

Charles I gave permission to Alexander Cuninghame of Barns to erect a lighthouse on the Isle of May to assist the fishers of the Forth. In 1636, John Cuninghame built a tower, forty feet high, vaulted at the top and covered in flagstones, where, all the year round, there burned a coal fire.

The fuel was supplied from the pits in Wemyss because of the hardness, durability and the clearness of the light. The beacon burned approximately one ton of coal on a summer's night, rising to nearly three tons in the dark of winter. This was the first permanently manned lighthouse in Scotland. Cuninghame was drowned while returning to the mainland in a storm, supposedly raised by an unhappy old woman called Eppie Laing, who was consequently burned as a witch. The fire was not without its dangers and, in 1791, the keeper, his wife and five children were suffocated by the sulphurous fumes. The main light was installed in 1816; in 1989, the modern high technology equipment was made to operate in a fully automatic mode.

Whaling

From 1757, a new era of fishing started in the East Neuk of Fife, with many able-bodied men and boys sailing as masters, harpooners, steersmen, line managers, seamen and apprentices in whaling ships out of Dundee and Aberdeen.

In 1817, men and women left the harvest fields crying, 'A ship a-fire!', as a tug, the first steam-boat to enter the Forth, sailed in and tied up at the pier at Anstruther. She was bringing back sixty-nine men from between St Monans and Crail employed in whaling. A coastal trader, her skipper had struck a deal to give the men passage 'with sea-chests, at eighteen pence [7½p.] per head'. The whalers were not always as lucky as to have transport home. Many had to walk the 'road and the miles tae Dundee' to secure a berth, and then to walk home again at the end of the long weary months or even years of voyaging. Nor did they have the advantage of the Tay Bridge, which did not open until 31st May 1878.

Sales, Couping and Smoking

The St Monans fishing scene is depicted, by the Reverend Gillies, in the *Old Account* of 1799:

> Formerly there was a very plentiful fishing upon the coast here, consisting of cod, ling, haddock, rowan or turbot, skait. [Sibbald recorded in 1803 that sturgeon was a prize catch in the Firth]. St Monance used to be one of the principal fish-towns upon the coast. But within these 4 or 5 years the fish have in a manner quite defeated these places, (particularly the haddock) and none are now caught but a few cod, rowan, and skait. Before, fish of all kinds were in great abundance, and at an easy rate, but now are very scarce, and high priced; not one haddock being taken in a whole year. There has been no sufficient cause as yet assigned for this remarkable change. The shoals of herring which used with great certainty to frequent the coast, particularly in the autumnal season, and likewise in the spring, are now become very precarious, and of no consequence. This great decrease of the fishing is a vast loss to this part of the country. For as fish was a principal part of the support of the inhabitants, other provisions have greatly advanced in price; and as great quantities of herrings, over and above the home consumpt, were cured and exported, trade has suffered much. Besides, the fishers are threatening an emigration to other places; though as yet only one man and family have left the parish this spring and gone to the town of Ayr, on the west coast.
>
> The common market for the fish is Edinburgh. They are bought up by the fishers of Fisherrow, who attend with their

11. Lassie gutters and drivers.

boats, purchase at sea, and carry them off. [This process became known as 'couping'.] Formerly the practice was, that out of the fleet of boats belonging to the town, two were obliged in their turn to come in to the harbour, and offer market for two hours, for the supply of the inhabitants. But that good regulation being now overlooked, the fishers have wholly laid it aside. This has enhanced the price of fish here, that it is but little below the market at Edinburgh, and they are difficult to be obtained. The lobsters are commonly taken in contract from the fishers by a Company, and carried alive to the London market and other places in England. In 1789, tens of thousands (20,000 from Crail alone) were sold in England at the sum of £12 10*s.* (£12.50p.) per thousand. The boats used in the fishing consist of a larger and smaller kind; of the former there are about 14, and of the latter about 20. The small are used both in summer and winter, in what they term the white fishing. Each of these require four men for the oars, and one steersman. With them, they fish with great and small line, for cod, rowan, haddock, and with nets for skate. The larger are used only in the herring fishing; and their complements of men are some six, some eight, according to their size, with a steersman. But besides these, there are a number of yawls, with which, through summer, they fish with the hand-line for the tanny cod, (or red ware cod, as they call it,) among the rocks and seaweed. The hands used in these, are commonly a man and boy, and sometimes only one man. Of the number of hands used in the fishing here, only such as are advanced in life hold close by it. The young men engage to the ships employed in the whale fishing; return when the herring fishing comes on in autumn; and, when that is over, engage themselves in voyages in private ships, in different places, during the winter season. By this means St Monance becomes a good nursery for sea men.

The nineteenth century ushered in a change of fortune for the Scots. Most of Catholic Europe bought its herring from Scotland; thousands of barrels were transported by rail into deepest Russia, forming, with potatoes, the staple diet of the peasantry. The

Napoleonic Wars found bread and meat very expensive, but fishing in the Firth of Forth brought a superabundance of herring in several successive years and a fleet of three hundred and sixty large boats and twelve hundred small ones had a bonanza. Harbours were improved, curing techniques refined, the 'Scotch cure' rivalling the Dutch; a board of commissioners was appointed and fishery officers employed. The summer of 1862 saw over a thousand boats in Wick for the herring.

Couping became highly organised and although cadgers (hawkers) and fish merchants from St Andrews and Dundee were to be seen regularly at the pier during the landing of the catches, gradually the couper, or cooper as he became known, was the great merchant of the coast. (This term is distinct from the same word cooper meaning a barrel maker.) Dispatch to the markets of London, Liverpool and Glasgow saw the use of larger boats, sailing under the flags of the Union Company and the UC Company.

Keeping the fish in prime condition was always a problem. Salting and pickling in brine had long been used but a new outlet for the East Neuk fishers was opened up by an Anstruther grocer, one Robert Taylor. His sailing by packet steamer from Edinburgh to Fife having been delayed, he took a walk into the High Street. The mail coach from Aberdeen had just arrived and he saw the guard deliver a package of Finan haddies, remarking as he did so, 'Haddies are dear nowadays in Finan.' Taylor's reaction was, 'Why not send smoked fish from Fife?' Experimenting in a hogshead barrel in his own backyard in Cellardyke, he quickly mastered the technique and had special premises built on the Brae. Fifty years on, the smoking trade was a thriving industry in the East Neuk. On 9th January 1869, deep-sea-going boats landed over fifty tons of what would become 'caller haddies'. Selling at ten shillings (50p.) per hundredweight (50 kilograms) 'smeekit haddies' were confidently shipped around the United Kingdom. Despite this success, by the end of the nineteenth century, smoking on a large scale had all but ceased. Today's smokies are once again largely the product of the small local fish merchants.

The *New Account* of 1845 showed the advances in fishing in the village over fifty years:

12. Local gutters at Peterhead circa 1925.
Back Row L-R: *Kate Bowman (Foreman); Maggie Thomas; Janet Cargill (Fyall); Bella Thomas.*
Front Row L-R: *Nina Fyall (Tarvit); John Thomas*, Maggie's son; unknown; Helen Taylor (Pittenweem); Ann Fyall (Buchan)*
**John was lost at sea in World War II.*

This is one of the principal fishing stations on the east coast of Scotland, and, including men, women and children, it may afford their chief occupation to about 300 individuals. The children, before they are able for harder work, go in great numbers, and to a distance of some miles, to gather bait. The women bait the lines. The men, including boys from fourteen to eighteen, go a-fishing. The herring-fishery is the great concern with our people. There is a partial herring-fishery, comparatively near to our own shores, in the winter and spring months. But it is the Caithness or north country fishing which forms the great object of attention to our people. From the latter part of June, and to the middle of July, they are in a bustle of preparation. The number of the boats fitted out is twenty-six, at fifteen tons each. The complement of men for each boat is five, in all 130 for twenty-six boats. St Monans does not furnish that number. There may be two men to each boat, strangers finding employment in our boats. These are

13. Mending the nets. Author's mother, Janet Lindsay and grandmother, Jenny Easson.

called half-deal men, from the limited proportion they receive of the profits, which is reasonably so limited, because, while they furnish their own nets, they have no property in the boats. The following may be taken as a tolerably accurate statement of the cost of fitting out one of our principal boats for sea. Boat with all her tackling and appurtenances, L. 85; 20 nets at L. 4 each, L. 80; provisions, L. 30. Every net is about 50 yards long, and fifteen score meshes wide, 32 meshes in the yard, the mesh 1¼ [sic] inch. The engagement which our people enter into with the fish-dealers is for six weeks; but the bargain is understood to have been implemented by the fishers of any one boat when they have caught 250 barrels, in howsoever short a time.

Cod-fishing for export is carried on to a considerable extent here. The packing furnishes employment and maintenance to many females. This fishing, however, is of very limited duration. When the herring disappear in the end of winter, it ceases of course, as it is with herring-bait that the cod are taken.

The cod, when cured, are sent to the London and Liverpool markets. Haddocks, turbot, cod, are, in their several seasons, sent in great quantities to the Edinburgh market, and also supply our own adjacent country by means of cadgers and fish-women.

Lobsters have been selling for five shillings [25p.] per score but the price has risen to twelve [60p.] and there is excited speculation that they might even fetch a shilling [5p.] each!

Besides 26 boats of about 15 tons, there are perhaps 14 yawls of 7½ tons. In 1858, the herring landings, in crans, at Anstruther and Cellardyke, Pittenweem and St Monans were 6,676, 1,263 and 1,316 respectively.

Navigation: There are two trading vessels belonging to the port; a schooner seventy-eight tons old register; a sloop belonging to the same owners, forty tons old register. These vessels are chiefly employed in the coasting-trade. It is very seldom that we are visited by foreign vessels.

The Fleet

The role of fishing in the economy of the East Neuk is well illustrated by reference to the First Annual Report of the Fishery Board for Scotland for 1883. Anstruther had become one of the twenty-six fishing districts into which the coast of Scotland had been divided. There were no fewer than 830 boats listed between

14. Preparing the gear in the Coal Wynd 1930s.

Buckhaven and St Andrews. They were classified by keel length: first class over 30 feet, second between 18-30 ft., and third under 18 feet. The report reads: 'The first-class boats of this district have an aggregate tonnage of 9,646 tons, the second-class, 838 tons, and the third-class, 179 tons – the total tonnage of the 830 boats being 10,663 tons. The number of fishermen and boys employed that year was 3,491; there were 46 fish-curers, 76 coopers, and other persons connected with the industry were estimated at 2,362, bringing up the total number of persons employed to 5,975. The value of the boats was estimated at £66,960, the nets at £95,584, the lines at £14,132 – making a grand total of £176,676.' Although the number of boats was only one eighteenth of the whole of the Scottish fleet, the tonnage was one eleventh and the value of boats, nets and line, was one eighth. By 1894, the number of boats had dropped to 686, the tonnage to 9,613 and the crews to 2,980.

The Steam Trawlers and Drifters

The era of steam trawling lasted exactly a century. On 2nd

November 1877, the first catch by a steam trawler, the *Messenger*, was landed at North Shields and was worth £750. One hundred years later, the *Northern Sceptre* reached the end of her useful life, when she was towed to the breakers at Medway.

Captain William Purdy of North Shields first thought of trawling with a steam paddle tug, when the local shipping industry was going through a lean time, as the railways were taking away trade. His idea was considered 'hopeless, impractical, absurd and new-fangled'.

However, Captain Purdy bought a trawl from Grimsby for ten guineas, paid five guineas for trawl heads to be fabricated, spent another three pounds ten shillings on trawl beams and fitted the gear to a jib crane near the mid-ship's funnel. Built of wood, the *Messenger* was some thirty four years old and developed twenty five horsepower. On 1st November 1877, she sailed out with just two experienced fishermen in her crew to handle the beam trawl, Alexander Fyall of St Monans and Thomas Thomlinson of North Shields. Their success was followed by more tug conversions. The advance was not welcomed by line boat fishermen, who showered the trawlers with stones if they went into 'stranger' ports. Soon purpose-built craft were made to order and the *Bonito*, the first launched on the Tyne, was taken to sea by, now, Captain Fyall. Having first sailed as cabin boy and cook in his father's sloop in St Monans, he made a name for himself among the trawling fraternity, becoming commodore of the big Irvin Company.

By 1890, a great fleet of steam trawlers and drifters were operation, the first of the latter in the East Neuk appearing in Anstruther in 1892. Both types of vessel were to see sterling service in the two World Wars. The Anstruther fleet of nineteen drifters in 1938 had dwindled to three in ten years. Now, like the old steam trawlers, they have disappeared from the fishing scene.

Salmon Fishing

The abundance of salmon in the Firth of Forth saw the arrival, in the summer months, of itinerant fishers, with their oar-propelled cobles and special nets. The sandy 'goats', or ravines between the rocks, made the coast from the Lady's Rock to Newark's beehive doocot, a favourite spot for their operations. The nearby grassy banks were festooned with frames for drying the salmon nets in the sun and wind.

However, more profitable salmon fishing was often found by local fishermen on the Tyne. Licensed by the Tyne Board of Commissioners at five pounds per boat, the two-man craft carried long float nets as employed in herring drift netting but of greater mesh size. Their permitted areas were from low-water mark to three miles seawards. In a good year, catches worth £250 per man were common.

Decline of the Industry

The serious decline of the Scottish fishery started after the Great War. In 1913, there were 32,678 fishermen with 52,338 dependent jobs. By 1937, the numbers had dwindled to 19,327 and 35,063 respectively; the corresponding numbers for vessels were 8,534 and 5,217. In stark contrast, in Norway, the number of fishermen rose from 63,000 in 1913 to 120,000 in 1936 and vessels from 59,000 open and 7,000 decked, to 63,000 and 12,000 respectively. Denmark and Sweden showed similar increases but advances in Iceland and the Faroes were even more remarkable.

By 1929, crisis point had been reached. A government investigation resulted in the passing of the Herring Industries Act in 1935 and the establishment of the Herring Board. The White Fisheries were covered by the Sea Fishing Industry Act of 1938. This willingness by government to help constructively saw renewed vigour in the industry but the outbreak of war in 1939 effectively destroyed all possibility of real recovery.

Despite enemy action, limited fishing did take place in both wars. It is interesting to note, from the *East Fife Observer* of 1917, that herring fetched a record 286 shillings (£14.30p.) per cran. The total landing, in rough weather, was 4¾ crans! Before the start of the conflict in 1914, the newspaper had noted the landing of twenty-seven crans at St Monans by the *Ruby*, KY448; the sale price was 28 shillings (£1.40p.) per cran! The fisherman of Crail, working in-shore with smaller boats, kept going through the war. In the week ending 1st June 1915, they shipped '626 barrels of partons [crabs] and 56 bags of whelks'.

15. Landing the catch – 1920s.

A cold job for one of the youngest workers at Yarmouth. Henry Guthrie (14), of St Monance, distributing ice among herring which have been landed on the Yarmouth quayside.

16. A cold job at fourteen. Henry Guthrie at the Herring at Yarmouth.

In the second World War, out of nearly 17,000 Scottish fishermen, no fewer than 10,000 served in the Royal and Merchant Navies. The Admiralty commandeered 671 Scottish fishing vessels, many of which never returned to the fishing. Sadly, every Scottish harbour lost someone.

The statistics of the following table show the drastic decline of the East Neuk fishing industry in ten years.

Not only had the numbers of boats and men diminished, in the case of St Monans by two thirds, but the herring shoals had to all intents and purposes disappeared. The higher catches at Anstruther and Cellardyke and the lower ones at Pittenweem were largely due to the size of boat.

Fishing Statistics

	Boats	*Tons*	*Men*	*Herring (cwt.)*	*Price (£)*	*Other Fish* (cwt)	*Price (£)*
St Monans							
1938	42	1,216	276	35,070	11,079	22,977	4,623
1948	17	242	92	46	48	4,454	9,047
Pittenweem							
1938	37	459	161	11,760	3,009	10,117	11,119
1948	30	390	157	17	11	9,173	21,276
Anstruther & Cellardyke							
1938	33	992	252	97,769	30,225	389	375
1948	22	441	131	32	37	5,642	12,823

St Monans Fishing Vessels (1920)

Registered in Kirkcaldy

Steamers & Drifters

KY	Owner	Tons
4 *Pride of Buchan*	J. Wood (Allan) and Julian Wood	86
69 *White Rose*	F. J. Offard	42

143 *Camelia*	P. Aitken (Hutt), R. Aitken (Dunn)	85
164 *Diligence*	T. Adam (Davidson) & Andrew Adam	85
172 *Lucy Mackay*	Robert Mackay, Wm. Mackay, J. Mackay (Smith) and P. Marr (Mackay)	94
208 *Ocean Angler*	Wm. Duncan and Alex. Hutt (Allan)	84

Sailing Boats

1 *Mary Duncan* (Motor)	James, George, Mary and Dav. M. Duncan	45
38 *Elspeth Smith* (Motor)	J., A., & M. Smith	56
51 *Celtic* (Motor)	Jas. Mackay	40
146 *Chrysanthemum*	Andrew Davidson & David Irvine	40
213 *Balmoral*	James Smith	39
280 *Linaria Alba* (Motor)	James, Alexander, & And. Innes	40
286 *Alice*	Philip Smith	40
421 *Gleaner*	D. & J. Marr	50
448 *Ruby*	J. & W. S. Bonthron	51
592 *Busy Bee*	J. A. Davidson	35
599 *Vigilant*	Thos. Adam & A. Adam	36
615 *Children's Trust*	Wm. Reekie	36
640 *Vesper* (Motor)	Alex. Reid	40
658 *Fyalls*	P., T., & T., jnr., Fyall	55
661 *Sunshine*	Wm. & Jas. Innes	54
665 *Promote*	R. Scott (Duncan), D. Scott (Allan)	52

Registered in Methil (ML)

Steamers & Drifters

122 *Lizzie Hutt*	Jas. Hutt, Chapman Innes & Eliza Hutt	27
123 *Christina Mayes*	John Mayes	26

Fishing

125 *Mackays*	D., Rbt., Alex & D. Smith, jnr.	30
126 *Janet Reekie*	Wm., Rbt., David, Alex & Chas. Reekie	26

Sailing Boats

9 *Pansy*	Rbt., Wilson, R. jnr. & John Reekie	41
15 *Harvest Moon*	Wm., Alex, James & G. Gowans	40
20 *True Vine*	David Marr	53
30 *Ann Cook*	Alex & Andrew Fyall	38
41 *Marjory*	Charles Mackay	48
48 *Verbena*	John Fernie, Jas. & Robert Wilson	39
50 *Agnes Irvine*	Alex Irvine	52
63 *Clan Mackay*	Rbt., Thos. & Jas. Mackay	51
80 *Endeavour*	John Cargill	42
84 *Chrysophrase*	Tom, Dd., John & Janet Morris	40
97 *Trust On*	Chapman Lowrie, Th. Anderson & David Irvine	40
117 *White Heather*	Alex, David & Andrew Morris & T. Gay (Morris)	43
198 *Lively Hope*	J. Allan, snr. & J. Allan, jnr.	41
217 *Renown*	Chapman Fernie	40
241 *Celerity*	James Mayes & John Smith	42
245 *Carmania*	R. & W. Smith	45
271 *Celandine*	Alex. & Andrew Innes	45
280 *Protect Me*	Robert Marr	47
285 *Annie Mathers*	Chapman, John & William Mathers	48
290 *Vine*	Alex. Balfour	47
487 *Condor*	Jas. Lowrie & Allan Smith	47
488 *Celerity*	John Hughes & George Allan	47
489 *Children's Trust*	Rbt., Chas., Dd. & Alex. Reekie	41
494 *Gratitude*	Wm. Ovenstone	43

Chapter 13

Lost at Sea

EVERY MARITIME COMMUNITY is constantly aware that the sea, the symbol of Eternity, upon whose bounty it depends, often exacts a terrible repayment. While there have always been tragedies of individual seamen, washed or fallen overboard and drowned, often dragged down by the great weight of solid leather thigh boots, or killed by swinging booms, derricks, falling masts or rigging, or by machinery, the sinking or wreck of the boats themselves, often with entire crews, are major disasters in the tightly-knit fishing villages.

St Monans is no exception and time has left a sobering roll-call of losses of men, gear and boats. Typically, on 20th February 1833, a dreadful storm caught a fleet of East Neuk boats fishing the Forth for herring. They had shot and hauled their nets, catching four to eight crans each, when the tempest hit at midnight. The craft scattered, some making haven in Elie, Pittenweem or Cellardyke, but a St Monans yawl, skippered by Alexander Reekie, was lost with all five of the crew. Yet another, the *Rose in June*, was a little more fortunate. The skipper, Andrew Davidson, and his mate, John Allan, were drowned, but the other four hands were saved. Again, the Reverend Robert Swan recorded that, at that point in his ministry of thirty-three years, no fewer than twenty-seven men had perished at sea. He actually held office for forty-five years, dying on 16th November 1849.

Mid-century, the *East Fife Record* reported

> ... the loss of the schooner, *Rival*, of Goole, under which command of the owner, Captain Drury, sailed from St Monance with a lading of 670 barrels of cured herrings for Hamburg. The schooner was wrecked in the island of Inist, and, as none

of the crew were heard of, it is supposed that they had all perished. When the *Rival* sailed from St Monance, there were on board, besides the crew, Captain Drury's wife, two sons and a daughter and it is now definitely reported that all these have met with a watery grave. A striking incident is further reported in reference to this melancholy disaster, as we learn that Captain Drury had a son and daughter who survive him. This daughter, it is stated, had intended going with her parents on the voyage, but, at the last moment, she determined on stopping with some friends at Leith.

Yet the blackest day in the history of East Fife fishing was Friday, 19th November 1875. The herring season at Great Yarmouth and Lowestoft, which lasted, nominally, from October through November, had been started in 1863 by a single boat, appropriately named the *Hope*. By 1875, no fewer than eighty-two sailing 'Fifies', many built in the St Monans yards, had ventured south. Two-masted, clinker-built with two lug-sails and a jib, measuring forty to forty-five feet overall and of fifteen to eighteen tonnage, some were half and others three-quarter-decked, the aft end being entirely open for the working of the drift nets. The St Monans fleet, numbering thirty, were joined by forty-three from Cellardyke and nine from Pittenweem.

Some set sail for home in the first week in November and arrived at their destinations without incident. However, the majority left on the morning of Friday the nineteenth, and were caught in a week of hurricane weather. No fewer than five boats, three from St Monans and two from Cellardyke, were lost with all hands.

The first casualty was the *Quest*, KY221, out of St Monans, a craft of keel length thirty-nine feet, which foundered and was driven ashore, a broken and dismasted wreck, at Blakeney on the coast of Norfolk, with the loss of all seven crewmen. They were: David Allan, skipper, married, six children; Alan, his son, unmarried; William, his brother, married, five children; Alexander Irvine, married, seven children; and Alexander Hutt, Alexander Latto and David Easson, all single men. From the loss of seven men were left, three widows and eighteen children.

Eight days after the storm, the steamer *Sea Nymph*, making

passage from Hull to King Lynn, recovered the *Beautiful Star*, KY1298, of St Monans, keel length forty-three feet. In the water-logged hull were found the drowned bodies of the skipper and four hands. The former had suffered a fractured skull and the others appeared to have been below, rendering him assistance, when tragedy struck. Examination of the wreck suggested that the heel of the twenty feet high mast had come out of the step and, falling aft, had crashed across the cabin entrance, making escape impossible. Two other crew members were missing, presumed drowned.

Next, a Trinity House cutter sighted the top of a mast on a half-tide scalp, or mussel bed, near Boston Deeps on the Wash. It proved to be a third St Monans boat, the *Thane*, KY1071, with a keel length of forty-one feet. She had obviously been run down as eight strakes of planks were cut through. On the wreck being towed ashore, there were found the bodies of Thomas Lowrie, Alexander Duncan and Thomas Fyall, those of the skipper, also Thomas Fyall, and the rest of the crew being missing. The skipper was married with two children, his brother Lawrence, unmarried, David Lowrie, married with five children, the afore-mentioned Thomas Fyall and Alexander Duncan, both married, the latter with three children, Thomas Lowrie married and Andrew Allan, a bachelor. The boat was owned by the skipper and David Lowrie. From Cellardyke, the craft lost were the *Janet Anderson*, KY1176, owner James Murray, senior master James Murray junior, with a keel length forty-one feet, and the *Vigilant*, KY1214, owner and master Robert Stewart, with a similar keel length.

In all, thirty-seven fishermen had perished, leaving nineteen widows and seventy-two orphans, besides a number of elderly relatives who depended on the seamen's support.

In St Monans, one unfortunate woman, Mrs Patterson, lost no fewer than nine of her kin: her husband, son, two brothers, three nephews, a brother-in-law and a cousin. Another, Mrs Allan, then about seventy years of age, lost two sons, two nephews, her son-in-law and two grandsons.

The mass funerals were held at the Borough Cemetery on Hardwick Road, Kings Lynn. Three of the fishermen had belonged to the Guiding Star Lodge of Good Templars, from Cellardyke, and no sooner was this known than the Lynn Lodges undertook the pious duty of the burials. Two hundred and fifty fishermen from the Royal Naval Reserve joined some nine thousand mourners in the singing of the final hymn, 'Safe in the arms of Jesus'.

A memorial in Kenton stone was erected, six feet two inches in length, weighing one-and-a-half tons, and set on a five-and-a-half ton pedestal. A representation of the *Beautiful Star* in the wrecked condition in which she was salvaged by the *Sea Nymph*, it was modelled on the memorial to Grace Darling in Bamborough churchyard. Daughter of the lighthouse keeper of the Farne Islands, she was the heroine who rescued a woman and four men from the wreck of the steamer *Forfarshire* in 1838.

The memorial is inscribed thus:

On the boat:
Beautiful Star KY1298 St Monance.

At the bow:
This monument erected by public subscription to the memory of eight Scotch fishermen drowned on the Norfolk coast in the November gale 1875.

Beneath the stern:
Life, how short! Eternity, how long?

On the pedestal:
Starboard side:
David Allan born 28 August 1827
Alexander Duncan born 7 June 1829
Thomas Lowrie born 3 October 1854
Thomas Fyall born 27 June 1851

Beneath:
When the shore is won at last,
Who will count the billows past?

Port side:
James Patterson born 18 July 1826
David Davidson born 1 February 1852
William Patterson born 18 January 1836
son Robert Patterson born 31 October 1857

17. 'The Beautiful Star' memorial. King's Lynn, Norfolk.

Beneath:

While we linger on the shore of life,
A wave wafts us to eternity.

The complete monument cost thirty pounds, with eight pounds for cemetery fees and installation.

A poet of the time penned the following lines:

Twas bleak November and the nineteenth day,
They left the port their season's labour done,
Brilliant with hope that they again should see,
Those friends they loved so dear, their friends at home.

Swiftly she glides across the raging main,
The 'Beautiful Star', with all her manly crew,
Destined, alas that they should never gain
Those shores for which they steer and billows plough.

The East Neuk rallied to the relief of the bereaved. Lady Anstruther personally comforted all the distressed and Sir Robert convened a meeting in St Monans Town Hall. He proposed to form a committee to start a Common Fund for the relief of widows and orphans in St Monans and Cellardyke. The trustees appointed for St Monans were the Chief Magistrate, Nicol by name, together with Messrs Robert McFarlane, James Robertson, James Trainer, George Bridges, David Hutt, Thomas Murray, and John Lockie, minister of the Free Church.

Events to raise funds were held all over Fife. In Colinsburgh, a bazaar, hosted by Lady Lindsay of Balcarres, raised £346 6*s.* 8*d.* (£346.33p.), the final total reaching £7,206 15*s.* 3*d.* (£7,206.76p.). Widows were allocated four shillings (20p.) per week with one shilling and sixpence (7 ½p.) for each child; their school shoes and books were also paid.

This terrible calamity had one good effect. From that time onwards, the boats fishing in the area were much larger. In the following ten years, sixty foot fully-decked boats were being used and, by the turn of the century, seventy foot boats were almost standard.

In retrospect, the disaster had been effectively predicted, some six or seven weeks earlier, by an article in a Norfolk newspaper. Reproduced in the *East of Fife Record* of 8th October 1875, the opening paragraph referred to the relative frailty of the craft:

> The Scotch Fishermen at Yarmouth – *The Yarmouth Independent* of Saturday last, in a lengthened notice regarding the herring fishing now commenced there, gives the following complimentary remarks on the appearance and exemplary behaviour of our fishermen, when fishing on the English coast;- 'The Scotch boats are doubtless good sea boats but not so large as our own, and less able therefore to stand against very rough weather. They must therefore wait for a favourable change when they will put to sea, and as they fish close by home we shall then hope to have some fresh herring. While referring to the Scotch boats it may be mentioned that the sailing powers of these boats were displayed in a very remarkable degree in their passage from the north to this port. One boat called the *Favourite* sailed from Anstruther to Yarmouth, a distance of over 300 miles, in thirty-two hours and, for the last hundred miles of the journey, she and her fellow countrymen kept pace with the steamers, plying between the

north and London. Of course, the wind was fair for sailing, but under the most favourable circumstances, the passage was an extraordinary rapid one. We are glad to see the Scotch fishermen amongst us again. They are an example to our own fishermen, and we hope they may have a beneficial influence upon them. It is a pleasure to see the Scotchmen, clean and respectably dressed, walking about the streets of the town, and enjoying themselves at national amusements, keeping clear of the public houses and low company and conducting themselves in a respectable and orderly manner. On Sunday, too, most of them attend some place of worship, thus showing that regard for the Sabbath Day, which is so characteristic of their people. If our fishermen and smacksmen would imitate their Scotch brethren, they would be better men, better servants and better off pecuniarily. The publicans would have less of their money and their wives and families would be better provided for. Many of our fishermen earn a large amount of money during the herring fishing, but are little better off for it. To quote the oft-repeated saying of Mr J. Hammons, 'they earn their money like horses and spend it like asses'. This cannot be said of the canny Scotchman. He is too wide awake to put his earnings into the pockets of the publican or spend it in other foolish ways so well known to our fishermen. He values his own respectability and the comfort and happiness of his wife and family too much to be entrapped into such dissipations, and, like a wise man, when he earns his money, he takes care of it.'

In 1906, Mr James Miller, the local boat-builder, sent a post-card to his wife, then on holiday in Ceres. Taken at the West Shore, the scene shows the maternal grandfather of Willie Miller, Alexander Irvine, one of the crew of the *Quest*, who was drowned. He is seen carrying a plank of wood and may have been preparing for the ill-fated trip. He left a wife and seven children, one of whom was Willie's mother, Janet Irvine. The card was discovered by Willie's daughter, Mrs Jenny McDonald of Picton, New Zealand. She made the following comment: 'That particular scene looks very similar today except that you would be hard pushed to find a horse

18. Setting off for the fatal drave of 1875.

and cart, or a woman wearing a mutch. The tall masts have vanished too; in fact, there are few masts of any size in what was once a busy and thriving port.' She added the following charming anecdote of her innocence as a wee lassie at the time of her great-grandma Janet's funeral, her only memory of the lady. 'I asked my mother [Jeannie Bowman], "What dis God dae wi' a' the empty boxes?"'

On the hundreth anniversary of the disaster, a descendant of Thomas Lowrie of the *Thane*, Mrs Jean Jenkins of Brundall, Norfolk, discovered an interesting sequel to her maternal great-grandfather's boat. As was the custom, the wrecks were sold as salvage, part of the proceeds going to the cost of the burials and the monument and the residue to the East Neuk Fund.

It transpired that the *Thane* and the *Beautiful Star* had been repaired; the latter had her name changed to *Jacobina*. In the 1910s, they were used to bring shingle for the building trade from Snettisham Beach. The *Thane* was laid up on the west side of the river Great Ouse in the 1920s but was then transferred to Heacham harbour and used for summer holidays. With the rest of the boats moored there, she was swept away on the extraordinary floods which inundated the east coast of Norfolk in 1953.

Following the directions given her by an elderly gentleman,

who, as a lad, had sailed on the refurbished *Thane* with his father around 1910, Mrs Jenkins, with her husband Joe, searched the area and found the keel and timbers, deep in rushes and almost covered in silt. A description given to Willie Miller, the St Monans boatbuilder, of the shape of the timbers and the positions of the dowel pegs, confirmed that it was, indeed, the *Thane.*

The whaling too was a hazardous occupation. In 1830, as many as nineteen Scottish whalers were wrecked in the Polar seas, victims of storm, iceberg and the ever-menacing crush of pack ice, as happened in 1836 to the *Thomas* out of Dundee. Gripped fast in the ice for months, many died of scurvy, frost bite and malnutrition.

In both World Wars, many local boats were commandeered by the Admiralty. However, the nation had to be fed and unarmed fishing vessels were prey to German surface raiders, U-boats and aircraft. On 6th July 1916, the St Monans boat *Watchful,* owned by Alexander Aitken, was sunk by submarine action while fishing off Shields. Fortunately, the crew were saved. Many fishermen joined the Naval Reserve in 1914–18, being engaged in patrolling, mine sweeping or other naval duties.

Over three hundred men were called to the Colours, some one hundred and fifty of them serving in the Army in Gallipoli, Egypt, Mesopotamia, Salonica and France.

The Second World War again saw the ready response of the men and women of the village to the three Services, the Women's Land Army, Air Raid Precautions and other duties. The war memorial in the upper churchyard of the Auld Kirk records the sad cost.

Chapter 14

The Harbour

Originally, the fishing boats or creers were hauled up onto the foreshore of the village. The approach was difficult and dangerous, being a narrow opening, or 'goat', between two ridges of rock, with the bottom very rough. By the mid-fifteenth century, the vassals of Baron Newark were set to erect a bulwark, which took two years in the building. On the site of the present Middle Pier, it was of poor construction but, after erosion by tide and gale, was improved and extended. In 1682, the great hurricane, which destroyed the early windmill, did much damage. A hundred years later, harbour walls had to be erected to prevent the ingress of sea water at high-tide into the houses of the feuars on the front. Like the Tolbooth, this improvement was paid by public subscription.

In 1816, a storm from the south-east breached the pier, again threatening houses on the north side of the market place. 'Notwithstanding the solemnity of the Sabbath', every townsman rallied to repair the damage; the threat to the livelihood of the village superseded the demands of the church.

The burgh records for 1859 report the negotiations for a loan from the Government to improve the harbour. This request 'to obtain a harbour of refuge' was denied, with an indication that help to Anstruther was favoured. The harbour had been surveyed in 1851 by Messrs Stevenson, the Engineers of the Fishing Board, who estimated that the necessary alterations would cost £8,000. The following significant reasons had been forwarded for the work:

1. There were now 85 boats whose tonnage was 1,275, plus 32 yawls. With the movement of the herring shoals further afield, the open-decked Skaffies, which had dominated the scene for

19. The early harbour.

years, were being replaced by the newly-designed Baldies, Fifies and Zulus.

2. There were 425 men employed.
3. The estimated value of the boats with their gear was £100 each and of the yawls £25 each.
4. The fishermen were making a weekly collection of £300 to consolidate a fund.
5. The Town Council were prepared to help and would underwrite a loan. Together with the fishermen, they would raise £350 per annum to pay off the principle and interest.
6. The upkeep of the harbour would come from Town Revenue.
7. There was an immediate need to increase the harbour accommodation. There was barely room to berth 30 boats. In bad weather, much damage was caused by overcrowding, craft often having to move to Elie or Pittenweem for safety. At the Lammas Drave, with all the fleet in use, twenty landed their catches regularly in Pittenweem, with subsequent loss of harbour dues. Others had to lie off and be accessed only when earlier boats had discharged their catch and come outside the harbour limits. On 26th July 1860, the records quoted the cost of enlargement at £2,850, including the straightening, strengthening and extension of the old pier westwards, by approximately half its length again; the new pier would measure 800 feet.

The fishermen agreed to pay two thirds and the Town Council pledged to raise £1,000. By 20th October 1860, this estimate had been rejected and a new one of £4,000 made. The National Bank of Scotland was asked for, and agreed to, £3,500, the Town Council signing on behalf of the fishers; the sum was subsequently raised to £4,500. The proposal to extend the railway to St Monans at that time would obviously enhance the importance, and increase the marketing profitability of the village. Anstruther and Pittenweem fishers became aware of the competition and they took up the challenge. Seven estimates, ranging from £4,933 14*s* 10*d.* (£4,933.74p.) to £8,699, were offered against the specification. The second cheapest, £5,066 18*s* 8*d.* (£5,066.93p.) plus a contingency of £133 3*s.* 4*d.* (£133.17p.) totalling £5,200, was accepted from Alexander Kinghorn of Leith; monies would be paid in stages by Messrs Stevenson but, as a safeguard, thirteen per cent would be kept back from the contractors. Agreements had to be obtained from the Lords of the Admiralty and from the Commissioners of Her Majesty's Woods and Forests! The former's condition was that the Commander of Coast Guard, or persons duly authorised, would have the authority to inspect, whenever necessary, for the conservation of navigation and the protection of the public. The latter's requirements were to be informed of the proposed tolls and harbour dues. It was reported on 22nd July 1861 by the Town Clerk, John Bowman, that these sanctions had been granted, albeit there were still problems as to the ownership of lands at the shore-line, which the new harbour would now encompass.

On 29th November 1861, it was announced that Messrs Stevenson had appointed as inspector, Mr David Matherr. He had just finished a contract as inspector at Buckhaven harbour and the new lighthouse at St Abb's Head. Although he had been paid ten shillings per day plus lodging allowance at the latter site, and despite the Town Council's offer of two pounds for his six-day week, a flat rate of eight shillings (40p.) per day was agreed.

Temporary accommodation for the workers was erected on the Mair. The work began in June 1861, but was brought to a halt because of lack of funds and a strike for higher wages. The stoppage was reported in the *East Fife Record* of 12th April 1862 as follows:

> The New Harbour Works – A commencement has at length been made in the erection of the new harbour here, for which the resident fishermen of St Monance, aided by a few influential persons, have so liberally agreed to tax themselves. The contractor of the works commenced about a fortnight since to excavate rocks where the new basin is to be, which is immediately to the east of the present harbour. Already, however, a partial stoppage has taken place, owing to a number of the labourers having struck for an advance of wages. This is only the case with regard to the labourers employed, the masons not having struck, but are still busy hewing the stones as they are excavated. The masons are paid by day wages, while

> the labourers work by the tide, at so much an hour. This temporary stoppage, we hear, is likely soon to be remedied, and the work will go on with all despatch. It is expected that they will be so far completed as to allow the new harbour to be used by the fishermen at the Lammas fishing of next year. There appears to be an abundance of block of excellent large stones on the spot, and already a great many of these have been excavated, dressed and ready for being placed.

By June 1862, Kinghorn, the contractor, reported that the stone being excavated from the harbour was not enough to complete the work. Furthermore, the great bulk of the face-work of the sea wall and quay must be obtained elsewhere. He proposed that the use of Carlinnose greenstone for the outer facing would give a much superior job.

This change of material would raise the costs by at least £650, the price of the Carlinnose being thirty-four shillings (£1.70p.) per yard, that from Grange and other quarries, fifteen shillings (75p.) per yard. The original estimate had been based on ten shillings (50p.) per yard. This increase provoked hostility in the fishermen and the threat of a lawsuit against Kinghorn.

However, the foundation stone was laid on 10th March 1863, this date being chosen as it was a national holiday on the occasion of the wedding of the Prince of Wales, later King Edward VII, to Princess Alexandra, daughter of King Christian IX of Denmark. Although seldom, if ever, used nowadays, it was named Alexandra Pier. The ceremony was recorded as follows by Baillie William Marr.

> On the eventful morning, baillies and councillors marched in procession from the Town Hall towards Pittenweem, Freemasons bringing up the rear. They were accompanied by the greater proportion of the inhabitants, all in high spirits and displaying a goodly number of flags. At the eastern boundary of the parish, they were met by a similar concourse of people, from Pittenweem, Anstruther and elsewhere, headed by the Anstruther Volunteers Brass Band and many Freemasons, mostly from St Adrian's Lodge, Pittenweem. They turned back over the new railway bridge, proceeding through the

village and down to the pier, near low water mark, the band playing all the while a variety of lively airs. John Williamson, Right Worshipful Master of Lodge St Adrian, and Depute Grand Master for the occasion, laid the stone with due masonic ceremony. Eight lines of the 'Auld Hunder' were sung, the Chaplain gave an appropriate prayer and the large stone was lowered into position. In a receptacle beneath it, had been placed a bottle, sealed with the village's second motto 'Grip Fast' and containing coins, newspapers and a document, descriptive of the work. A copy had been read aloud during the earlier proceedings and the pier now named, was soon baptised by the pure ocean wave. During this solemn, imposing scene, the utmost stillness pervaded the whole of the vast assembly of people. Nothing was heard but the voices of the officiating speakers, except, of course, the roar, at regular intervals, of the wild waves, dashing on the rocks a few yards distance and the occasional peal from the two-pounder cannons, stationed at the head of the pier to grace the occasion and manned by a party of our Naval Coast Volunteers. After the ceremony, the masons and magistrates adjourned to the Parish schoolroom, where a substantial lunch stood in readiness. Suitable toasts and speeches, followed by appropriate airs from the band, formed the principal feature of the proceedings there.

Shortly after, the masons and other strangers began their march homewards, accompanied a considerable part of the way by the magistrates and inhabitants, all of whom felt highly indebted to them for their hearty co-operation and interesting visit. The whole proceedings terminated amicably and to the entire satisfaction of all concerned.

The special stone was brought from the quarry near Inverkeithing in the sloop *Blossom* but, initially, progress was slow. The finishing of the local railway track in 1863 released a considerable work force and the task was completed on 16th January 1865, except for some rock to be removed in the spring. Exactly a year previously, Kinghorn had pulled out of the contract, claiming that he was not being paid appropriately. Two years later, he was dead and his executors were demanding payment, claiming to have shipped in 1,444 yards 2 feet 4 inches of greenstone at 30*s* 4½*d.* (£1.52p.) per yard. The total demand was for £2,249 1*s* 4*d.* (£2,249.7p.) but the arbiters in the dispute granted only £680.

The eventual total settlement required was £1,250, so the council and skippers met on 17th October 1868 and signed a joint pledge to clear the debt.

The attendees and signatories	
Members of Council	*Skippers*
Bailies:	David Hutt
Peattie	John Ovenstone
Small	Thomas Aitken
Marr	Philip Scott
Councillors:	David Easson Jr.
I. Ovenstone	Thomas Wilson
David Marr	Robt. Reekie (Simpson)
Robt. Macfarlane	John Fyall
John Fulton	William Duncan
Henry Guthrie	David Allan (Gowans)
Robt. Reekie (Simpson)	Robert Allan
Robt. Mackay	James Hutt
James Trainer	John Reekie (Bowman)
James Paterson	John Innes
David Latto	Chapman Mathers
	Thomas Aitken J. (Marr)
	Philip Aitken
	David Allan
	James Paterson
	Wm. Mathers (Hutt)
	Wm. Meldrum

Bailie Peattie in the chair.

20. The harbour from the Neuk.

Proposed in June 1877, started in 1878 and completed the following year at an estimated cost of £5,000, financed by the fishermen, was the construction of new Middle and West Piers, the latter 435 feet long. In the event, with a bond on the skippers, the National Bank lent £7,500. A concrete breakwater to shield the entrance was also built at that time.

The piers were designed by Thomas Stevenson (1818–87). His father, Robert (1772–1850), was the pioneer of pier and lighthouse building, among his achievements being the famous lighthouse on the Bell Rock. Thomas ran the company with his brother David, also an engineer and designer. His son, Robert Louis Stevenson (1850–94), the author of such classic novels as *Treasure Island, Kidnapped* and *Catriona,* spent holidays in St Monans, while his father supervised the construction of these Victorian piers.

In March 1879, a bid for a slipway at the upper end of the new West Pier, to cost £207, was rejected as being too expensive.

Reported in the *Fife News* on 11th October 1879 a memorial stone was erected on the West Pier. There was no ceremony like the splendid occasion of 1863, but again a bottle was entombed, 'containing coins of the realm, a few *cartes-de-visite* of some of the harbour promoters and the newspapers of the day, including the *Fife News,* with details of the construction.'

The contractors were John Jackson & Co. of Glasgow, the manager, Edward Challoner, the inspector, John Nicholson and the engineers, again David and Thomas Stevenson.

Space had been left for a 'Public Necessity'! On 22nd May 1880, the Council ordered immediate estimates for construction in wood or iron. They were still considering this '*Clochemerle*' on 3rd May 1884! John Anderson's bid was £6 *5s.* (£6.25p.) for a roof of wood and £7, if in iron.

The construction of the pier had had its problems, the contractors regularly threatening to sue the fishermen for their boats colliding with, and demolishing, scaffolding on nearly every tide. In the *Annual Report of the Fishery Board for Scotland* for 1883, it is stated that:

> The fishermen of St Monance, to their great credit, unaided by any public grant, erected a good harbour there, at a cost

> of about £15,000. The increased size of the boats now engaged in the fisheries rendered it absolutely necessary that some rock should be excavated, and the outer entrance channel to the harbour widened, but the fishermen were quite unable to raise the amount required for these additional works. After having made full enquiry into the whole circumstances of the case, we resolved that, in the event of the fishermen paying us £500, we would expend an amount not exceeding £2,000 in all towards carrying out what was required. This £500 was sent to us, and we had the gratification of ordering the works to be proceeded with.

A year earlier the Board had reported that on the whole east coast of Scotland there were only four really good harbours for fishing boats, namely, those at Aberdeen, Peterhead, Fraserburgh and Cluny harbour at Buckie.

The Burgh Records of 12th January 1884 noted the above, adding that a bond, subscribed by thirty-nine skippers, pledged that every sea-going fisherman would contribute ten shillings (50p.) to the National Bank of Scotland.

Over the years, the repairs of many breaches of the sea walls were paid for by the Town Council.

By 1899, Fishery Board grants were being based on the weight of fish landed at each harbour. The following table summarises the allocations.

Harbour	*Landing in hundredweight (50 kilograms)*	*Grant (£)*
Elie & Earlsferry	1,195	518
St Monans	25,499	9,749
Pittenweem	9,807	3,588
Anstruther & Cellardyke	143,223	51,068
Crail	1,831	728

The Burgh Records, for 7th June 1902, noted plans to improve the harbour and deepen the basins. The cost of approximately

21. Matthie's monument.

£5,230 would be subsidised by a grant of £3,750 from the Fishery Board of Scotland, if £1,500 could be raised locally. Again the Bank approved the loan, albeit there was still a debt of £5,398 14*s* 9*d.* (£5,398.74p.).

Finished in 1905, the work was accomplished under David Stevenson's son, Charles. There were no pneumatic drills nor electricity and Willie Miller, who became the Director of his ancestors' boatyard at the harbour, recalled, as a boy, the blasting, the removal of material by horse-and-cart and the men working under the light of paraffin flares.

The *East Fife Observer* of 1936 recorded: 'A notable event was the redemption of a debt of £8,000, incurred by the fishermen in connection with harbour improvements in 1878. The final discharge after long-overdue debt was accelerated by the Bank, writing off £225.' The accolade of the Fishing Board had been somewhat misplaced!

At the top of the West Pier, on the previous site of Walter Reekie's shed, a slipway to accommodate boats for refurbishment or painting was built for Millers in the 1970s. Stones from the old railway station at Anstruther were used in the construction of the winch house.

Today, between the harbour mouth and the west breakwater can be seen a concrete block on which is mounted a much-rusted metal pole, the structure being known as Matthie's Monument. This was an aid to sailing boats, when adverse weather made leaving the harbour hazardous. The technique was to secure one end of a rope around a paul or mooring post on one of the piers. The other was passed around the pole and the slack wrapped around the boat's steam-driven capstan. The vessel was then winched out clear of the harbour mouth into calmer waters. Boats would often have to wait in a queue to avail themselves of this primitive but effective facility. The name came from Matthew Peattie, who owned Craigie Wells farm and several other properties around St Monans. When it was decided to build a beacon on the rocks at the harbour mouth, Matthie, as he was known locally, defrayed the costs. The Peattie Family still live in the village; he was a great-uncle to Tom and Jean (Mrs James McKenzie).

In the absence of radio (invented 1895), television (1926) or the telephone (1876) (the first recorded use of the last in St Monans was by a council official on 15th March 1910), weather forecasting was based on local knowledge and the traditional folk-lore of 'A red sky at night ...' and such-like prophecies. Although an embryonic Meteorological Office was established in 1854, the first official daily forecast was given on 3rd September 1860, but was only available in London-based papers, such as the *Daily News*.

The mercury barometer had been invented by Torricelli, a pupil of Galileo, in Italy in 1644. However, poor fishing households could not afford to buy such an instrument or even the cheaper aneroid system. Accordingly, the Town Council decided to install a mercury version for common consultation. The minutes of 18th June 1870 recorded the condition of its use as follows:

> In respect that a barometer for the use of the inhabitants of St Monance generally was some time ago placed in the East Gable of the House in the Square belonging to Robert Robertson and that the placing of it there was granted as a favour by him, it is hereby recorded for the satisfaction of the said Robert Robinson [sic] and his successors and for the information of all concerned that the use of the said Gable for the purpose mentioned shall not at any time hereafter be founded on the part of those interested in the said Barometer, it being therefore admitted that the exclusive right of the said Robert Robertson to the said Gable remains.

Again, on 24th September 1870:

> In regard to the barometer on the Gable of Robert Robertson's property it was agreed to allow him a rent of one shilling per annum for the privilege; it being understood that if the Barometer is removed at any future time, the Town Council shall restore the Gable to its former state.

The minutes of 8th November 1894 record that the barometer had been damaged but had been replaced. Responsibility for it was then passed to the Harbour Commissioners. The casing was vandalised and the instrument stolen sometime in 1997. The great-grandson of Robert Robertson, Henry Guthrie, himself an ex-merchant seaman and Coastguard officer, who was born and had lived in the house for many years, has no knowledge of the rent ever having been paid in his grandparents', parents' or his own lifetime.

The harbour needed repairs in 1922, 1923 and 1929. In 1937, a meeting of the Harbour Commissioners was told that a grant of £3,213, mainly for the extension of the East Breakwater, had been promised by the Development Commissioners, following a recommendation by the Fishery Board. The sum was later increased

22. Old Timers.

because of rising building costs and the year closed with the scheme nearing completion. In 1996, extensive repairs were made to the west breakwater.

Sometimes a harbour belies its name and becomes a place of danger. The sea is ever a natural hazard and accidental duckings are not unusual, particularly at periods of high activity. Two dramatic rescues from very dangerous situations in St Monans harbour deserve mention. On 21st April 1890, Jock Fyall of the East Backgate, who was both blind and severely crippled, was saved by Henry Guthrie, grandfather of the aforementioned Henry. A cooper by trade, he was well known locally for his powerful swimming; the Royal Humane Society awarded him their Bronze Medal.

In the 1930s, Alex Scott, also of East Backgate, then a pupil at the local Primary School, while fishing, slipped headlong off the East breakwater. The incoming tide swept him into the harbour-mouth. He was saved from almost certain death by a passing visitor from Glasgow, James MacKechnie, who had sprinted from the East Shore to the end of the middle pier before diving in to the rescue. The local council honoured his bravery with the presentation of a wallet and a sum of money. Alex now lives in happy retirement with his wife Ena, née Bett of Cellardyke, in Melbourne, Australia.

Few fishing vessels use the harbour today, unless they are being winched ashore on the slipway at the West Pier for painting. There are several local yawls pursuing line-fishing and shooting creels for crab and lobster, but for St Monans, the fishing industry, once the mainstay of the economy, is no more.

Chapter 15

The Railway

THE ENHANCEMENT OF TRADE for the fishing community, by the introduction of steam locomotion to the area, has already been mentioned.

According to James K. Corstorphine in his book, *East of Thornton Junction*, the Fife Coast Line was constructed in six stages, by four separate companies during a thirty-five year period from 1851 to 1887. The first section to be opened was the Leuchars to St Andrews railway in 1852, closely followed by the Thornton to Leven branch in 1854. The line between Leven and Anstruther was built in two stages; the first to Kilconquhar was completed in 1857, with Anstruther being reached six years later. In 1883, the line was opened between Anstruther and Boarhills, but it was to be another four years before the Boarhills–St Andrews link was completed.

While the line terminated at Kilconquhar, East Neuk passengers had to walk, ride or take the stage coach, plying four times daily from Anstruther, to make their connections. The opening of the line onwards to Anstruther was initiated on 1st September 1863. The impact of this extension had been debated in the Town Council. The *East of Fife Record* for 5th November 1862 noted that, although the Council had not been approached, they were content that the provision of a suitable bridge to cross the turnpike road below Craigiewells Farm would accommodate all coach, farm and other traffic.

Apart from transport for their catches, one great advantage to fishermen was the ability to send torn and damaged nets back from distant parts, their wives and daughters mending them and then returning them to the boats by the same means. Very often, the husband or boy-friend sweetened the task by wrapping safely in the net, a fairing or gift from shop or market. Typical offerings would be a 'cheenie dug' (china dog) or a pair of tingaleeries, as they were known locally, elegant stalked china bowls, festooned with beads and prisms in glass. Broken ones were much treasured by children for producing rainbow spectra.

James Corstorphine adds the following pawky tale to his railway saga. The 'occasion' of a trip to Edinburgh was recalled by a passenger who witnessed an elderly lady, fully laden with her day's shopping, attempting to alight from a train at St Monans station. Seeing that the weary traveller was encountering some considerable difficulty in doing so, a smartly-dressed and well-spoken gentleman offered to lend a hand with her parcels. When the struggling passenger and her shopping were successfully disembarked, the woman thanked the gentleman for his kind assistance. 'Don't mention it,' he said, stepping back on to the train. Came the reply, 'Wha? Me? Ah'll no tell a sowl!'

Yet another local was quoted in the local newspaper on the occasion of her first ever excursion by train. 'Am wan a ticket,' she told the booking clerk. 'Certainly, madam. Where to?' 'What business is it o' yours, whaur am gaun tae?' came the sharp reply.

The *East of Fife Record* for 7th June 1882 stated that St Monans Town Council had petitioned the Houses of Commons and Lords

23. St Monans railway station.

to support a Bill, amalgamating the North British, the Edinburgh, Perth and Dundee and the West of Fife Railways. The North British eventually controlled the Fife Coast Line until New Year's Day 1932, when they all became part of the London and North Eastern Railway, the famous LNER.

The railway staff of the day took great pride in their station, keeping buildings, platforms and adjacent track in immaculate condition. Prizes were given for 'Best-kept' and St Monans figured regularly on the winners' lists. Summer saw wonderful displays of rose-beds and all manner of floral artistry, with every gas-lit lamp boasting magnificent hanging baskets. In the forties, such stalwarts as signalmen Sam McGregor and John Robbie, with booking clerk Marjory Aitken, kept the tradition alive.

Being given such magnanimous prizes as five shillings (25p.), they raised most of their own plants, supplementing them with cuttings supplied by regular travellers. Cold winter mornings at the station were cheered by bright coal fires in the waiting rooms, using, of course, the best 'Dunfermline splint', as fuel.

Post Second World War, the new Labour Government determined on the Nationalisation of all rolling stock, lines and properties, leading to the formation of British Railways on 1st January 1948. Again, the station was vital to the massive influx of summer visitors, mainly from Edinburgh and Glasgow, which could double or even treble the population. Whole local families would decamp to the attic for seven or eight weeks. The village fairly buzzed with activity; swimming galas, putting competitions, dances, whist-drives and concerts were the order of the day. Often, several generations of families would make the pilgrimage to St Monans from over the Forth and from the West, year after year. The car was a luxury as were holidays abroad and flying almost unknown, so rail travel was the primary conveyance for most people. Local boys supplemented their pocket money by plying as porters, conveying luggage on their fathers' net-barrows.

In September 1965, the 'axe' of Dr Richard Beeching fell on the Fife Coast Line and, with many others, St Monans Station was closed. Notable among those who tried to oppose such drastic action was Provost James Braid of St Monans, who, with Provost Andrew Scott of Elie, urged that 'every possible protest should be lodged by the people living between St Andrews and Leven.' Always a doughty fighter for the rights of the community, Provost Braid's pleas of the loss to tourism and the lack of transport for some hundred pupils travelling daily to Waid Academy, Anstruther, fell on deaf ears, as did his imaginative plans for restructuring the services to minimise costs.

A founder member of the Steering Committee of what became the Scottish Vigilantes Association, Jimmy had campaigned tirelessly throughout Scotland since 1963 to stop the closures. He likened the threat to Scotland's prosperity to the Romans' attempted invasion of Caledonia, quoting the historian Tacitus. 'They make a desert and they call it peace.'

In addition to the active campaign, a veritable 'paper war' erupted in the columns of the *East Fife Observer*, early in 1964. The Vigilantes had chosen as their mascot and logo, a suitably be-tartaned train, called MacPuff. One of the Provost's main antagonists was the local schoolmaster and his fellow councillor, Fergus Young. This often acrimonious exchange of views and opinions was summarised in a delightful parody of the ballad, 'The Holy City', by two young St Monans men, William J. Gowans and Christopher Rush, then working in Edinburgh. William, sadly, was killed in a mountaineering accident on Ben Oss, near Tyndrum, on 18th April 1977. Chris has gone on to be a leading Scottish writer and poet. (see Chapter 22) Carefully wording their letter to avoid any possibility of libel action, they concluded as follows:

The Ballad of MacPuff

Last night I lay asleeping,
I dreamed a dream so fair,
I stood in old St Monance,
Down by the harbour there,
I heard the Brethren singing,
And ever as they sang,
Methought the voice of Provost Braid
From the Council Chambers rang.

Chorus:

MacPuff! MacPuff! MacPuff! MacPuff!

Don't close the railroad down,
    But let it continue
Through old St Monance town.

And then methought my dream was changed,
I hear another tongue,
The Provost's glad hosannas
Were hushed by Fergus Young,
Whose speech began with merriment,
But soon it turned to woe,
When Dr Beeching's axe appears,
The branch will have to go!

Chorus:

    MacPuff! MacPuff! etc.

And once again the scene was changed,
Along came Aitken Fyall,
And, with the help of Robert Burns,
Brought Mr Young to trial.
But now we've all heard of MacPuff,
Let Fergus Young go free,
Although he may not have a chance
To write for STV.

Chorus:

    MacPuff! MacPuff' etc.

The attractive lattice metal footbridge connecting the north and south platforms and spanning the goods yard, together with the signal box, all the buildings and the road bridge were demolished. Today, it is the site of an industrial estate.

Chapter 16

Boat-Building

FISHING AND BOAT-BUILDING are mutually dependent activities and the latter trade existed in the village from earliest time. Mention has already been made of the seizing of boats from St Monans by the marauding English in 1544. Locally-built craft have ever been highly regarded by the Scottish fishing community.

Apart from the mention of '1 boat-builder' in the *Old Account*, neither that report, nor the *New*, gives any detail of the industry. It may be presumed that, as both authors were gentlemen of the cloth, whose stipends depended mostly on agriculture, they simply neglected to mention the boatyards. Nor were they welcome anywhere near the harbour as the superstitious, albeit religious, fisherfolk considered their presence there to be bad luck.

However, what is recorded elsewhere is that, by the turn of the twentieth century, no fewer than eleven companies were building boats in St Monans, Pittenweem, Anstruther and Crail. The oldest of these was the firm which became James N. Miller and Sons Limited.

Established at Overkellie in 1747 by John Miller, the company transferred to St Andrews in 1768 before being finally set up in St Monans in 1779. Seven generations of the family ran the business until it was sold to the Liverpool-based firm of McTay in 1976, although keeping its title.

In addition to Miller's, St Monans had the yards of Walter Reekie, established in 1872, of R. Reekie and of T. Robertson Innes. The last was located at the top of the Coal Wynd, now Forth Street, on the corner with Hope Place. The completed hulls were transported down the steep incline to the harbour on wooden rollers, a truly hazardous task. The author's grandfather, Andrew Fyall, then a shipwright, before becoming skipper of the motor-boat

24. Miller's yachts.

Ruby, lost a finger in such an operation. Man-handling the craft was eventually assisted by a traction engine. In addition to carpenters and joiners, the yards were supported by blacksmiths and sailmakers, the last of whom were John Allan, with his smiddy on the Broad Wynd and Jimmy Main, with his loft in the Maltbarns.

Walter Reekie succeeded his father-in-law, J. Robertson Innes, as head of the firm. The yard encompassed a whole gamut of craft as an early advertisement illustrates: Coasters, Tugs, Motor Launches, Passenger Boats, Cruisers, with Fishing Craft a speciality.

A description of the development and achievements of the Miller Yard is best given by a direct quotation from the speech delivered by the then joint managing director, William P. Miller OBE, on the occasion of the celebration of his firm's bicentenary in 1948.

> It can be safely assumed that the first Miller-built boats were the type used on the local beach. It is worthy of note that this same type of boat survived until quite recent times. At this point a description of these boats would be appropriate. They varied in length from 16ft. to 40ft. with a beam exceeding one third of the length and of comparatively shallow draft. In design, they were sharp ended, with both stem and stern rounded under water, the depth of the boat being slightly more forward than aft. Internally, the boats were open from stem to stern and fitted with cross seats or thafts. These were spaced wider at the stern and had a short platform underneath to carry the nets and fishing gear. A single mast, with dipping lugsail, was fitted in skegs forward. Four or six oars were carried and extensively used. It has been known for this type of boat to be rowed continuously from Wick to the Firth of Forth. From this prototype, all East Coast fishing boats have been fashioned. As you can imagine, the improvements took place over a long number of years. First, a short deck was fitted forward to provide sleeping accommodation. The deck was gradually lengthened until the boat was decked all over. Then a mizzen mast was fitted. There is no doubt that this type of boat was the forerunner of the present-day National Lifeboat.

At this period, machinery began to make its appearance in the form of the 'Iron Man'. This was a hand-driven winch, fitted abaft the mizzen mast and used for hauling in the nets. An old account book of 1850 shows that these boats were being built for just under £1 per foot. A 30ft. boat cost £25; as a comparison, a present day boat of the same dimensions would cost £950 without engine. A record of 1851 shows that my grandfather, John Miller, built five boats ranging in length from 36ft. to 39ft. for the towns of St Monance, Pittenweem and Buckhaven.

Until my father, the late James Miller, took over the business in 1888, it remained a purely local concern, building only for the Fifeshire towns. He, however, considerably extended the work and had yards building both in St Monance and Anstruther. He built a large number of the 50 to 80 foot sailing Fifies. When steam entered the fishing industry, he immediately started building the steam long liners, and, later on, the early steam trawlers, considerable numbers being built for North Shields and other fishing ports. Both types measured 80ft. to 90 ft. in length with 19ft. to 20ft. beam. These were followed by the steam drifters, which were 75ft. to 85ft. in length and fitted with compound steam engines, which were made in Leith.

A 100ft. cargo boat was built for the sugar trade in Cuba and steamed out under her own power. Then a fishery inspection ketch was built for the late King Albert of the Belgians. At this period, the first Miller yacht was built. This was an 80ft. steam-driven vessel with the clipper bow and long overhung stern, which was popular at that period. From then onwards, Miller boats have been sent all over the world.

When the internal combustion engine was introduced early in this century, he again took a keen interest and was concerned in some of the earliest experiments carried out. One of the most interesting was an experimental semi-diesel 2-stroke engine made by the late Professor Peck of Edinburgh, and fitted into a 65ft. Fifie sailing boat, very aptly named the *Wave.* This interest has been retained and greatly enlarged on to this present day. In 1908, an event took place which has had considerable influence on the Miller business. This was the building of a 40ft. yacht to the order of the late Sir Robert Brooke. This boat was fitted with a four cylinder Kelvin paraffin engine. The efficiency and simplicity of this motor engine so appealed to my father that he undertook to become agent for them, an agency which we still hold. From that first engine, many hundreds of Kelvins have been fitted to the boats built in the yard and also to the local fishing fleet.

During the first World War, there was a large demand for motor launches for service in the Near East; a speciality was made of this work, and this type has been built ever since. After the first World War, when the fishing industry, and trade generally, began to feel the effects of the slump, the firm again launched out into a new line. That was the building of yachts. In the period between the two wars, sixty-six were built. These included all types, motor, sail and auxiliaries. While quite a number of these were designed by the firm, some were also built to the specification of such famous designers as G.L. Watson, W.G. McBryde and Robert Clark.

It must be recorded here that, in 1921, an entirely new type of fishing boat was built for use on the West Coast of Scotland. This was a boat with cruiser stern and rounded forefoot and of medium draft, fitted with a motor engine and sail, and built to the order of that pioneer of ring net fishing, Robert Robertson of Campbeltown. This type of boat proved so successful that it has now become the standard for the British Isles. Our record during the late war is also one of which we can be proud. Employing some 120-130 personnel, altogether 58 boats were built for the various services. These included 29 of the 112ft. submarine chasers. (Miller's set a record by building one of these boats in seventeen weeks, from the laying of the keel to its commissioning.) Since the war, we have once again reverted to the building of fishing boats, and a good number have already been launched.

In the early 1920s, when the motor engine became the accepted thing in fishing boats, a demand arose for a motor-driven capstan. After some experiment, a very successful

> version was produced, given the name of '*Fifer*', and fitted into a considerable number of fishing boats, both in Scotland and in England. In 1944, it was recognised that the modern fishing boat must be able to prosecute every type of fishing, and for this reason the firm designed the new '*Fifer*', which would be suitable for all fishings with equal efficiency. This machine has proved a great success and production has been to capacity during the past three years.

Willie Miller's daughter, Jenny (Mrs MacDonald) relates two stories of the time of building the motor-launches, one remarkable, the other amusing. The first submarine chaser built, ML 108, caused great excitement in the village. The approach to the East Pier had been sealed off with barbed wire and a naval picket, with rifle and fixed bayonet, kept guard. Secrecy was obviously vital, as this warship was being fitted – with wooden guns!

Jenny also recalls her first and only brush with Royalty. She was invited to an afternoon recital by the famous Polish singer Jan Kiepura, in Earlsferry Town Hall. There were many Polish troops billeted in Elie and their orchestral concerts became an entertainment feature of wartime East Neuk. Her escort was a young naval lieutenant, Battenburg by name, whom she describes as 'a real chinless wonder type, with a monocle, a silver-topped cane and a little dog'. Gentleman that he was, he made her walk, there and back! No, it wasn't Prince Philip!

Walter Reekie's yard, too, made a magnificent contribution to the 1939-45 conflict, building many 120 foot specialised mine sweepers. In contrast to the light sectional cross-ply construction of Miller's craft, these were heavily-built boats and very demanding on the workmen. The main timbers were of oak, with planking of larch, two-and-a-half inches thick. The bilge was also in oak of four-and-a-half inches. The constructional detail suited each type of vessel's purpose; the submarine chasers of Miller's were lightweight, sleek greyhounds, while Reekie's were robust enough for their task of pulling heavy mine-clearing gear at relatively slow speeds.

Albeit the boat builders were exempt from military service, they had a long working week of 8 a.m. to 8 p.m., Monday to Friday, and 8 a.m. to 4.30 p.m., Saturday and Sunday. Wednesday was the only tea-time finish but many of the workers were recruits in the Local Defence Volunteers, latterly the Home Guard, and were expected to mount guard duty for one night, every week.

Post-war, Miller's was busier than ever. Between 1948 and 1960, their output was 97 fishing vessels, 77 Miller Kelvin launches, 28 yachts, 12 pilot boats, several mine-sweepers and Dark Class torpedo boats, besides many capstans and winches of the Fifer series and other items of boat's equipment.

On 26th October 1949, the village and the whole boat-building fraternity of the United Kingdom were shocked by the death of Walter Reekie. His latest launching, the *Pride o' the Clyde*, built for Tarbert owners, was practically ready for her sea trials. Boarding her at the West Pier, he missed his footing on the ladder and, falling to the deck, struck his head on the gunnel, being killed outright. His yard was taken over by Miller's in 1951, but closed two years later.

A temporary lull in orders had seen the conception, design and building of the first Fifer, a thirty-three foot yacht. Jimmy Hutt, for many years chief engineer at Miller's, described the tremendous care and dedication in workmanship and in the selection of materials. 'It was virtually hand-built, much of the interior wood-work being to cabinet-making standards.' An instant success at the Boat Show at Earls Court, London, it was sold to a journalist on the press preview day and the firm took another eleven orders. By the time of Willie's retirement, over fifty had been built, one for the Peruvian-born comedian Michael Bentine. The prototype was called the *Royale Fifer* and is still very much afloat. In 1997, the author, with his wife June and friends Shirley and Sonny Corstorphine from Cellardyke, were visiting Swansea Marina. Sonny, a one-time keen sailor himself, recognised a Fifer. Yes, it was the *Royale Fifer*, still in beautiful condition. They were shown over her with great pride, by her present owner, a spry, septuagenarian Welshman, Tewdyr Watkins, and there in the wheel-house was the Miller plaque. Her credentials were checked with St Monans, so now Tewdyr is even prouder to have a craft of such distinction. The author also knows of an elderly Miller's vessel still fishing the waters of Cardigan Bay, Wales.

25. Reekie's Boatyard 1945. L-R: Tommy Morris, William Reekie, John Ovenstone, Willie Doig.

Willie Miller records that, in 1913, wages in the boatyard were sixpence (2½p.) per hour or twenty-eight shillings (£1.40p.) for a 48 hour week. After the Great War, they rose to three pounds per week, then to £1 7*s.* 6*d.* (£1.38p.) per hour after the Second World War and to £2.50p. per hour in 1988.

In his life story, he also remembered a period of great activity at the Kelvin Works. While still an apprentice, he had been put on piece-work, building seven horse-power engines, at seven-and-sixpence (37½p.) each. Managing to complete four in a week, he felt like a millionaire!

On his retirement in 1970, the yard continued its success, under the very able stewardship of his nephew Jimmy, also a designer and son of his brother Tom, for many years Willie's co-director. The company secretary was Jimmy's sister Jessie.

The yard, under McTay, closed in 1992, bringing to an end two hundred and forty-five years of outstanding boat building and the sad demise of the major source of the village's economy. The Miller family's contribution to village life is featured in Chapter 21.

Chapter 17

Farming

General

WHEN JAMES VI OF SCOTLAND described his Kingdom as 'a beggar's mantle with a fringe of gold', that fringe was the East Neuk of Fife. As an alternative, Orr claims that the quotation was actually 'the golden fringe of a worsted petticoat'.

In 1770, Pennant, an English traveller, described Fife as 'fertile in soil, abundant in cattle, happy in collieries, in ironstone, lime and freestone, rich in manufacture.' The *Old Account* of 1799 recorded for St Monans: 'The nature of the soil is a light loam, and friable, with very little clay, all quite free of stones, and very fertile and manageable. It is peculiarly well adapted for green crops, but yields all the usual crops in abundance.' An old saying was: 'Ae crook o' Forth is worth an earldom in the North.'

Again, Tucker, in his *Report to the Commissioners of Scottish Customs* in 1856, noted 'one of the best and richest counties in Scotland ... more from the goodness and fertility of the soil than any traffic,' which 'made it the residence and seat of many gentry, who have wholly driven out all but their tenants and peasants to the shore-side.' Obviously, the landlords made up their own rules and their word was law.

The lands of St Monans are no exception and they constitute some of the finest agricultural areas in Britain.

Methods

For centuries, the only implement used in the cultivation of major tracts of land was the old Scots plough, of very heavy and clumsy construction. It was drawn by two oxen and two horses or by four oxen and one horse. It was with such a plough that Scotland's Bard, Robert Burns, toiled on the sour soils of the farms of Mount Oliphant, Lochlea, Mossgiel and Ellisland.

By the 1780s, this was replaced by the smaller English plough, with an iron mould board, then by a lighter Scots version and again by yet another model, partly English, partly Scots. The English version was considered to make a neater job but was not good on stony ground, whereas the Scots plough answered all terrains.

Normally, these lighter versions would be drawn by a pair of horse, but if arable land was being reclaimed from grass, three or even four horses were yoked. Farriers and blacksmiths were in great demand. Harvesting grain was done by scythe, with the women binding the sheaves by hand.

The main crops were hay, wheat, barley, oats, potatoes, turnips, peas and beans. Vast quantities of the last were shipped to Glasgow and its neighbourhood, trade being improved significantly by the opening, in 1790, of the Forth-Clyde Canal. In the reign of Charles II, a scheme had been proposed to link the Firths of Forth and Clyde but, like many another major undertaking, official commitment see-sawed between enthusiasm and apathy. The writer Daniel Defoe saw this shilly-shallying as deplorable. In his book *A Tour Through the Whole Island of Great Britain* in the 1720s, he maintained, 'It must lie till Posterity, yet the rising Greatness of their Commerce, shall not only feel the want of it, but find themselves inclinable, as well as able, to effect it.'

By 1759, the Magistrates of Glasgow had the improvement of the harbour and the waters of the Clyde enabled by an Act of Parliament. The opening of this important link between the North Sea and, effectively, the Atlantic Ocean was symbolised by an official deputation, sailing from Port Hamilton to Bowling and pouring a hogshead of water from the Forth into the Clyde. The Continent, particularly the Lowlands of Holland and Belgium, was the destination of much of the potato crop. This trade continued, albeit to a much more limited extent, in the 1930s, when Dutch ships were loaded in St Monans harbour.

There was a great deal of livestock and the area was famous for its fattened cattle, much sought after by butchers from Edinburgh and Perth.

Fertilisers

A major source of fertiliser for the land was seaweed. In St Monans, it was collected from the 'kelp shore', between high and low-water marks, usually after gales from the north-east, east and south-east. Additionally, some ten tons were cut and gathered from the rocks, every three years. Much of the kelp was thrown up below the Auld Kirk; the ruts cut in the sand-stone by the iron-shod wheels of the carts can still be seen on the shore, between the Dawzie (in the nineteenth century, Dassey) and the mouth of the Inverie Burn. Every aspect of the seaweed industry, gathering, drying and kilning, was arduous, unpleasantly wet and often noxious.

In the west of Scotland, the kelp industry had dominated the lives of rural communities. After the Highland Clearances of 1782 to 1820, the price of alkali soared because of foreign wars. The landowners hurriedly checked the mass migration to the colonies by having Parliament pass a Navigation Act, which made sea-passage to the Americas too expensive. They established village communities, committed to the kelp trade. During Napoleon's Iberian Peninsula campaign, the usual sources of fertiliser from Spain and Portugal were cut off by the blockade of British ports by the French Navy.

Although the rich landowners of the East Neuk did not look to the calcined ash as a major economic factor, the burghs often did sell the seaweed harvests. Typically in 1694, an Englishman offered four pounds per annum for the privilege of cutting and burning the kelp for a year. The council eventually accepted the bid with the proviso that the burning should take place at the west end of the town and only when the wind blew from the east. Environmentalists were active even then! Despite this source of fertiliser, potato yields were only some two to three tons per acre, scant return by today's standards.

For the west of Scotland's nobility, the kelp harvest provided a source of wealth, rivalling the wool trade. Local landowners were ever eager to claim the seaweed, albeit their domains could only extend to the high water mark. Below that were territorial waters, ostensibly belonging to the Crown and the people. Nor was its significance lost on Sir John Anstruther, who, in 1875, found himself in dispute with St Monans Council, as he was claiming all foreshore rights.

The *East of Fife Record* gives a most vivid account in the 1880s of a typical incident as follows:

> War or no Ware: On Tuesday last, our peaceable and law-abiding community might have been witnessed under a state of intense excitement, bordering on absolute furore and the scene it gave rise to, partook so much of a ridiculous element as to deserve a passing notice. The only noteworthy element of the storm here being a large accumulation of drift seaweed in the harbour, the opportunity was not to be lost of turning a penny and it was accordingly immediately taken possession of by our juvenile population, a squad of whom were told off to collect it in heaps, while the others went about negotiating for its disposal amongst the non-privileged farmers, one of whom pays them at the rate of 2*s.* 6*d.* [12½p.] per load. The heaps having caught the eye of an adjacent farmer, always wide-awake, he, it is said, in ignorance of their origin, and ascribing to a tidal freak the tempting mounds that covered the beach at once despatched carts and men to remove them, meanwhile rejoicing at his luck in being the first to discover this unusual phenomenon. All unsuspicious, the men set about their task, while hundreds of eyes looked on with a vacant stare, not a listless indifference, but rather of incredulousness, as if the audacity displayed, being so enormous, their minds could scarcely be brought to realise what was transacting before them. At length, a tangle, thrown with unerring aim at the head of a ploughman, broke the spell, also – his pipe, and was the prelude to a storm of oaths and objurgations, which increased in volume as the elders mingled their voices with the protesting youngsters. Law and lairds, factors and farmers, all came in for their due portion of abuse and defiance, while the well-directed tangles gave both men and horses a foretaste of what their share would be in the impending conflict. By this time the whole inhabitants seemed to have turned out, and became active participants in the row, when the ploughmen, thinking that:

'He who fights and runs away,
May live to fight another day;
But he who is in battle slain
Will never rise to fight again.'

wisely determined to leave the field of ware and, turning their horses homewards, left the town amidst the hooting and jeers of the crowd – a favourite mode of reception here for distinguished visitors, which was the next day afforded to Mr Jamieson, factor, who, with a *posse* of farmers visited St Monance, to make enquiries, it is supposed, with a view to legal proceedings. The carts, with those of others, subsequently returned, but confined themselves to the weed lying loose on the beach. We understand that there is at present a case pending in court testing the right of an inhabitant carter to collect and sell seaweed from St Monance shore.

By the twentieth century, the burning was omitted and the raw seaweed was ploughed directly into the land. Today, the evolution of industrially produced chemicals, combined with intensive, low-labour farming techniques, has virtually eliminated the exploitation of kelp as a fertiliser, although it is still used in industries such as glass, soap, cosmetics, pharmaceuticals, textiles and medicines.

Crops and Wages

Prior to the nineteenth century, there had been a great deal of flax grown by the villagers, who hired ground from the tenant farmers. However, the price of seed and high rents reduced this trade. Consequently, the number of weavers in St Monans fell from six in 1799 to four in 1837.

Wool was sheared from the local flock, carded, spun and woven into cloth for everyday wear.

As with the fishing, a major factor dominating the prosperity of the farming community was the vagary of the weather. Food shortages with consequent rise in costs had ravaged the parish in 1558. In 1782, the harvest was late because of heavy rains throughout the summer. There had been snow and severe frosts from the end of September through the whole of October. Famine threatened as grain prices rose rapidly to one shilling and threepence (6p.) per peck. From 1st February 1783 to the end of May that year, the Lord of the Manor, Sir Robert Anstruther, made supplies available at the reduced price of one shilling (5p.). Rationing of foodstuffs was not a new phenomenon as experienced in the two World Wars of the twentieth century. The twice-weekly distribution was controlled by the requirement to produce the necessary ticket. Relief came with the early arrival of considerable cargoes from the Baltic States, occasioned by a premature thawing of the ice-floes.

In 1845, if he provided the manure, a cottar would pay a farmer two shillings (10p.) for a row measuring one hundred yards, for the planting of potatoes. The fee was raised to four shillings (20p.), if land, labour and manure, costing five shillings (25p.) per cart-load, were provided by the farmer.

A good labourer received from one shilling and fourpence (6½p.) to one shilling and sixpence (7½p.) per day. Lifting potatoes earned one shilling (5p.) per day and dinner. Harvest wages were also one shilling and sixpence per day from breakfast. If men were fed for the whole harvest, the pay was two pounds, with 'bounties', such as potatoes and flax, and supper; women were paid one pound thirteen shillings (£1.65p.).

Mechanics, such as wheelwrights and masons, had a minimum of a florin (10p.) per day, rising to half-a-crown (12½p.) in summer, with the longer hours of daylight.

The common wage for a farm servant was ten pounds per annum with a cottar house, six-and-a-half bolls of oatmeal (430 lbs. – 216 kilograms), three chopins of milk (6 quarts), presumably daily, again with ground for potatoes. Female servants were paid three pounds per half year, 'exclusive of tea money'! Such low wages would be supplemented by allowances of potatoes, a 'biling in a poke', to be taken home, a perk afforded to tattie-howkers to the present day.

By stark contrast to these rates, a hard-working collier was already earning eighteen shillings (90p.) per week, nearly fifty years earlier.

The staple diet of the peasant was oatmeal, potatoes, fish and, in the country parts of the parish, pork from their domestic pigs.

In 1845, fuel was expensive, coal, exclusive of any toll (a penny per load), or tax, being one shilling and threepence (6p.) per load of 22 stones (140 kilograms). Most of it came from Earlsferry, four miles away, but Sir Ralph Anstruther had opened a mine locally, bringing the price down to one shilling (5p.). A cart-load delivered would cost eight shillings and five-pence halfpenny (42p.), whereas it could be bought at the pit-head in Earlsferry for four shillings (20p.).

A Cameo of Farm Life

Andrew Peddie, the second generation of his family to own Coal Farm, now retired, with his son Peter carrying on the tradition, has set down his reminiscences of the farm and the St Monans that he has known from childhood.

> My father, Donald Peddie, came to Coal Farm in November 1930 from the Crieff area. The farm was 275 acres at that time and the rent £350 per annum. He employed three horsemen and a cattleman and the wages were around £1 1*s.* (£1.5p.) to £1 2*s.* (£1.10p.) per week.
>
> In 1933, Dave Lumsden, who drove the second pair of horse, was paid £1 1*s* 6*d.* (£1.7½p.) per week. He had three sons, and at that time, lived in a two-roomed house with no inside water and an outside toilet. All the men also got one ton of potatoes every year and half a boll of oatmeal (70 lbs.) every month. They all had a pigsty, or 'crave' as they called it, and most of them bought a piglet twice a year. In the 1960s, I asked old Dave Lumsden how he had managed to bring up a family on such a small wage, and his reply was, 'It was as easy then as it is now. We had oor meal and milk and tatties and a garden, and killed a pig twice a year, so if anybody came in you aye had a ham hanging from the ceiling to gie them, and if we were gaun onywey, we walked.' The men had no statutory holidays and worked both Christmas and New Year's Days, but got one day off for St Andrews Market, or Lammas Fair, on the second Tuesday of August, and a day on Hansel Monday, the first Monday after New Year's Day.

I can remember that, during the winter herring season, father always bought a barrel of salt herrings, which lay in the cart shed, and the men helped themselves, whenever they felt like it. Father started to retail milk in St Monans in 1931, and my elder brother Peter and I went out with him twice a day, at 7.30 a.m. and again at 6 p.m., so that, after a year or two, we knew everyone in St Monans. If father went to Glasgow to sell sheep, he was always late home so he got Willie Tarvet, the local garage proprietor, to drive the car, while Peter and I delivered the milk. It was *3d.* (1p.) per pint and eggs varied from 11d. (5p.) to 1*s* 6*d.* (7 ½p.) per dozen.

We always had a squad of about twenty-four women and children gathering potatoes and I recall one woman raging at father, because he only paid them 3*s.* 6*d.* (17 ½p.) per day, while someone else paid 3*s* 7*d.*

I can remember that, when the boats were leaving for Yarmouth or Peterhead, the fishermen all came along to Coal Farm to fill their mattresses, or 'chaff tykes' as they called them; they only wanted oat chaff.

During the winter season, we ate a lot of herring, because there was a continual stream of little boys coming along with their 'scrans', and mother could not say 'No' to them. One thing you may not have heard about is the 'Molly Cooper Trust'. This Miss Cooper had died and left a sum of money, the interest from which was to be divided among three or four indigenous spinsters or widows over the age of sixty-five and resident in St Monans. The trustees were the Church of Scotland minister, and the farmers of Coal Farm, Newark, Abercrombie and Stenton. It was paid in December, and, for a month beforehand, father had a constant stream of old ladies, asking for a share. Usually there were three or four beneficiaries and they got £1 10*s.*, (£1.50p.) or £2 each.

By the time father died, and I became a trustee, things were more prosperous, and some of the ladies were insulted at the thought of being given charity: Even when I was a trustee, there was only £7 or £8 to hand out, and eventually the trust was wound up and the capital given to charity.

I remember Walter Gordon, the Auld Kirk minister, telling

us that, when the boats were going to sea, the fishermen would cross to the other side of the road rather than meet him. Old Tam McBain, one of our orramen, used to tell us some of the other superstitions. It was unlucky to stick a knife in the mast, and the word 'pig' was never uttered on a boat.

When Walter Gordon was newly married, around 1935–6, he thought he would support some good cause, and took his wife to a whist-drive. This caused a great 'stishie', and he had to appear before the Kirk Session to explain himself, for playing cards were instruments of the Devil.

My recollection of the trade in St Monans in the 1930s was of the number of shops there were: At least four bakers: Jimmy Ferguson, Miller Terrace; Willie Ferguson, Broad Wynd; Jimmy Redpath, or Rippit in the local dialect, the Neuk, and Sandy Reekie in East Backgate. Several grocers: Guthrie, Miller Terrace; Walter Reekie, Mid Shore; Gerrard, West Back Gate; Norrie Birrell, Broad Wynd; Meldrum, Virgin Square; Boyter, West Shore, and probably more; two chip shops: Jock Mathers, West Shore; and Jimmy Wood in Virgin Square. Gerrard sold papers as did Ivy Easton, Coal Wynd, who also offered stationery, watches etc; two clothiers, Tammy Lindsay, East Street and Willie Summers in George Terrace; two shoe shops, D.I. Black, Broad Wynd and Eck Dunn, off Virgin Square.

The streets were lit by gas lamps and the 'leerie' went round with a lit taper at dusk, to light them, and round again at dawn to turn them off. The street refuse was lifted daily by horse and cart, and the contractor had to put in a tender each year. Mostly it was a Peattie as I remember, but sometimes Andrew Dunn. The refuse was dumped on an unsightly heap on the common, where the caravan site is now. The rest of the common grew rough grass and whins, with net drying poles scattered about, but eventually, during the war, father was asked to plough it up. He cultivated about seven acres for three years, two years oats and one year potatoes, then it was sown down to grass and handed back to the council.

The author recalls, as a student, planting and lifting potatoes there and forking the field of oats to horse and cart, driven by two of Dave Lumsden's sons, John and Davy. This, the battlefield of 1548, is now the site of the excellent local Bowls Club.

Potato gathering was a vital source of revenue every autumn, with the casual labourers, faced with a 7 a.m. start, walking to the fields of the other surrounding farms of Newark, Craigiewells, Balbuthie, Abercrombie and Ardross, often a distance of several miles. During the Second World War, the absence of many of the women-folk, in the Armed Forces, the Land Army and the local camouflage-net factory, meant that the only source of labour was the youngsters. Accordingly, the school summer holidays were split into two periods, the second coinciding with the potato lifting. Once the fields had been finished, farmers would permit locals to glean ungathered potatoes or to follow the plough as the land was prepared for sowing the next crop. In this way, many homes were amply stocked, often for the whole year. Indeed, the housewife would choose the daily meals from a selection of bags. The varieties, Golden Wonder, Kerr's Pink, King Edward and Home Guard would be preferred for boiling, while Majestics undoubtedly made the best chips!

Chapter 18

Salt-making, Mining and Milling

WITH THE READILY-AVAILABLE SOURCE OF SALT and its importance in everyday life and in the fishing industry, it was not to be wondered that the inhabitants of St Monans made every effort to retrieve it from the sea.

Early primitive techniques using salt pans, or 'bucket pats', cut from the solid rock, were superseded by the erection of a salt-works at the east end of the town. Called St Philip's, it was built between 1772–4, by the Newark Coal and Salt Company, a joint venture, established in 1771 by Sir John Anstruther of Elie House, who owned the land, and his partner, Robert Fall.

The windmill, which pumped the sea water up to the pans, lies on a direct line from Balcaskie House, then the residence of Sir John's cousin, Sir William Anstruther, through a long avenue of trees across the estate to the distant Bass Rock. Nine buildings held the cast-iron pans, which measured twelve feet long, by six feet wide, by one foot high. The housing of the workers lay immediately adjacent. Most of the salt-makers, some twenty in number, had been experienced in other works on the Fife coast, notably at Wemyss and Dysart. Each pan had a salt-master and two assistants.

Still visible is the channel hewn through the rocks to low-water mark, with a rock-cut settling tank about halfway along its length. This retained sufficient water at low tide to ensure a continuous supply to the pans. Sand and weed were allowed to sink to the bottom of the tank before pumping commenced. The salt water was boiled over coal fires, which were kept stoked twenty-four hours a day. The water was clarified by the addition of lime or ox blood, until all superfluous matter could be skimmed off as scum or evaporated. The saline particles remaining were then

26. The Windmill – East Braes.

drawn into the consistory to cool, previous to being stored in the girnel.

The production of one ton of salt required between five and seven tons of coal to fire the pans. At peak output, some two thousand tons of salt per year were extracted, necessitating the mining of well over ten thousand tons of coal annually for that purpose alone. Known as panwood, this low grade coal had the advantage of being mined at the colliery set up, again by the company, at Coalfarm. The pit, which was situated at the corner of today's stackyard, provided employment for some thirty-six miners and boys. Unlike the slave labour in the collieries of West Fife, all were free men. The shallower reserves of coal having been exhausted, a new shaft was sunk to two hundred feet, just across the main St Monans–Pittenweem road from present-day Coalfarm. There were no farm buildings there at that time. Deeper mining was made possible by the installation of a steam-driven beam engine for the extraction of water, which was pumped up to the thirty-foot level of the old mine. Thence it ran, through an adit or passage-way, into St Monan's Well, or 'the meeneral', and so to the sea. This adit was tunnelled and built of stone, being large enough for a man to crawl through for maintenance purposes. After mining ceased, generations of tenants and farm-workers used the mine shaft for the disposal of sewerage and all manner of rubbish. It was eventually sealed off in the mid 1940s.

A ramp, still visible by the fall of the land to the east of the windmill, marks the beginning of the waggonway used to transport the salt to Pittenweem. Consisting of a wooden railway track along which horse-drawn, side-tipping trucks moved coal and salt, this link ran inland across what is known as the Waterless Road, curving around the back of Pittenweem to avoid the high ground of the Taft Hill. It then wended its way down present-day Abbey Wall Road to a new pier, constructed at Pittenweem harbour for the purpose of shipping the salt to other parts of Scotland and to the Continent. On the journey back, fuel for the salt pans was loaded at a number of small coal-mines, some above the Waterless Road and another on a spur line serving Balcaskie. Both the waggonway and the pier were financed by Sir John. In return, Pittenweem Town Council reduced his harbour dues significantly and gave his shipping priority over other craft.

Because of the high proportion of impurities, the salt was not suitable for curing, so the fish trade still had to rely on better quality foreign imports. Tax on salt was high, often reaching

27. *[This page and opposite] The Salt Pans (courtesy Fife Council).*

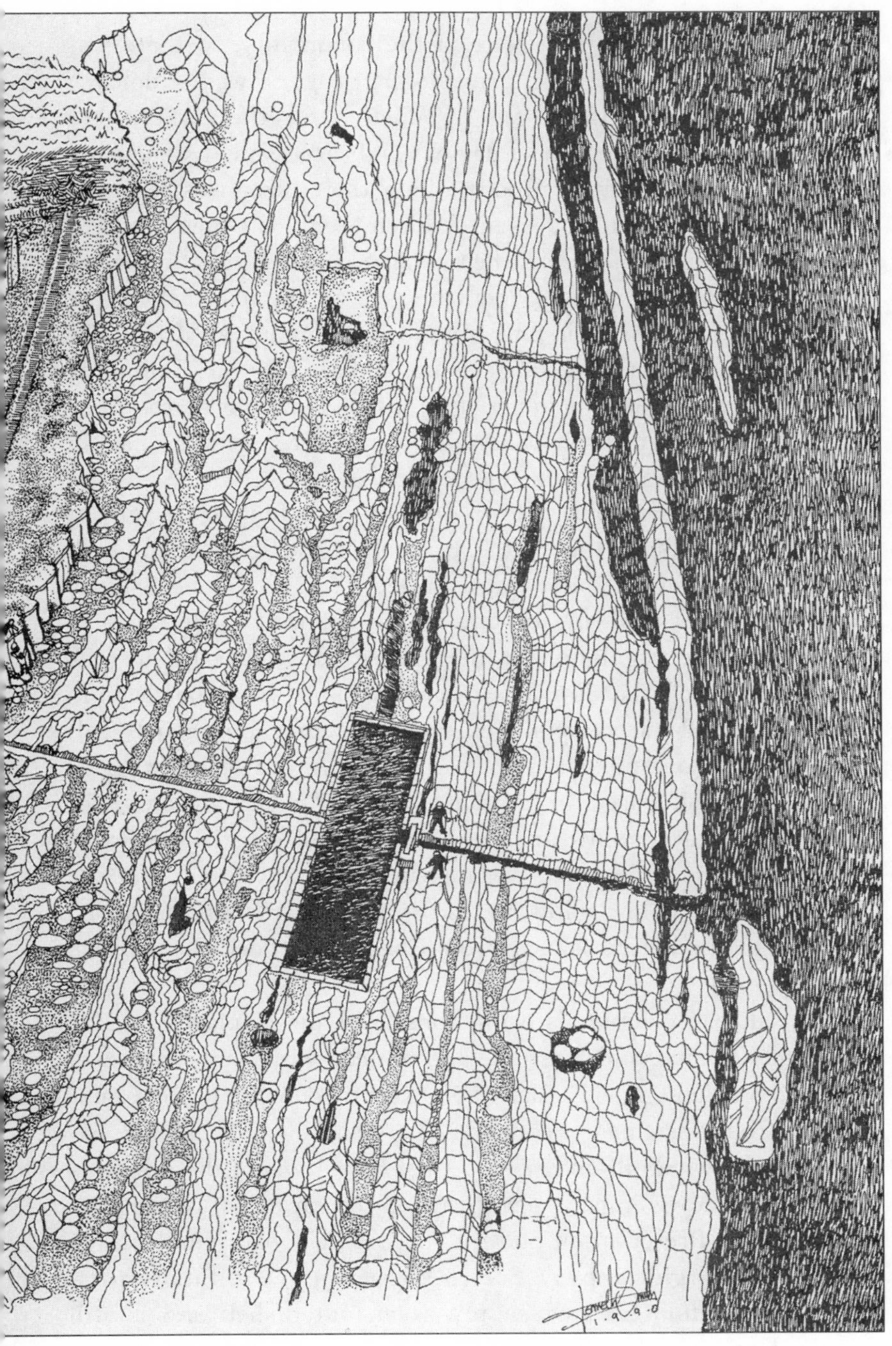

eighty per cent of the sale price of the commodity, so there was great temptation to steal it. Cruizers, or gaugers, were employed by the government to oversee production for the owners, but experienced salters were most devious and successful at smuggling out substantial quantities. Hoodwinking the cruizer was regarded as an accomplishment and even children would fill their pockets.

In 1794, a disastrous fire at the Coalfarm colliery, possibly caused by the ignition of firedamp, methane gas, by the naked flames of the miners' candles, their only source of illumination, drastically reduced coal output. The safety lamp, invented by Sir Humphrey Davy, was not in use in mines until 1815. Pumping at the mine stopped in 1803; the salt-pans are variously reported as having been abandoned in 1823 or 1844.

An article in the *East of Fife Mail* of 20th June 1822 set out the requirements of the Salt Tax. 'Salt made in Scotland will not be charged with duty, but a license of £1 is to be paid by each salt-maker, and an account of the quantity made is to be kept under the regulation of the Excise. English salt, or rock salt, upon which the duty has been paid, is to be imported into Scotland for all purposes; a countervailing duty upon Scotch salt is to be paid on importation to England. A drawback is to be allowed on fish cured in Scotland with English salt only, for foreign exportation only, under the direction of the Fishery Board and the Excise.' The duty on imported salt was lifted in 1823. This was a crippling blow to the local industry as it allowed cheaper, high quality rock salt from Cheshire to flood the Scottish market.

The salt-pan complex is being conserved and displayed by Fife Regional Council and East Neuk Limited, with the support of Historic Scotland, North East Fife District Council and the Countryside Commission for Scotland. The project which, so far, has restored the windmill and started the excavations of the salt-pans and workers' dwellings, is being carried out on behalf of the East Neuk of Fife Preservation Society. The work is being undertaken by the Edinburgh company, Scotia Archaeology. Until its restoration, the windmill existed simply as an outer shell and is still known locally as the Roondel.

It must be a matter of some regret that the restoration does not encompass a far older and much more significant relic, the Well of St Monan, lying scarcely one hundred yards from the windmill.

Little is known of the demise of coal-mining after the 1845 census, apart from the notice, in the *East of Fife Mail* of 2nd May 1873, that a new coal pit was being sunk, one and a half miles north of the village at Scot's quarry, where a colliery had been in operation forty years previously.

As in many villages on the shores of the Forth, 'sea coal' was often revealed by storms. The *East Fife Observer* of 10th June 1926, reported:

> Mining operations were resumed out St Monance way last week. Dotted along the sea shore are several seams of fairly good quality coal, which, however, can only be worked at low tide. A number of miners arrived at the 'dry' town and commenced operations and succeeded in augmenting their depleted finances by the sale of coal recovered from the shore seams.

The 1799 census reported on ironstone as follows:

> Ironstone is found in considerable quantities upon the beach. There are regular bands or bars of ironstone imbedded in the till; but it is chiefly found in the form of small stones, of one or two pounds weight. The proportion of iron to the whole of the ironstone is from 18 to 12 cwt. in the ton. The tacksman of the ironstone receives for it, when shipmasters take it as ballast, 9*s.* (45p.) per 24cwt (1220 Kg).

Other than for ballast, nowhere is there an indication of any use being made of the ironstone. The nodules or ribs seem to have been just physically separated from the shale, fireclays and coal in which they were found; no attempt was made to extract the element, iron. The absence of roasting ovens and blast furnaces in the area would appear to confirm that extraction was not considered commercially viable.

In Scotland, native ironstone had first been smelted using coal-fired furnaces, at the Carron Iron Works. Opened in 1759, the year of Robert Burns' birth, it was later celebrated by him in lines written on the window of the inn at Carron:

We cam' na here to view your warks
In hope to be mair wise,
But only lest we gang tae hell,
It may be nae surprise.

An earlier windmill, for the grinding of flour, located in the Overtoun, possibly on present-day Station Road, was destroyed in the great hurricane of 1682. The arms broke their fastenings and spun so rapidly that the bearings overheated, setting fire to the fabric and demolishing the mill. The miller told the Superior that a wife, possessed of supernatural powers, had died and so evil spirits were abroad. He therefore demanded that she be buried as soon as possible. Thereafter, a water-mill was erected on the Inverie Burn and was in use for over a hundred years. Originally, grain was threshed by hand, using flails, but mills driven by horses became universal. By 1837, steam engines had been introduced, with the prediction that they would oust horse power within fifty years.

As stipulated in the St Monan Charter, the mill on the Abercrombie lands still required, in 1799, that 'all tenants are thirled for such grains as are mealed for the use of their families and pay multure', the toll taken by the miller. 'Thirled' or 'bunsucken' meant that the tenant was bound by his lease to grind his grain at the leasor's mill. The *Statistical Account* of 1845 makes no mention of the existence of a mill.

Chapter 19

Other Occupations, Trades and Businesses

A NUMBER OF YOUNG PEOPLE were employed making fishing nets, at a wage of ninepence (4p.) per day. The first net-making machine was patented in France in 1778. However, it had a cardinal design fault in that the knots slipped easily and it was not until 1835 that Walter Richie of Musselburgh devised a mechanical method of making an ordinary hand-knot. Previously fashioned from hemp or, on the Continent, from coarse Persian silk, the nets were now produced in cotton twine. The advent of these machine-made nets signalled the end of manual production, until the Second World War saw a revival. The dexterity of local women in mending fishing nets was recognised by the establishment of a factory in the Malt Barns, now the Maltings, in what used to be known as Johnstone's Close. These nets however were not fabricated to catch fish but to assist in the camouflage of trenches, tanks, radar sites, gun emplacements and other military installations and equipments. Of a much bigger mesh size than most fishing nets, they were fashioned on a hand-held mould or slim rectangle of wood. The coarse twine used was often creosoted for weather protection, a practice much disliked by the workers because of the persistent smell and fouling of their clothing and persons. However, this activity afforded a source of income and made a most positive contribution to the war effort.

In 1779, the village supported the businesses of four bakers, three brewers, two blacksmiths, five fleshers or butchers, four general merchants, one wright, one boat builder (Miller), two masons, two sieve-makers, two flax dressers, one shoemaker, five tailors, four weavers and one gardener. The rest were fishers, pier workers and gutters, general labourers, ploughmen, shepherds, farm workers and employees in the coal mines, quarries and salt works. There had, at one time, been some interest in the extraction of cod liver oil but never on a scale to make it commercially viable. There was no railway and roads were minimal and often in a poor state of repair, so the distribution of goods was predominantly by sea.

By the *Third Statistical Account of Scotland* in 1952, the businesses listed in the village were: six grocers, four drapers, three painters and decorators, two newsagents, four bakers, eight fishmongers, one fish salesman, two plumbers, four joiners, three cobblers, two electricians, two garages, three builders, two ironmongers, one greengrocer and restaurateur, two cycle agents and radio dealers, two blacksmiths (one at Abercrombie), one chemist, one butcher and one hairdresser. The rest of the working population were mostly fishermen, and shipyard and farm workers.

There were also three branches of national banks. The impact of modern society with more affluence, changing ecological conditions, and the advantages of technology over that one hundred and seventy-three years is evident. Mechanisation had drastically reduced the number of farm workers and the fishing industry had suffered catastrophically with the disappearance of the herring from the Forth and elsewhere.

The next forty-five years to 1997 saw even more radical changes: drapers, bakers, cobblers, cycle and radio dealers, ironmongers, blacksmiths, the chemist, the butcher and the restaurateur all disappeared. Two banks had closed, the one remaining operating on a part-time basis. Such boat-building as existed was sporadic and the number of grocers was halved. The count of plumbers, joiners and electricians was virtually unchanged and the village now had a florist and a diving centre, specialising in underwater repairs.

Perhaps the most remarkable statistic is that, despite the almost complete absence of fishing, although a number of seamen, engineers and skippers still worked from other ports, the nine businesses dealing with the domestic sale of fish escalated by three hundred per cent to twenty-seven, often with rounds extending many miles beyond St Monans, even to Perth, Edinburgh and Glasgow.

Chapter 20

Language and Education

Little is known of the first languages spoken in Scotland but it is clear that neither Scots nor Gaelic can be claimed as the original tongue. When the Gaels or Scotti arrived in Argyll from Ireland around the fifth century AD, followed by the Angles, who came to the East of Scotland in the seventh, they found that, in both the Pictish North and the Cumbric South, there were tribes speaking in a British Celtic language, similar to modern Welsh. The Welshmen inhabited Lothian and Ystrad Clwyd or Strathclyde. There seems to be little doubt that Welsh was the first ancestral tongue. The name Wallace (de Walles) means man of Wales, although by the time that the Scottish hero William Wallace was born in 1296 in Elderslie Castle near Paisley, the local speech was Gaelic under the influence of immigrant Irish.

In tenth century Scotland, five languages were spoken: the Gaelic of the Western Highlands, the Pictish of the North East, the Norse of the Isles, the Welsh of the Central and Western Lowlands and the Inglis of the South-East. The last eventually became known as Scots and is the forerunner of the languages of Lallans and Scottish English, spoken by all Scots today. Celtic scholars tend to think that Welsh survived until about the eleventh century in some parts of Lothian.

Recognising the civilising influence of Norman culture on ideas of government, laws and literature, David I and his successors granted lands in Scotland to such French noble families as Bruce (de Bruys), Balliol, Grant and Fraser. These immigrants spoke Norman French but the mass of the people of lesser rank who accompanied them spoke the Northern dialect of Inglish. This became the common language, so the local Gaelic-speaking population had to learn to speak it to participate in commerce.

Being great traders, the Scottish people absorbed words from many sources. From the twelfth century, the eastern parts of Scotland had much in common with the Low Countries, where they established colonies in such places as Bruges and Middleburg. The Scots, in turn, encouraged Flemish craftsmen, particularly wabsters, or weavers, to settle in the expanding boroughs, hence such names in St Monans as Fleming from Flanders and Bremner from Brabant.

The other major trading partner and military ally was France and so the language was also influenced by the Norman French of the twelfth century settlers and by the Central French of the Auld Alliance, which joined the two countries in commercial and diplomatic co-operation from the late thirteenth to the mid-sixteenth centuries. The administration of the borough was carried out by the provost (French *prévôt*) and the baillie (*bailli*).

Latin had been the language of the Church and the Law in the Middle Ages and, before the end of the fourteenth century, both Latin and French were used in scholarship and private correspondence by the few who could write. By 1424, Scots had replaced Latin as the official language recording the statutes of the Scottish Parliament.

In small communities such as St Monans, limited education and lack of intercourse with the world outside led to the development of a distinctive local dialect, now, under the influence of travel and the media, slowly disappearing. Other East Neuk inhabitants still refer to the 'Simmininsers' as 'droners'!

One of the great accomplishments of King David I was to organise the Church to make all the people of Scotland believe that they belonged to one nation, as they all adhered to the same faith, Roman Catholicism. He increased the number of bishops from four to nine, charging them to ensure that there were a sufficient number of churches in each diocese. More importantly, in connection with both monasteries and churches, there were established schools, where children were taught to read and to sing, although most of the pupils were boys who aspired to become monks or priests.

King James IV also paid much attention to education. He passed a law requiring all barons and the gentry to send their sons to school from the age of eight until they became proficient Latin scholars. The young men were then to attend college to study law. At that time, Scotland had three universities, St Andrews, founded in 1411, Glasgow, 1451 and, in James' reign, Aberdeen, 1495. The last Baron Newark, having three daughters but no male heir, had, therefore, no obligations to fulfil in the field of education.

Much of the good done for the people by David I, and the monarchs who followed him, had disappeared by the time that Mary, Queen of Scots, came to the throne in 1542. The bishops, priests and monks had neglected their churches and nowhere more so than in respect of education.

The fall of the old church and the establishment of Protestantism in Scotland with the Reformation saw the clergy tackle learning with the preparation of a document entitled *The First Book of Discipline*. Its mandate was clear: 'Seeing that God hath determined that His Church here in earth shall be taught, not by angels but by men ... of necessity it is that your Honours be most careful for the virtuous education and godly upbringing of the youth of this realm.'

It was the hope of John Knox and his fellow reformers to use the wealth of the church, particularly that of the monasteries, to establish a regular system of primary, secondary and university education. However, the Crown and the nobles seized the bulk of the financial resources and Knox's scheme never came to fruition. But it was not forgotten and the Revolution Parliament, by an Act of 1696, decreed that every parish should have a school. The heritors or chief landowners were adjured to 'provide a commodious house for a school and the salary of the headmaster'. Despite this edict, in the eighteenth century, there were many districts in Scotland with no school. Yet, for its size, Scotland had more schools than any other country in Europe and earned the praise of foreigners on that account.

Notoriously, dominies were paid little more than the wage of a labourer. The Education Act of 1696 set a maximum stipend of 200 and a minimum of 100 merks (£10-£5) in return for which the schoolmaster would be expected to teach mathematics, Latin, grammar, arithmetic, writing and singing.

Such penury often forced the abler and more ambitious

28. *The old school. Today's Town Hall. Net "barking" in the foreground.*

pedagogues to leave teaching for work in merchant houses and as clerks in the East India Company. Others struggled to maintain their families by keeping small shops or taking on other parish tasks, such as clerk, beadle or gravedigger.

The texts in common use were the Spelling Book, the Bible, Mason's *Collection of Prose and Verse* and Fisher's *English Grammar.* It was taken for granted that the pupils would memorise the best-known hymns.

In St Monans, the Act of 1696 had been anticipated by fifty years, the north transept of the Auld Kirk being the venue for the first organised school in the parish, opening in 1646. The position in 1799 as stated in the *Old Account* was: 'There is no schoolhouse in the parish but the heritors allow the interest of the money, appointed for building a school and a house for the master, to hire one.' The dwelling house, still standing at the end of East Shore, was built as the parish school in 1826. Its status was detailed by the Reverend Robert Swann in the *New Account* of 1845.

> *Education.* – We have one parochial school. The average number attending was given in at last examination at 51 boys and 35 girls = 86. The schoolmaster has the legal accommodations, and the maximum salary. His fees are reading, per

29. Primary school class (1912).

quarter, 2s. [10p.]; writing, 2s 6d. [12½p.], arithmetic, 3*s.* [15p.], Latin, 5s. [25p.]; no additional charge has hitherto been made for English, grammar or geography. The fees may amount to L.25, or L.30 a year. The parochial schoolmaster carries on, efficiently and acceptably, a Sabbath evening school. There is another school in St Monan's upon the teacher's (John Jack) own adventure. I do not understand his fees or the branches taught to be different from those of the parochial school. He is of the Established Church, his numbers 67. There has been recently established in the parish by Lady Anstruther of Balcaskie, an infant school, which is also supported by her ladyship, and promises to be of great benefit to the place. None of the children at other schools in the parish, cost less than 2s. [10p.] per quarter, none more than 5s. [25p.]. There is no quarter of the parish so distant from school, as to be a bar to attendance. There are no additional schools required. But a *sewing school* might possibly be of advantage. From the irregular attendance of children at school the people here might be thought less alive to the benefits of education than they really are. But they are so dependent upon the services of the children in some of the fishing departments, that they are constrained to keep them from school when they would be glad that they could attend it. Many parents, however, are culpably remiss in enforcing attendance.

The last observation could be echoed all over Scotland at that time for, despite the Acts in favour of Education, thousands of children did not attend any school.

A new school, now the Town Hall, was built in 1866, but the premises at East Shore continued in use for some time; Standard II was taught there and senior boys from the new building attended for lessons in cooking.

The Education Act of 1872 laid down that all schools should be managed by boards, elected by the ratepayers and not by the Church, as had been the previous practice. In the case of St Monans, the Church implied the heritors at Balcaskie. However, the latter continued to take an interest in education in the village and, on 27th December 1923, Sir Ralph Anstruther opened a new

30. Primary school class (1997).

school, almost immediately adjacent to the old one, bordering on the Mair.

That, in turn, became dilapidated and inadequate by modern teaching standards and the present school was opened on the same site in 1987. Coincidentally, the number of pupils in 1997 was almost identical to those attending the parish school of over 150 years ago. However, significantly then, the private school of John Jack had a roll-call of 67. The numbers attending the Infant School started by Lady Anstuther are not specified but it may be premised that there were twice as many children in the parish at that time. Many youngsters were already working by the time that they were twelve years old. Again, secondary education was not available in the district until the opening of Waid Academy, Anstruther on 6th September 1886, albeit the minimum age for entry was ten. Originally conceived in 1800, but never realised by its founder and benefactor, Lieutenant Andrew Waid, as Waid's Orphan Academy, where boys would be prepared for entry into the Royal Navy, the school has expanded significantly, both in the curriculum offered and in premises, particularly since the Second World War. The founder's instruction 'to make special provision in the teaching of mathematics and navigation' was honoured and became vital to aspiring seamen, officers and captains of the East Neuk.

Although entrance to Waid Academy was limited, St Monans pupils could attend the local school, usually until the leaving age of fourteen. An extension of a further year could be given to attend a supplementary course. The author has the Certificate of Merit awarded to his mother in 1919. It states, rather grandly, 'The Lords of the Committee of the Privy Council on Education in Scotland, have been pleased to sanction this Certificate of Merit, in terms of Article 29 of the Code … to Janet Fyall, a pupil over fourteen years of age in St Monance Public School.' The subjects, which, with character and conduct, were all rated as Very Good, were English, Arithmetic, Handwriting, the Laws of Health, The British Empire, its history, growth and trade, Singing, Drawing, Drill and the Special Subjects, selected under Schedule VI of the Code. The last was a Household Management Course of Cookery and Sewing. The Headmaster of the day was James Steele.

Chapter 21

Everyday life

General

BEFORE THE MIDDLE OF THE FOURTEENTH CENTURY, St Monans appears to have been almost buried in obscurity. The coaching road between Pittenweem and Colinsburgh effectively by-passed the village. This isolation led, inevitably, to considerable inbreeding. One unkind historian wrote, 'It has been unhesitatingly affirmed that there are more imbeciles in St Monans in proportion to the extent of the population than any other town in Britain'! Yet another quoted, 'If a stranger cam in wice [wise] at the tae end of the toon, he'd gang oot daft at the tither'!

Being so cut off, St Monans was not unlike the nearby village of Bucklevie or Baclevie, the 'town of the sword', which lay between Elie House, home of the Anstruthers, and Kilconquhar Loch. The settlement disappeared in 1760, when Sir John Anstruther bought up the feus, evicted the tenants and flattened their dwellings, to please his wife! She simply did not like the look of the hamlet, so had it destroyed. Happily, St Monans, although also owned by the Anstruther family, did not suffer such a dire fate.

By the eighteenth century, with boats being built bigger and more sea-worthy, and with the fishing fleet expanding, more skippers ventured outside local waters. Others joined voluntarily, or were press-ganged into, the navies of the day, including those of foreign powers, to sail the seas of the world as fighting men, merchantmen, whalers and even pirates. The story of the establishment of the penal settlement in Australia in 1788 records that the convict barque *North Briton,* of four hundred tons burden, under its master, Captain Thomas Fyall of St Monans, arrived at Botany Bay, now Sydney, after a passage of one hundred and five days from Dublin.

Intermarriage with other communities and even foreign nations was inevitable and obviously enhanced the local stock. The villagers, however, kept a somewhat cold reserve to 'outsiders', and even by the middle of the twentieth century, any person marrying into a St Monans family from any other place, even as close as Pittenweem or Cellardyke, was regarded as an 'incomer'. It has been said that continuous residence for forty years might just qualify for acceptance!

The specification for a fisherman's bride is clearly stated by John Orr in his *Handy Book of the Fife Coast.*

> The wife of a fisherman must be born amongst the remains of cod, herring, and lobsters; her first drawn breath must be largely composed of odour of tan and herring pickle; she must understand from girlhood the meshing of the nets, the oiling of monstrous boot, the baiting of lines, the mending thereof, and in fact, all the ins and outs of fisher life. And such a wife must come of a fisher stock – hence the choice is necessarily restricted to their own community, and thus a village in the course of time repeats itself, so to speak – a natural consequence which physiologists declare to have a deteriorating influence on the mental capacity of a people.

Another basic requirement was to be able to knit competently, usually on four needles. Guernseys, often with distinctive individual patterns, were everyday and even Sabbath-wear. The long, solid leather thigh boots were worn over one or two pairs of hand-knitted stockings, known locally as 'buit hose', and the full length drawers or Long Johns were also in wool, usually pink!

The antipathy between peasant and fisher, combined with the former feeing locally twice a year because of the problems of transport, meant that the rural community did not have the benefit of an influx of new genes for their betterment.

Much of the life-style of the villagers is best chronicled in the three *Statistical Accounts of Scotland,* which have already been quoted.

The *First* or *Old Account* was published in 1799, the *Second* or *New Account* in 1845 and the third in 1952. The consecutive contributions recorded therein as 'The Parish of St Monance', 'The

31. Her Majesty, Queen Elizabeth, is welcomed by Provost William Dunn.

32. Her Majesty, Queen Elizabeth, The Queen Mother, with Cllr. James Braid, OBE, JP.

Parish of Abercrombie and St Monans' and, again 'The Parish of St Monance' were authored by, respectively, the Reverend Mr Archibald Gillies, the Reverend Robert Swann, Minister, and Sidney B.F.F. Gowans, MA, a native son, together with Wilfrid Skelding, MA, the Headmaster of the Primary School.

After the visits by King James III in 1482 and King James IV in 1503, 1505 and 1506, there appears to have been no more Royal occasions until the middle of the present century. The first was by Elizabeth of Glamis, as the then Queen of King George VI, and the second in her role as the Queen Mother. These two events are linked by a touching, if somewhat amusing, incident. The first time, an old lady, dressed in her widow's weeds and black shawl, ignoring the arrayed dignitaries and avoiding the vigilance of law and security officers, pushed forward. Confronting Her Majesty, she asked anxiously, 'Hoo's yir man?' The King had been ill for some time; the two ladies had quite a chat. On the second visit, many years later, the Queen Mother remembered their dialogue. 'Last time, a dear soul asked most kindly for my late husband but I expect she is gone now.' Auld Margit Innes, from the Backgate, would have been well pleased!

Leisure

Long working hours, heavy manual labour and the imperative demands of the church for committed attendance left but little time for the pursuit of leisure. Even for the youth, their simple pleasures such as swimming, fishing or playing under the gas-lit street lamps were confined to week-days; the Fourth Commandment, 'Remember the Sabbath day and keep it holy,' was paramount. Sundays consisted of attendance at bible-class and church, dressed in best clothes, family lunch, an afternoon family walk, and sitting around, almost motionless, for most of the time. The advent of newspapers, radio and eventually television provoked hostility, as these worldly pleasures were considered by many to desecrate the Seventh Day. The growth of newspapers was remarkable; in 1782, there were only eight in the whole of Scotland but, by 1790, the number had risen to twenty-seven.

News and gossip, local and external, was avidly exchanged at

33. 'Gies yir crack.'

pier-end, street corner, tavern, market place and at the church door. The Reverend Doctor E.R. Ramsay, Dean of Edinburgh, in his book *Reminiscences of Scottish Life and Character*, tells how housemaids, expected by their employers to attend church diligently but to return immediately to cook Sunday lunch and to continue with the household chores, often demanded time for a chat before and after the sermon. One would-be servant was told that such latitude would not be permitted. Her retort was to the point. 'Then I canna engage wi' ye, mem, for 'deed I wadna gie the crack i' the kirkyaird for a' the sermon.' Traditionally, the weekly market had been held on Friday but, in 1705, was changed to Tuesday – 'Sir Alexander Anstruther of Newark to receive all tolls and customs.'

By Leighton's account (1840) and that of the Reverend Swann (1845), the nearest market town was Pittenweem, which was also the post town. The London and Edinburgh mail arrived there, at 'half-past six o' the clock' every morning, departing again at seven in the evening. However, by 1886, Hay-Fleming records that there was now a post and telegraph office in St Monans.

The Balcarres coach started at Anstruther for Pettycur at 'eight in the morn', on Mondays, Wednesdays and Fridays throughout the year; it left from Number Two, Princes Street, Edinburgh for Anstruther, every Tuesday, Thursday and Saturday. There was a daily coach from Anstruther to Largo, where a steamer from Newhaven arrived twice daily. Many ships plied a coastal trade over to Edinburgh in the summer months. Goods carriers operated from Crail to Edinburgh and from Pittenweem to Cupar, the county town.

The *New Account* also details nearly two miles of turnpike road, running along the north-east boundary of the village and about the same distance along the shore. There is no mention of the costs of the tolls.

The most celebrated social gathering in the East Neuk was the Fair at Anster Loan, immortalised by William Tennant, a local man and Professor of Oriental Languages at the University of St Andrews, in his narrative poem, 'Anster Fair', published in 1812.

People flocked in, not only from the surrounding district but, according to Tennant, from the length and breadth of Scotland:

St Monance, Elie, and adjacent farms,
Turn their mechanics, fishers, farmers out,
Sunburnt and shoeless schoolboys rush in swarms
With childish trick and revelry and shout;
Mothers bear little children in their arms,
Attended by their giggling daughters stout,
Clowns, cobblers, cotters, tanners, weavers, beaux,
Hurry and hop along in clusters and in rows.

From John O'Groat's house to the border-meads,
From Isle of Arran to the mouth of Don,
The Islanders, piping they come, unshav'd, unbreech'd,
unhos'd.

Anster harbour would be filled with boats carrying visitors, bringing all manner of goods and drink to enhance and enliven the celebrations.

From clean-skied France and muddy Zuyder-Zee,
From Flushing port, the palate-biting gin,

Some from Garonne and bonnie banks of Seine,
Transport, in pipes, the blood of Bacchus' berry.

So important was the event that it was graced by the presence of the King of Scotland, James V and the Royal Court, who included in their number, 'Young Newark, vap'ring in his scarlet coat'. The gentry joined them for feast and ball at Anster House.

The poem, one hundred and thirty seven cantos long, gives a wonderful panoramic view of the commercial activities and social customs of its times.

Tennant mixed the actual event with myth and the magical legend of Rab the Ranter, the 'Border laird of good degree' and 'bonnie Maggie Lauder', the local beauty. Tradition has it that the character of this lady was actually based on a brothel-keeper, who lived in East Green, Anstruther, sometime before 1650.

Maggie's hand in marriage was to be the prize of the outright winner of a series of competitions: riding an ass, a sack race, bag-piping and humorous story-telling – a bucolic Olympic Games! The list of would-be suitors ranged from the nobility, including Newark, to the gentry, local farmers and merchants. Needless to relate, Maggie did not end up in the castle at St Monans, but was won by Rab. He had been secretly aided by a fairy, Mistress Puck, and by Sir Michael Scott of Balwearie, the Wizard of the North.

Although every stratum of life might be represented at such public gatherings, the upper classes lived on quite a different level from the rural simplicity of the peasantry. A visit to the East Neuk by King James V started an association of gentlemen in Anstruther, which was as notorious as the Hellfire Clubs of eighteenth century England, such as the so-called Monks of Medmenham Abbey. The King, or the 'Gudeman o' Ballangeich' as he was popularly known, would disguise himself as a piper and wander around his kingdom to get better acquainted with his subjects.

On one occasion, making his way to Dreel Castle in Anstruther, he found his progress barred at high tide by the Dreel Burn in full spate. However, a local, buxom, 'gaberlunzie' lass, a tinker, hoisted her skirts and carried him over on her back. Her reward was a gold sovereign, in return for which she gave him her benison or blessing.

May your purse naer be toom,
And your horn aye in bloom.

Dining at the castle that evening with Earl William Anstruther, or 'Fisher Willie' as the locals nicknamed him, James is reputed to have proposed the formation of 'The Most Ancient and Puissant Order of the Beggar's Benison and Merryland'. The records of this erotic club, which are now preserved in the private Kavanagh collection in the USA, exist from 1732 to 1836, when it was disbanded.

This pseudo-knightly Order, limited to thirty-two members, met twice yearly, at Candlemas, 2nd February, and St Andrew's Day, 30th November, under the auspices of the Anstruther family in Dreel Castle; the room was known to initiates as the Temple. The *Fife Herald* for 20th November 1823 carried the following notice. 'The annual meeting of the Knight Companions of the Most Ancient, Honourable and Puissant Order of the Beggar's Benison will be held within their chamber at Anstruther on Saturday, being the 29th of the present month of November. Dinner on the table at 4 o'clock precisely. By command of the Sovereign. A.J., Recorder'. A.J. was probably Andrew Johnstone. Alan Bold, in his introduction to the 1982 edition of the Records of the club, states, 'In its ritualistic detail and sexually explicit symbolism, the Beggar's Benison Club was remarkable.' Its favourite toast was 'To the beggar maid and joy.' As Prince of Wales, George IV became a member, joining the local aristocracy, including Lord Newark, Sir Charles Erskine, the Earl of Kellie, every laird between Cambo and Largo, David Anstruther, who married the heiress of Newark, grand-daughter of General Sir David Leslie, shipbuilders, baillies, magistrates, councillors, lawyers, surgeons and customs officers. With few exceptions, successive parish ministers of the Four Eastern Boroughs, Anstruther Wester, Crail, Pittenweem and Kilrenny, were installed as knights. Bishop David Low of Pittenweem requested the last Recorder to delete his name from all existing records. A noted raconteur of ribald jokes, he had attended fifty meetings! Teenage strippers were featured in many meetings, although Bold states, 'Actually the ongoings were relatively harmless and if the attitude to local girls was cavalier, then it was all done with the best of intentions in the most morally unstable of societies.' Anstruther had led the fleshpots of London's Soho by centuries!

With neither radio nor television, local entertainment was essentially home-spun. Apart from the kirk choirs, there were musical societies and, for many years, St Monans had a fine fiddle orchestra. The tradition continued into the 1930s, when the lynch-pin was Sandy Reekie, a violin maker living at Number 1, Hope Place just opposite today's Town Hall. It was there with his wife Jean, as piano accompanist, that he held his rehearsals. Among the group were Walter Reekie, boat-builder, and his very talented son, Walter, who later played first violin with the Scottish Orchestra; Andrew Allan, the local Registrar of Births, Marriages and Deaths; Tom Lindsay, local tailor and haberdasher; and a young John Ovenstone.

The last was to feature in village entertainment for the whole of his life. At the time of writing, he is aged seventy-six and still bringing happiness to audiences, not only in the community, but all over Scotland. Born into a musical family, including his father who was a fisherman, he was taught, at the tender age of three, by his mother to play a small melodeon. Progressing to penny whistle and saxophone, and still, by his own admission, unable to read a note of music, he mastered a bewildering spectrum of instruments: continental accordion, with buttons instead of keys, bagpipes, trumpet and even the humble wood-saw, a tool of his trade, became part and parcel of his repertoire. One of his joys was to play the trombone which he had inherited from his uncle, Willie Ovenstone, who had performed in the village Brass Band. The key to his success, despite the lack of any formal tuition, is his talent of having perfect pitch. Apprenticed in Reekie's boatyard, after leaving Waid Academy, he soon formed his own band, Sonara, organising dances to raise money for war weapons, typically for *Spitfire Week* and *Guns for Russia.* Later, keeping his day job as a site agent in the building industry, John steadfastly refused to turn professional despite many offers. 'I'd rather do it for charity,' he opines 'It wouldn't be fun any more!' His son John followed in father's footsteps, as did grandsons Gary and Ian, the latter a professional piano tuner.

34. The Musical Ovenstones. John, Ian, Gary, John (Snr).

Several homes had little bellows-operated organs, around which families and friends would gather to sing the well-beloved Scottish songs and hymns. Concerts were always well attended, particularly in the winter months, when a crowded church-hall was warmer than the fireside. Solos and duets were much in demand, with tuneful renderings such as 'The Crookit Bawbee', 'Leezie Lindsay', 'When ye gaen awa, Jimmy', 'The Auld Maid in the Garret' and 'John Grumlie'. Recitations ranged from complete renditions of Burns' 'Cottar's Saturday Night', 'The Twa Dugs', 'Tam O'Shanter' or Longfellow's 'The Wreck of the Hesperus', to the short and pithy 'East Neuk Lassies'.

> The lassies o' the Ferry
> They busk braw, [dress]
> The lassies o' the Elie
> They ding a', [beat down – smash]
> The lassies o' St Monans,
> They curse and ban, [reproach or 'cast up']
> The lassies o' Pittenweem
> They do the same,
> The lassies o' Anster,
> They drink strong yill, [ale]
> There's green gress in Cellardyke
> And crabs intil Crail.

Penny readings were also a source of entertainment and the *East of Fife Record* of 31st January 1868 gives the following account:

> Penny Readings: The great popularity to which these amusing entertainments have risen in many places throughout the country, has, at last, inspired some of our leading townsmen to introduce these into our town also. A number having some time ago formed themselves into a committee, a series of readings are, we understand, to be given every Saturday evening, this being the only evening during the week that the fishermen of the place can have an opportunity of attending these entertainments. The first series took place within the Union Hall, on the evening of the 16th inst., but intimation

of the meeting not having been properly given, and the arrangements for it having been hurriedly gone into, the whole affair came off with little or no success. Better preparations having been made for the second series, Saturday evening last was appointed, when the hall was crowded, there being nearly 250 present. Mr Robert Lindsay, tailor, occupied the chair, and in a long and compact speech, adverted to the popularity of these readings in other places, and he had no doubt that they would become popular here also, if all things went on right. A number of duets, songs &c. were given throughout the evening by Messrs W. Ferguson, Morris, Brodie and others, all of which were well executed. The readings during the evening comprised, 'The Hen-pecked Husband', given by Mr Dickson of Elie, and 'Astronomy' by Mr John Ross, station agent here, both of whom were, at the close of their respective readings, warmly applauded. By the next occasion, the audience had swelled to 380, being entertained to a reading by Mr Brodie, a carter, of 'Hail Smiling Morn'. By the Fifth Reading on 6th March, 1868, no less than 408 were present to be regaled with the recitation 'Buy your own goose' and glees sung by Misses M. Fyall and M. Easson and Messrs Ferguson and Morris.

The return of the fleet from the fishing grounds was always an important occasion, with news of the catches anxiously awaited.

O joyfu's the din when the boats come in,
When the boats come in sae early,
When the lift [sky] is blue an' the herrin' nets are fu!
An the sun glints on a' things rarely.
When the wives buskit [dressed] braw and the bairns an' a',
Come linkin' [joining arms] doun tae the quay, o
An the very fisher dugs, pu' each ither-by the lugs, [ears]
An join in the general glee, o.

Yet another distraction was the training of part-time soldiers, the early Territorial Army or Home Guard of their days. Again, the *Record* gives the details:

Third Fifeshire Volunteers. – This company of volunteers, of

> which a good number of the young men of this place are members assembled here for company drill on Wednesday evening. A special arrangement having been made with the railway company, the main body of the volunteers was brought from Anstruther by the train leaving there at 7.20 p.m., which halted at the station here. Having formed themselves into marching order, they proceeded from the station through the town, and went to the Town's Muir, where they were put through several movements by Captain Roger. There was a large turn-out of the inhabitants to witness the manoeuvres, it being the first occasion of a volunteer drill here. Owing to the eagerness of the spectators to watch the different movements of the company, the drill had to be gone through with great caution.

Albeit a sport mostly patronised by the aristocracy, cock-fighting parted many a commoner from his hard-earned pennies. The *Cupar Herald* of 28th March 1822 carried the following announcement:

> Cock Main. – The main of cocks will be fought at Cupar on Wednesday and Thursday, 3rd and 4th of April, betwixt the Gentlemen of Fife and the Gentlemen of Angus for two hundred guineas the Main, and five guineas a battle, consisting of thirty-one Mains and nine Byes. To commence at 11 o'clock each day.

The *Cupar Herald* of 12th September 1822 shows that there were lotteries long before the 'innovative' National Lottery introduced by the Tory Government in the 1990s. The claim was made that 'This is the only lottery for more than thirty years past in which the whole of the prizes have been left floating [today's 'Roll-over'?] and more fixed for particular days; the prizes were 3 of £20,000, 2 each of £10,000, £5,500 and £2,000, 10 of £1,000 and 100 each of £500, £300 and £200.'

Coursing too, was an attraction and the *East of Fife Record* for 1875 advertised a match at Stenton Farm, St Monance, the property of Sir Robert Anstruther of Balcaskie. He sponsored the event 'to keep alive the spirit of coursing, presently at a low ebb in Fifeshire'. There were to be '12 grand runs' with 'excellent dogs'. Poor hare!

Sir Robert and Lady Anstruther were, however, mindful of the happiness of their tenantry, affording them a gala occasion early each year as the following excerpt from the *East of Fife Record* for 18th January 1869 relates:

> Festivities at Balcaskie. – On Thursday last week, Sir Robert Anstruther Bart. M.P., with his accustomed liberality and benevolence, gave his annual entertainment to the tenantry, household servants, workpeople and tradesmen engaged on his estate. The servants' hall, dining room and saloon, were superbly and tastefully decorated with evergreens; and beautifully coloured and appropriate mottoes were pendant on the walls, festooned with holly and laurel leaves, doing credit to the artistic taste of their designer. The tenantry dined in the afternoon and the tradespeople were entertained to supper in the evening. At a little past eight o'clock, the large party including both tenantry and servants, entered the saloon which was fitted up *pro tem* for a dance. Here, they were cordially welcomed by Sir Robert and Lady Anstruther. Mr Anstruther, Mr Henry and Miss Anstruther commenced the programme by dancing, very nimbly, some pretty steps in Highland style.
>
> Sir Robert, with Mr Anstruther, led off the first reel. The party then engaged with great enthusiasm and spirit in the general dance. During the banquet, the healths of Sir Robert, Lady Anstruther and the family were drunk, and gracefully responded to by Sir Robert. A number of excellent songs were then sung by Mr Symington, Colinsburgh; Mr Grubb, Pittotter; Mrs Harrison, the housekeeper; Mr Summers, Colinsburgh; Mr Troup, Balcaskie, and by Sir Robert himself. With song and dance, the greased hours on downy pinions brought nigh 'the wee short hour ayont the twal', when the last dance was announced. Sir Robert, as a finale, sung 'Auld Lang Syne' in capital style, the whole company standing with hands crossed in a circle, and joining in the chorus; and, after thanking the company for their attendance and good behaviour, all separated, highly delighted with the entertainment. Great praise is due to Mr Finnie, the butler, Mrs Harrison and Mrs Earth, for their endeavours to make their guests

comfortable and happy. The music was supplied by Mr Alex Burgess, teacher of dancing and Mr Troup of Balcaskie.

The following week, the Laird and his Lady provided a 'grand entertainment' in the Infant and Parish Schools for more than 150 children. Christmas trees, beautifully decorated and illuminated by coloured wax tapers, bore a gift for each child. A large number of parents were admitted to enjoy the novelty of the trees, the first they had ever seen since the tradition had been introduced to Britain by Albert, Prince Consort to Queen Victoria. There was also cake and fruit for each scholar to take home. Sir Robert complimented the classes on their good behaviour, explaining that the treat was to encourage them to be diligent in their studies and to attend to the instructions of their teachers and ministers.

His popularity was exemplified by the actions of the villagers to have him elected to the County Council in November 1868. A large proportion of the electorate decided to have a grand demonstration in his favour. A crowded meeting, mainly of fishermen, was unanimous that he should have all their votes. There was no need for him to canvas 'on the stump'.

All boats stayed in harbour on polling day, there was a village holiday and a great procession, complete with band, marched to Anstruther to record the votes. Sir Robert topped the poll and the multitude turned their steps back to Balcaskie by torch-light, with yet another band swelling the celebrations. When Sir Robert appeared at the gates of his estate, the villagers unyoked his horses from the carriage and drew him to Balcaskie House in triumph. In a speech of thanks, he explained that, throughout the campaign, he had been taunted as not being on good terms with his neighbours. The warmth and generosity of their support had proved otherwise. His staff then dispensed refreshments to all present, who were well contented with the day.

Lady Anstruther had instituted a Parochial Library in 1843 and the St Monans Burgh Records of 11th May 1867 noted her donation of another 627 volumes – 187 to the Female School, 50 to the Reading Room in the Town Hall for the use of fishermen and the remainder to the Parochial School. A charge of one penny per month was levied to pay for binding, repairs and new books.

She had set up an Infants School and a Sewing School and organised and ran a Clothing Club, which provided warm garments for over thirty of the poor and aged. Throughout her life, she was a great benefactress of the village and Thomas Mathers, St Monans' fisherman poet (Chapter 22) dedicated his book to her, in recognition of her good works.

In a talk to the Auld Kirk Women's Guild, Willie Miller and Tom Ovenstone, both born before the turn of the nineteenth century, recalled the amusements of their boyhoods. They instanced the much anticipated Sunday School treats to Balcarres Woods; the song 'I see Balcarres with trees all around' was sung for decades. In the early days of the twentieth century, the 'jaunt' was by corn carts, decorated overall, as were the horses. They remembered Pinder's Circus, the Big Top pitched on the Mair and the parade through the town of elephants, lions and performers, followed by excited children. As befitted a future engineer of distinction, Willie was more entranced by the massive steam engine with its great brass pillars. Dick's Cinematograph, with the first moving pictures seen in the village, was featured in a wooden booth, erected outside the present Town Hall. Hitherto, such entertainment had been restricted to lime-light pictures and slides on the 'magic lantern'. Jack Drew's Pierrots usually set up their stage in Coal Wynd, opposite the present newspaper shop, then the premises of William Easton, one of Scotland's foremost photographers. The village was visited by German bands, barrel organs, dancing bears and one-man bands. Travelling auctioneers had their pitch just off Virgin Square, and sold everything imaginable, including china and watches, timed, as Tom Ovenstone told it, 'to a minute a month'.

Post First World War, an Ex-serviceman's Club with 228 members was formed; the Secretary was Willie Miller. As the American Forces Base at Crail was being disbanded, the canteen building was offered free of charge. Re-erected on the site of the present bowling green, and opened on 19th February 1921 by Colonel T. D. Murray DSO, initially it proved to be very popular, with dances, whist drives, concerts and other local functions. However, the management of 'the Hut', as it was known, ran into serious financial difficulties. Support had dropped off as many members had to seek employment outside the village and its transportation from Crail and rebuilding had cost a considerable sum. In 1934, the club was disbanded and the Hut, which had become an eyesore, sold for agricultural use to George Hain, who farmed at Craigiewells, where it was used as an implement shed for many years.

At a Town Council meeting in May 1936, it was proposed to build a swimming pool, financed by public subscriptions, at the East Braes. This was agreed and the necessary land purchased from the owner, Mr Baird of Elie. However, doubts were expressed as to the choice of the site. Its proximity to the windmill raised concern about the possibility of underground working for coal and other structural defects, allied to the salt-making operations. Fishermen favoured the West Sands, just beyond the Lady's Rock, as the inclination of the skellies to the shore would minimised construction costs and have the added advantage of having the water replenished afresh on every tide. Despite these misgivings, the pool, costing £2,000, was opened with a floodlit gala on 17th July 1937. Buckhaven Amateur Swimming Club assisted the venture with a fine display of diving and swimming on 23rd July. The attendant was paid two pounds per week and the refreshment hut was let for one pound ten shillings (£1.50p.) for the season. Children under ten were charged one penny.

Not unnaturally, with fishing and boat-building being the main commercial activities of the village, there was a popular model yacht club. It was run on the proverbial shoe-string, the gross takings for 1938 being £3 4*s* 0*d.* (£3.20p.). Members kept their craft in the changing rooms at the swimming pool over the winter for a fee of one shilling (5p.).

Football has long been a favourite sport in St Monans. On 9th June 1922, the Town Council agreed that the St Monance Swifts Football Club could have a pitch on the East Common (the name Mair or Muir had been dropped) at an agreed annual rent of ten shillings (50p.). They were empowered to erect a fence and to charge gate money. This decision was challenged immediately on the grounds that it was illegal to set ground aside for the sole use of one section of the inhabitants. The Charter of St Monans was invoked and the fence removed. For many years, the venue was Hain's Park at Craigiewells Farm, just across the road from today's

Auld Kirk manse. Grass-cutting was by courtesy of Geordie's milking herd and pre-match preparation often involved the removal of considerable quantities of rose fertiliser! The changing accommodation was in the Malt Barns at Johnstone's Close, a good half-mile from the pitch, and nobody owned a car!

The Swifts had their most successful season in 1935–6, when they won no fewer than six East Fife Amateur Football Association trophies: the Championship Shield, the Montgomery, Davidson, Janetta, McArthur and Scottish Midland Cups. This remarkable record was followed in the next season by scooping four more trophies. The committee of R. Cathcart, W. Doig, W. Pratt and J. Wilson saw a number of their protégés reach professional status. Willie Main played for Birmingham City and Bob Allan for Raith Rovers, while Willie Peattie, after winning a cap for Scotland as an amateur, went on to star with Dundee United and Raith Rovers. Willie Main's brother Alex played for Raith and Edinburgh City. Dave Ovenstone turned professional with Raith but, after four years, went south where he played for Queens Park Rangers, Cardiff City and Watford. He finished his career as player-manager with a non-league club.

As the local schoolmaster, the then Provost, James Gourlay,

35. St Monans Swifts 1920.

36. St Monans Swifts 1935-36. Back Row: W. Main, A. Wilson, W. Peattie, G. Budd, J. Wilson (Capt.), J. Hutchinson, R. Peattie. Front Row: W. Pratt (Trainer), G. Watson, A. Main, T. Archer, J. Birrell, J. Duncan, D. Wilson (Secretary, reserve goal keeper).

was a member of the Board of Raith Rovers Football Club, he arranged a Grand Charity Match with the Swifts to support the Bathing Pool Fund. It was held at Hain's Park on 6th September 1938. With entrance at sixpence (2½p.), the gate totalled £8 1*s* 9*d.* (£8.09p.)! Financial analysis of this sum defies description! Perhaps boys got in for threepence, although usually they had free entry.

The outbreak of war in 1939 saw the cessation of amateur football and the Swifts entered the ranks of the Juveniles under the guidance, among others, of Joe Ritchie (later a baillie), Alex Wood (later Provost) and Mr Fannen; the trainer was Alex McDonald.

By 1946, the Amateur leagues were re-established, with the Swifts again under Alex Wood and Mr Fannen. Ex-Provost James Braid joined the management team in 1952, but a financial crisis in 1959 saw the club dissolved on the advice of the Scottish Amateur Football Association. A new club, the St Monance Swallows, was launched under the committee of Robert Smith, Chairman, Jimmy Hutt, Secretary and Treasurer and members Chapman Mathers, John Gowans, and father and son, George and Alex Russell.

Jimmy Hutt recalled that the complete new strip for the whole team was bought for less than ten pounds. He also remembered an embarrassing incident when the first match of the season had to be played at Pittenweem. The centre of the local pitch, now on the Mair, obviously without objection to the violation of the Charter, was occupied by a large marquee. It had been erected by a company of Boys Brigade from Glasgow, frequent visitors to St Monans in the summer holidays. The *Glasgow Herald* newspaper carried an inflammatory banner headline, decrying the Swallows for attempting to have the Brigade thrown out of the village!

David Parker went on to play for East Fife, while the post-war team emulated the success of the earlier Swifts. In sixteen seasons, they won the Fife Amateur League on twelve occasions, reached the final of the Fife Amateur Cup four times, scoring three successes, being in the quarter finals of the Scottish Amateur Cup and scooping many local trophies.

From 1976, the club was run under the guidance of Jimmy Hutt, Lawrence Kinnear and Bill Ritchie. Jimmy's son, Bob, carried on

37. St Monans Swallows 1962–63. Back Row: Philip Gay, Bill Mathers, John Forgan, Bill Ritchie, Ted McLaughan, Ronnie Stevenson, John Allan.

Front Row: Jim Scott, David Parker, John Ritchie, Jim Wilson (Capt.), Alex Tarvit.

in 1981 and from 1990, management passed to another local man, Sergeant Andy Morris of the Fife Constabulary.

Over the years, team lists show great family participation, the Mains, Wilsons, Peatties, Cathcarts, Ritchies and others all contributing, season after season. Remarkably, Jim Wilson, popularly known as Jav, captain in 1963–4, was preceded by his father, John, captain in 1936. His maternal grandfather, William Dunn, was the goal-keeper of the 1920 side!

Robert Nee was yet another local lad who became a professional football player. Captain of the Waid Academy First XI, he also turned out for Wemyss Schoolboys, often following a Saturday morning school's fixture with an appearance for the local Swifts in the afternoon. He was in the side which won the Montgomery Cup in season 1946–7. In 1946, Wemyss schoolboys carried off the East Scotland Cup and the Fife Cup. In 1948, aged seventeen, Bob signed for Raith Rovers, making his debut against a Dundee side which included Billy Steel, a great Scottish Internationalist. Called up for National Service, he toured units in Korea with a British Army side based in Japan.

Demobbed, he thought to try his luck in English football so asked the Raith manager, Bert Herdsman, for a free transfer. Herdsman's reaction was to complain about the ten bob (50p.) a week that they had paid him during his time in the Forces! He played with Carlisle United and Brighton and Hove Albion.

Bob says that the scenes that have stuck in his mind over the years are the 15 to 20 a-side games, played on the Mair until it was too dark to see the ball! He also remembers the bruises from the heavy working boots!

John Ritchie, a pupil at Waid Academy, while a member of the Wemyss and District Schoolboys Football Club, was capped for Scotland against the Welsh Schoolboys in 1951, Festival of Britain Year, at Stark's Park, Kirkcaldy. The programme described him thus: 'an accurate passer of the ball and packs a fair shot.' The following month, again at inside left, an anachronistic term in these days of strikers and sweepers, he turned out at Chesterfield against England, in the Victory Shield match, and, in the words of the local newspaper, 'played a blinder'. In opposition that day were Duncan Edwards and David Pegg, both of whom went on to play

38. St Monans Primary 'K.O. Kids' 1969. Back Row: W. Horsburgh, J. Stewart, D. Redpath, R. Hutt, C. Young, I. Melville. Front Row: C. Montador, G. Webster, J. Falconer, J. Dunn, I. Hodge, J. Wilson.

39. Robert Nee (Football).

for the full English Senior Eleven. Tragically, as members of the youthful Manchester United team managed by Sir Matt Busby and known as Busby's Babes, they were involved in the Munich Air Disaster on 6th February 1958, when a British European Airways plane crashed during take-off from a snow-covered runway, killing twenty-three passengers, including David Pegg. Duncan Edwards, the English left-half, died in hospital fifteen days later. After school, John Ritchie spent nearly four years with Chelsea Football Club, then under the management of Willie Birrell, a native of Anstruther.

Following John Ritchie, at Waid Academy, Wemyss and Scottish Schoolboys was Philip Gay. After captaining Fife Schools in 1953, he had the distinction of playing at the Empire Stadium, Wembley, on the occasion of the English Schools Golden Jubilee International on 3rd April, 1954. For this prestigious Junior event, there was a record crowd for a boys' match of over 90,000 spectators. The occasion had the full pomp and ceremony usually only afforded senior football, with a Marching Display by the Massed Bands of the Royal Marines, community singing conducted by the famous

Wembley character, Arthur Caiger, and the presentation of souvenirs by the Scottish Member of Parliament, the Right Honourable Iain Macleod, then Minister of Health. These were plaques in oxidised silver, with a picture of the Empire Stadium in enamelled colours. The official match report listed among the outstanding members of the Scottish defence 'Philip Gay, their tall, industrious centre-half'. By the 8th May the same year, he was again on duty for Scottish Schools in the return match, played at Tynecastle Park, Edinburgh, home of the Heart of Midlothian Football Club. Listed under the 'Sons o' Scotland' was 'Philip Gay (Wemyss) Centre-half. Comes from St Monance in Fife. Thrives on hard work, is tall, very strong and is seldom beaten in the air. Places the ball well.'

National Service in the Army saw him stationed in Germany and, in 1961, adding a German League Winner medal to his collection of trophies; he had been invited to play for the local Paderborn 088–Football Club. The bonus for winning was a football tour of Holland. There were no official German photographs

40. John Ritchie (Football).

as the Cold War was in progress and the infamous Berlin Wall was dividing the country.

In 1961 and 1962, in addition to playing for the local club, he was a member of the British Army of Occupation on the Rhine (BAOR) XI, which competed against all the North Atlantic Treaty Organisation (NATO) teams in Europe. Demobilised in 1963, he returned home to St Monans to play for the local team. Jim Scott was leaving to join the Merchant Navy so Philip replaced him in his favoured position of centre-half. His only disappointment was that they did not win the Scottish Amateur Cup. His haul of trophies from 1963–70 gives some idea of the strength of the side. Philip lists medals from 3 League winners, 2 League Cups, the Lindsay, Usher, Montgomery and McArthur cups.

The principal breeding ground for these prominent players is the local primary school. In the spring of 1969, the school's XI set a record of scoring seventy-nine goals without conceding a single reply. Such was their prowess that, in a game against Elie Primary, while leading 14–0, they came under strict instructions from the bench. The Headmaster gave the order, 'When I wave my handkerchief, stop scoring!' Needless to say, they found it very

41. Philip Gay (Football).

hard to miss! The headline in the *East Fife Mail* read, 'Fishermen's sons have an empty net.'

The family Montador, of French extraction, has, for centuries, been a local 'clan'. One of their number, John, was one of Scotland's premier athletes in his day. An 'evens' man (10 seconds over 100 yards), he ran professionally at many athletic meetings and Highland Games, but, most notably, at the world-famous Powderhall Sprint. Regarded as the oldest professional event of its kind, the race was held over one hundred and thirty yards, at Powderhall, Edinburgh, every New Year's Day. With the rise of sponsored athletics in recent years, it has been discontinued. John's nephew Harry relates how his father Jimmy was so sure that his brother, tipped as the hot favourite, would win the coveted trophy and prize, that he backed him to the tune of one hundred pounds, a great deal of money in those days. Sadly – he lost!

Also worthy of special mention in sport is John Davidson, the only villager, and, indeed, the only pupil of Waid Academy, to be capped for Scotland at Rugby Union. The following description is taken from the programme from the Calcutta Cup match against England at Murrayfield in 1960.

> John Alexander Davidson of Edinburgh Wanderers, gained his first cap a year ago in the Calcutta Cup match when playing for London Scottish. During his three seasons with the club appeared for Surrey and previously played for Penryn and Wasps. Joined Wanderers this season on returning to business in Scotland. Chosen for the Irish match after being a reserve against Wales. Took part in the 1957 trials but in the early months of this season was unable to play owing to injury. Learned the game at Waid Academy, Anstruther, and played for North-Midlands two years ago against the Australian touring team. Made a first appearance for Edinburgh in January against the South. Third cap today.

During an overseas tour of duty with the Royal Air Force (1952–4), he captained the RAF Hong Kong XV, and the Combined Services XV. He also played for the Hong Kong Colony against the Fijians. John's athletic prowess had been marked earlier, when he was both Senior Sports Champion at Waid Academy and Scottish Schools

Triple Jump winner. In 1951, he represented Coastal Command in shot and discus at the Royal Air Force Athletics Championships at Uxbridge. The following year, he took both the hammer and discus titles at RAF Hong Kong.

The present village Post-master, Peter Marr, also had a distinguished athletics career. In 1958, at the Scottish Schoolboy's Championships at Westerlands, Glasgow, he won the senior discus competition with a record throw. He later represented Scotland against the North of England at Goldenacre, Edinburgh. Captain of both Rugby and Athletics at Waid Academy, he set a new Fife School Championship discus record as well as winning shot and javelin. He still holds Waid's shot and discus records, which he set in 1956, and also played representative rugby for the Midland XV.

John Guthrie achieved international status with the javelin. Success came early, when, aged fourteen, he became the Scottish

42. John Davidson (Rugby & Athletics).

Schools Under Fifteen Champion with a record throw of 51.88 metres, which stands to this day. He was awarded the F.J. Clegg Memorial Trophy in 1982 for the Best All-round Athlete at the Scottish Junior Championships. The Scottish Open Under Seventeen Championship was his next achievement and, later, he took the Under Nineteen event. Scouted to join Edinburgh Southern Harriers, he trained with Stewart Togher. The latter is now the US National hammer coach and one of his team took the Silver Medal at the 1996 Olympic Games. At nineteen, John was offered an American University Sports Scholarship but was dogged by injury. His first appearance at international level for Scotland was in 1983 at the Nike Classic meeting at Crystal Palace, London. He went on to win more than a dozen International vests. In 1984, he carried off the Northern Ireland title and followed this up in 1984, 1985, 1987 and 1988, by reeling off winning performances in the Scottish Senior Championships.

In 1986, he was chosen for the Commonwealth Games but again sustained a muscle injury and had to withdraw. He rates his best performance as being at the Amateur Athletics Association

43. Peter Marr (Athletics).

Championships of 1985, where he was placed seventh in a fiercely-competitive international field. The Olympic Silver medallist, Dave Ottley, smashed the championship record and the qualifiers included the UK Champion, Ronald Bradstock, and the Japanese ace, Masami Yoshida. Most of the top ten qualified to the Olympic standard. Second that day was Mike Hill, who competed for Britain in several Olympics and with whom John trained in 1988 in Leeds. Their very successful British National Coach was Wilf Paish, whose 'stable' has included such stars as Tessa Sanderson, five times Olympic javelin champion and Peter Elliot, the 1,500 metres runner.

With the close proximity of Elie Links, which spawned the legendary Earlsferry golfer, James Braid (1870–1950), five times British Open Champion, it seems only natural that golf should become a popular pastime in St Monans.

Few families can have had more success than that of Bill and Ruth Mathers, whose sons John and Alan have remarkable records of golfing achievement. Nurtured from the tender age of five by John Reekie, the then Elie professional, both were playing off scratch by the age of sixteen.

44. John Guthrie (Athletics).

45. John and Alan Mathers (Golf).

John, the elder, reached the last sixteen of the British Amateur Championship at Dornoch, beating Walker and Ryder Cup player David Giford in the process. Winning both the Scottish and the British Colleges titles in 1987, he also captained the winning British team. He broke the Elie Course record with a 64, only to lose it two years later to Alan, who carded a 63.

Alan was the first winner of the Scottish Under-16s' Golf Championship, inaugurated in 1983, and his many trophies that year included the coveted St Andrews Boys Open. By the next year, he had become the youngest ever player to be eligible for the Champion of Champions contest at Leven, finishing the 72 holes in a very credible seventh place, against a strong field of some forty top amateurs. Representing Scotland at Boys and Youth level, he became the Irish Youth champion. Both lads were regular Fife County players, participating in most Scottish and national events with much success.

Alan won the prestigious Boyd Quaich at St Andrews in three successive years. University Internationals saw him play in such exotic locations as Japan, America, Sardinia, Portugal, Spain and France.

In addition to his Elie success, he holds course records at Athlone and Golf Club de Bataille. He was a member of the full Scottish amateur team which played England at Royal Porthcawl in 1984.

In 1987, they completed a family double at St Andrews, Alan taking the Eden Trophy for match play, which he won again subsequently, and John, the Victory Cup for stroke play.

The village also has a very successful Bowls Club, opened in 1955 by ex-Provost James Braid and his wife, Alison. William Duncan, already a keen bowler who had contributed significantly to the realisation of the project and the establishment of the club, was elected first President. The Honours Board in the pavilion records the subsequent holders of the post:

1957–58 J. Braid

1959–66 J. Gowans

1967–68 J. Wilson

1969–71 S. McGregor

1972–73 W. Duncan

1974–78 J. Braid

1979–80 J. Ritchie

1980–83 G. Allen

1983–84 J. Braid

1984–86 H. Montador

1986–88 A. Cameron

1988–90 R. Anderson

1990–92 J. Hamilton

1992–94 C. McKay

1994–96 G. Barclay

1996–97 D. Davidson

1998– V. Bland.

The Miller Family

Apart from providing economic prosperity in their ever-busy yards, the boat-building family of Miller played a leading role in the welfare and social life of the village over more than two hundred years. Records of the seventeenth century identify early ancestors as Félipe, a fishing family from Brittany, again a relic of the Auld Alliance with France, hence today's Phillips. The *East of Fife Record* of November 1869, noted that Mr John Miller, Willie's grandfather, was taking a Sunday School Class for Young Ladies in the Union Hall. His sisters, Catherine and Isabella, were teachers in the local school. Willie Miller described the latter, his aunt Bella, as a 'born organiser', steering the Gospel Temperance, the Liberal Association and, in the First World War, the Red Cross and the Women Volunteers, who picked sphagnum moss, used for dressing wounds. She was Associate to Lady Mildred Anstruther's Branch Presidency of the Scotch Girls Friendly Society. One of the Society's aims was to recognise the role of many young women 'in service'. Their stirring mottos were:

> 'Seek ye first the Kingdom of God,'
> 'Bear ye one another's burdens,'
> 'Obey in all things your masters in singleness of heart, fearing God.'

The author has the Card of Merit, dated 24th June 1893, presented to his grandmother, Jenny Easson, 'for faithful service in the employment of Mrs Peter Fyall for two years'. Bella also headed the organisation of the Old Folks' Tea, a New Year's Day treat of food and entertainment for pensioners, held originally in the Union Hall and then in the Church Hall in Station Road.

On her death, her nephew Willie assumed many of her duties. With his retirement and until the event's termination in 1990, the convenor was his niece Jessie Miller, daughter of his brother Tom. The author is indebted to Robert Ovenstone, an elder of the Auld Kirk and chairman of today's Community Council for his description of the event.

The Old Folks' Tea was started over a hundred years ago. There was a committee responsible for organising this annual event, most of whom were members of the Free, Congregational and Auld Kirks. They supplied all the crockery, cutlery, table cloths, etc. All the best tea-sets, copper kettles, silver teapots came out and a local baker did the catering. Entertainment and speakers were organised; it was an enjoyable time for the old folk. It was held on New Year's Day until it wasn't possible to get catering on that day. It was then moved to the Saturday after New Year. My father, Tom Ovenstone, was on the committee. Some two months before the event, they got together to discuss things and identify all those who had reached the age to qualify for an invitation; all who had become widows were invited. These invitations did not just apply to St Monans folk living in the village but to one-time locals living elsewhere. Apart from the treat, the guests also got a gift to take home, usually a locally-baked sole pie, delicious steak in pastry, or tea and sugar. Funding was from donations and I believe the samples of herring from the boats, offered in the sale ring during the winter herring, were tipped into a barrel and the proceeds from the sale went to the Old Folks' Tea Fund. I have no doubt there would be another method of funding from the boats after the winter herring ceased in 1943. My father was on the committee up to the time he died in 1980 and I have heard him say it was becoming more and more difficult to decide who was entitled to an invitation. It was much simpler when everyone knew everyone in these villages. So many were coming from elsewhere to live here and it eventually became well nigh impossible to know whom to invite. It would not have been very nice or hospitable to invite local folk, who were known, and leave out some elderly person of whom the committee was unaware. It was eventually abandoned in 1990.

The same year, the Community Council discussed the situation and we felt the Old Folks' Tea, with its hundred years' history, was so much a part of St Monans, that it would be wrong to finish it altogether. It was decided, therefore, to try to keep it going, but not to issue invitations and to have it open to folk living in St Monans. The practice of giving parcels to take home was discontinued. This idea was excellent, when folk did not have very much and a little extra was much appreciated, but, we felt, it was not necessary nowadays. What we do now instead of issuing invitations is that, early in December, we put notices in the Post Office and at the Autumn Club, along with a list, inviting pensioners to enter their names for the Old Folks' Tea. This gives us an idea of how many will attend. The Haven at Cellardyke has done the catering since Guthrie's Bakery in Miller Terrace closed. We also arrange for a variety of entertainers. We invite the two local ministers and their wives: one minister says Grace at the start and the other gives a blessing at the end. The venue for the event is now the Town Hall instead of the Church Hall. It has been very successful up to now and all seem to enjoy it. We were fortunate, in the first year that we started, to receive £500 from the Mayview Hotel Charities to be used for the benefit of old folk. We also get donations from other sources, although the cost is mostly met from Community Council funds, which have been raised over the years.

Born in 1899, Willie Miller, who has already been quoted in Chapter 14, was a man of many parts. A Sunday School teacher, an elder of the Auld Kirk at age twenty-five, he was, for forty-one years, Session Clerk and convenor of the Old Folks' Tea Committee for fifty-six years.

Apprenticed at the famous Kelvin Engineering Works in Glasgow in June 1913, aged fourteen, he became a master of his profession, innovating and inventing, among other fishing equipment, the Fifer winch, a four speed motor-driven capstan, still used world-wide. In the First World War, then aged seventeen, he volunteered to join the Motor Boat Section of the Royal Naval Volunteer Reserve. Rapid promotion to Chief Petty Officer saw him serving in HMS *Glen*, a topsail schooner of about 150 tons, which had been converted to a Q-boat. This was one of the smallest of the vessels, posing as unarmed merchantmen, being used to decoy German submarines, which were wreaking havoc on coastal shipping. The *Glen* was originally the *Sydney*, out of Wicklow in Ireland. Many years later, Willie was surprised to see her sail into St Monans harbour to pick up a cargo of potatoes. After further service in Egypt, he was demobilised on 2nd July 1919 and returned to St Monans to pursue a brilliant career in engineering and ship-building.

He was a Founder and Vice-President of the Scottish Fishing Boat-building Association and National President of the Ship and Shipbuilders Federation of Great Britain in 1963. A member of the Institute of Marine Engineers, and Scottish representative to the United Nations Food and Agricultural Organisation, addressing congresses in Rome, Paris and Copenhagen, he became involved in many other national and international assignments. Despite such a work-load, he still found time for local community activities. Councillor, Baillie and Provost of the village, Justice of the Peace, co-founder and President of the Anstruther branch of Rotary International, he was invested, in 1956, with the Most Excellent Order of the British Empire by Her Majesty the Queen, for services to the fishing industry.

On his 89th birthday, he was presented with the Paul Harris Fellowship, the highest award given by Rotary International.

He was a fine historian, with a particular affinity for the annals of his beloved kirk. He had hoped to present a pulpit in the form of a boat's prow, which would be made in his yard, but red tape from the Presbytery and church hierarchy at Edinburgh effectively terminated his plan.

His daughter Jenny relates that, fastened above the lintel of the doorway of their home, the Miller family house, at Ivybank, Rose Street, was a piece of carved oak from Newark Castle. It had been there for many years, but during alterations was moved to her father's workshop. On emigrating to New Zealand, he had it placed in the kirk. Possibly part of the surround of some panelling, it is four feet one inch in length, two-and-a-half inches wide and some three-eights of an inch in thickness. Beautifully carved in a floral rose design, it would seen most appropriate to display it publicly, particularly in view of the ancient connection of kirk and castle.

Also in the Rose Street garden was a carved Viking head, which had been found on the beach by Willie's father. It was probably a

46. Willie Miller, OBE, JP, MIMarE.

relic of the bloody times of the Danish invaders. Prior to boatyard buildings being erected in Rose Street, the land had been the garden of a fine house. Owned by one Kate Bridgeford, it boasted a splendid, curved stone staircase. The entrance gates from the Coal Wynd (Forth Street) was wide enough to allow the passage of a horse and gig, and were flanked by two large stone pillars, on each of which was carved a large rose. Tradition had it that it was the White Cockade of Bonnie Prince Charlie and the Jacobite Rebellion. Nearby, in Willie Miller's garden at Ivybank, was a very old white rose, which, supposedly, had bloomed since the turbulent days of the Forty-Five.

Willie Miller lived to be a grand old man of ninety-four years, spending his last days in Picton, South Island, New Zealand, near Jenny's home. He was still very active mentally, designing aids for the aged.

Happily, despite the closure of the yard in St Monans, the Miller dynasty is being perpetuated as builders of fine boats in New Zealand. A cousin of Willie, Andy Miller, already ran the firm of Miller and Tunnage in Port Chalmers. During the Second World War, a young Chief Petty Officer from Christchurch, serving on HMNZS *Achilles*, and who knew of the connection, took the opportunity of a berthing in Scotland to visit the St Monans yard. There, Roger Carey met Jenny Miller, who was then on the office staff, and three years later, they were married in New Zealand.

After demobilisation, Jenny and Roger moved to Picton, on South Island, New Zealand and started their own boat-building business. Interestingly, their first family clinker-built dinghy was called *Inverie*. Today, son Phillip designs boats and son Jimmy builds them, big eighty-footers for inshore fishing.

The history of all the boats, which her father, an Associate Member of the Royal Institute of Naval Architects, designed and built, is faithfully recorded by their daughter Joan in her book, *By Boats We Live*. A talented artist as well as an accomplished writer, she has illustrated each craft in superb water-colours.

Revenue and Taxation

In the days of poor roads and no railway, much commerce was conducted by sea. A substantial portion of the town's revenue was raised from local tolls, anchorages and customs dues. Additional shore charges were levied on local and visiting tradesmen and merchants.

The schedule of these charges, as fixed and approved by the Magistrates and Town Council in December 1817 and October 1840, shows a most comprehensive list of activities. There were three levels of taxation: for freemen, for stranger burgesses and for unfree men, the last not enjoying the liberties of the other classes and being subject to paying excise. The table gives an excellent indication of the variety of goods and materials which constituted the commercial practices of the town.

Common charges were 'For each day selling Beef, Pork, Mutton, Lamb or Veal in Town – Twopence [1p.]'; 'for each boll [140lbs. – 64kg.] of Meat brought into the Town for sale, three farthings.' There were different prices for 'killing for sale in the Town, Ox, Cow, Calf, Sheep and Swine.' Raw materials such as 'Bark, Salt, Lime, Smithy Coals, Malt, Grain or Potatoes imported or exported by land or sea' were charged 'per chalder', an old Scottish measure of about one ton. 'For Ale, Beer and Porter,' the tariff was per 40 Scots pints [1 pint = 1 English gallon], while 'Whisky, Foreign Spirits and Linseed' were rated by the hogshead; 'Iron, Tow, Flax and Hemp' by the ton; 'Tar or Herring' by the last [a wagon load of about 4,000 pounds (1,800 kilograms)]; 'Slates, Bricks, Peats, wet and dry Cod, Ling, Haddock' per hundred; 'Hides' by the daiker [10], 'Butter, Beef, Grease, Tallow and Oil' by the barrel; 'Fruit, including Apples, Pears and Plums, Carrots or other Roots, Pewter or Tin Ware, and Mussels, imported by land to the town by the cart-load for sale – three farthings.' Charges were levelled for 'each horse-, ass-, or mule-load, or cart- or wain-load of any article of merchandise to be sold in, or go out of, the Town.' Cheese was charged per hundredweight (50 kgs.). 'For each day that stranger merchants Hawk through, or sell by Public Roup, in the Town – Threepence [1p.] (for un-freemen)'. Fees for 'Strangers' Boats' entering the harbour depended on whether they were 'Drave boats during the winter and Lammas Fishings' or at any other time. 'Ships or Vessels under 120 tons to pay one-half-penny per ton of Shore Dues.' Above that tonnage, the cost was 'a slump [a lump sum] of Five Shillings and Two Pence [26p.].' All vessels paid for 'Beaconage', according to tonnage. This was a contribution to the upkeep of a warning beacon for assisting entrance to the harbour, particularly in bad weather. It often consisted of tarred kindling in a cresset, or iron basket, set in a prominent position on high ground at the back of the village. Local boats only paid anchorage if they were loading or unloading.

Earlier records from the '*Curia Capitalis* [Court Book] *of the burgh of Barronie of St Monance holden in the town of St Monans* (note different spellings!) on 28th October 1719 by Sir Alexander Anstruther of Newark, Superior, show the following examples of Customs duty.

For each chalder of Foreign Salt	£0.6.8.	[33p.]
For each chalder of Corn or Salt	£0.5.4.	[21p.]
To each barrel carried out of the town	£0.0.8.	[3p.]
To each last of empty barrels	£0.2.8.	[13p.]
To each pack of Wool	£0.2.0.	[10p.]

There was great diversity in early Scottish weights and measures and matters were not resolved until 1661, when a Commission was set up by Parliament to recommend national standards. Exemplars were kept in different cities and burghs, the *ell* for lineal measure in Edinburgh, the *jug* for liquid capacity in Stirling, the *firlot* for dry measure in Linlithgow and the *troy stone* for weight in Lanark. The uniformity of weights and measures was established by Act of Parliament in 1824.

The Customs, Anchorage, the Town Yard, Braes and Refuse were put up for public roup each year 'at Twelve o' the clock midday'. From the year to March 1745, it was 'carried to Andrew Bains, Junior Baillie for Eightie Four Pounds'; in 1748 'to Andrew Kay, Baker, for £58 Scots' and, in 1776, 'to John Reekie, weaver for £53'. The figures for 1799 show the prime bidder as Andrew Roger at £3 16*s*. (£3.80p.) for Customs and Anchorage, one guinea (£1.5p.) for Braes and Sward and fifteen shillings (75p.) for street dung. The apparent radical reduction of tariffs was due simply to the switch of currency from pounds Scots to pounds Sterling, the latter being equal to twelve of the former.

The records for 26th April 1841 detail the roup of the Mair: '11 acres, or thereby, Imperial measure, with two acres being reserved for the feuars for drying and bleaching clothes, drying nets and tarring ropes.' The conditions of let were strict, entailing 'meeting the rules of approved husbandry', such as manuring. After the last crop of corn was harvested, rye grass and clover had to be sown. During the lease, in accordance with the Burgh Charter, Sir Wyndham C. Anstruther, Baronet, could still prospect for, and mine, coal, metals and all minerals, and could build waggon roads or aqueducts across the property. He undertook to indemnify the tenants, the arbiters to be mutually chosen.

Barrel stances and herring curing stations at the harbour were also rouped. The minutes of the Town Council for 1908 record that the former sites were still being let. Boat stances on the beach and on vacant ground by the East Harbour were also a source of revenue; the income for the year beginning June 1877 was £10. Boats were often hauled up the Coal Wynd (Forth Street), to stand on the Mair, the first use of a steam engine for that purpose being recorded on 23rd July 1869.

The town smiddy (blacksmith's shop) was leased on an annual basis; the Town Hall too added to the Common Good. In 1852, it was let to James Cochran for teaching evening school at a cost of 1*s.* 6*d.* (7½p.) for five nights; this was reduced to 1*s.* (5p.) the following year. However, in 1854, by a majority vote of the councillors, permission was refused to Teachers of Dancing on the grounds that such so-called entertainment was lascivious and lewd! In 1885, Mr James Reekie, boat-builder, applied for tenancy of space for a boatyard, sixty feet by twenty feet, at the West Pier. The rent was set at £3 per annum, with the responsibility of clearing the ground of ballast and other rubbish. This requirement seems somewhat at odds with the Council decree, three years earlier, that no ballast was allowed to be thrown out of any vessel unless the skippers bound themselves to take it away by the next tide.

In 1911, there was an application by Mr Walter Reekie to build a yawl in two months in the Coal Wynd; the charge was agreed at ten shillings (50p.).

The villagers did not always comply readily with the charges or the conditions of let. Typically, it is recorded that, in 1872, John Gerrard took a berth in the harbour let to another and 'he had so acted in the face of remonstrance by the Magistrates that he was to be charged eighteen shillings [90p.], twice the normal rate, or remove the boat, or legal proceedings would be initiated.'

The renting of the Mair also led to domestic squabbles. The

East of Fife Mail of 1908 recorded that Mr James Finlayson of Coal Farm had complained to the Town Council that straying horses from a tinker encampment were ruining his crops. He maintained that, as the Council charged the tinkers rent, so they should be obliged to fence off the Mair. The reply was one of regret but also a refusal to be associated with the situation. In 1910, the topic was again addressed. Baillie Fyall proposed that the letting of the common should cease, which was carried. This decision immediately raised the problem of how to redress the loss of income; there had been a scale of charges for circuses, camps, etc. The removal of the gypsies would solve the farmer's problem but this required some legal strategy. Although the Charter gave the Mair to the villagers, from time immemorial strangers had squatted (not a modern term) or encamped there, so it could not be considered as private ground. Again, it was not enclosed, so the law of trespass did not apply. However, it was an offence for anyone to encamp or light a fire on or near a private road or enclosed and cultivated land or any turnpike or statute labour road. The proximity of the Mair to the main St Monans–Pittenweem road meant that the squatters, complete with their livestock, had their marching orders.

In addition to local taxes, tolls and harbour dues, general taxation covered a bewildering spectrum of subjects. Typically, there was window tax (1748–98) for houses with more than seven windows. Householders often filled windows in to avoid payment. Old records for 1790 in the Parish of Cupar give: 'Lady Betty Anstruther, formerly 39 W, shut up 5 W.' The Inhabited House Tax of 1778–98 and the Shop Tax (1785–89), both applied to any house or shop with an annual value of over five pounds. From 1777–98, male servants (gardener, footman, coachman etc.) and female servants (scullery- and chamber-maids, cooks etc.) were subject to their employers paying tax on them. The Cart Tax of 1785–92 applied to two-, three-, or four-wheeled carriages, 'upon every Coach, Berlin, Landau, Chariot, Calash, Chaise-marine, Chaise, Chair, and Caravan, or by what name so-ever such wheel Carriages now are or hereafter may be called.' Horses too were covered; the Horse tax of 1785–98 applied to carriage and saddle horses and the Farm

Horse Tax (1787–97) to horses used in husbandry or trade. For one year only, 1797–8, there was a Dog Tax.

Clocks, and gold, silver or metal watches were taxed in the same year. From 1798–9, there was an all-embracing Consolidated Tax, 'covering value of houses, numbers of windows, male servants, carriages, horses and dogs.'

In late eighteenth century Scotland, spirit, beer and malt accounted for more than half the amount collected by the Excise. In addition to the items already mentioned, there was an astonishing array of taxable goods, commodities and processes. Every Excise Officer had to carry his Commission, listing all duties to be levied ... 'upon making of Soap, Paper, Pasteboard, Millboard, and Scaleboard respectively; and upon printing, painting, or staining of Paper, and upon printing, painting, staining or dying of Silks, Callicoes, Linens and Stuffs respectively; and upon the making of Starch, and of Gilt and Silver wire respectively; and upon tanning, tawing [kneading] or dressing of Hides and Skins, and pieces of Hides and Skins; and upon the making of Vellum and Parchment respectively, and upon Silver-plate and Manufactures of Silver respectively; and of the Inland Duties upon Coffee, Tea and Chocolate and upon making Malt and making and importing Mum, Cyder and Perry ...' Mum was a strong German beer, originally brewed in Brunswick.

As duty was mostly charged during manufacture, so the Excise Officer's time was largely taken up with inspections by day and night. Soap-boilers had to be visited every four hours, candle-makers every six. For the paper trade, there were no fewer than seventy-eight rates of duty, for the tanning industry fourteen, each skin and hide being weighed and marked with an excise seal. The malting process in whisky making, in which the barley, which had been steeped in water to allow germination to take place, was dried out, could last for a fortnight; a minimum of five visits had to be made during that time. Naturally, it was not unknown for the officer to be persuaded to skimp or even ignore his duties by a suitable donation in cash or kind.

Public Utilities and Health

Already noted in Chapter 3 were the early pilgrimages to the Chapel and the Well as cures for every ailment and disease, but, principally, the Black Death, the bubonic plague spread by rats, leprosy and smallpox. There were epidemics of the last disease in 1783, 1784 and 1786. On 14th October 1845, the Synod of Fife, which had met in Cupar, set aside Thursday the 18th, for 'humiliation and prayer in consequence of the prevalence of cholera in the land.'

The *Old Account* notes that 'If the contagion got in during the summer, when the air is much tainted with the refuse of the fishing, it is then peculiarly fatal, sweeping off from twenty to thirty children at a time.' However, by then, inoculation had been introduced and there was hope that the death rate would be much diminished.

The almost total lack of household sanitation, together with the inevitable detritus from the gutting and preparation of fish and the shelling of mussels for bait, created a far from healthy environment.

As already observed, rubbish removal was the subject of annual roup or auction. The Burgh minutes of November 1836 record the resolution that the street dung be cleared every fortnight; fish offal was to be removed every twenty-four hours by the owner, 'otherwise the same to belong to the Jacksman [a retainer of the Superior].

Inter-village rivalries and jealousies led to deprecatory statements such as that reported in the *Pittenweem Register* of April 1848:

> While the inhabitants of other parts of Europe are employed in pulling down Monarchies, setting up Republics, and struggling for liberty, the people of Bonnie St Monance ... are fighting for filth ... On Monday last, farmers' carts went through the town for the purpose of removing the middens, which stand on the street, and paying for the soil, but a number of the proprietors of the middens refused to sell, alleging that it would be more to their advantage to keep the dung until they had a full cart-load, and then they would get something worth while for the goods. The Magistrates and Board of Health would not listen to this arrangement, and

> carts, protected by Police, were next day sent to remove the nuisances without further ceremony. It was then that the hue and cry got up; and ... when they saw the carts approach, they fell to work, some had shovels but more had nothing but their fingers, and with an assiduity which could not be surpassed, threw every particle of dung into the sea rather than let the carts have the advantage of it ... While the work was going on, one of them was heard to say – 'By Gosh! I wad rather eat it than let them get it.'

St Monans, without the advantage of a local publication, had no means by which to retaliate.

The *Fifeshire Journal* of 1849 reporting a suspected outbreak of cholera states:

> Our Board of Health has been employed in going through every house and cellar in this town in purpose to see every house cleaned and whitewashed, and they have ordered cholera medicine to be distributed at three different houses in town should anyone be affected by the malady. Those who are unable to pay get medicine gratis. We are thankful to say that no case has yet occurred in the village.

In 1871, the paper again reported 'the removal of all nuisances, house by house'.

In 1852, the Reverend D. C. Foggo, minister of the Auld Kirk, proposed that there should be a supply of filtered water. Hitherto, water had been brought in barrels by cart from the Inverie Burn, an expensive and time-consuming exercise. The Session decided not to proceed at that time.

In 1866, the Parochial Council decided to send the dung cart round every day for refuse and ashes and to dispense with middens and ashpits, which were to be found in the streets, usually just outside front-doors. This resolution was to be enforced by the Nuisance Removal Committee!

Sir Ralph Anstruther again brought up the vexed problem of an adequate and healthy water supply. The piggeries on the Mair were 'dirty, ill-kept and overcrowded'. Considered insanitary, they were ordered to be removed. Previously, all pigsties had required planning permission before erection. The minutes of 26th November 1853 noted that the widow Duncan had built a sty without permission and was ordered to demolish it forthwith.

Such minor and comparatively trivial matters at least afforded the council, constrained as they were by the almost dictatorial will of the Superior at Newark, the opportunity of conducting some competent business, other than the annual routine election of officers and the rouping of public amenities and utilities.

In 1873, water supply was again debated, this time with more concrete proposals. The initial plan was to draw supplies from the Dreel Burn, the volume running in the Inverie being totally inadequate for the needs of the rising population. The Inverie was the outlet to the sea from streams rising near Kilconquhar Loch and Balcarres Mill. Tributary sources of the Dreel were from Kellie Law, Cassingray, Baldutho and other farms, flowing past Pittenweem and emptying into the sea at Anstruther. To be delivered through iron and clay pipes, the estimated requirement was thirty gallons per day per head of population. However it was pointed out that such a drain on the resources of the Dreel might lead to claims for compensation from the mills at Milton and Anstruther Wester and from the threshing mill at Balcormo.

The alternative scheme was to share the supplies of Pittenweem, whose consumption was thirty-three gallons per day for each of the population of eighteen hundred. The head count in St Monans being approximately the same, such a split would reduce the supply to sixteen gallons. Financial estimates varied from £2,100 to £2,800.

The opening of the waterworks and the supply of mains water became a reality in 1883, albeit mostly from communal street pumps, some of which were still in use in the 1940s. Domestic mains water was a luxury.

Hay-Fleming observed that 'many of the towns are far from clean' but then added, 'Nowhere are stronger, healthier-looking people to be met than in the confused and dirty streets of St Monance.' He attributed such rude health to 'the abundance of fresh air, which permeates every house and also the excellent supply of water, which had just been introduced.'

In 1883, Lord Lindsay offered £30 for the street manure, which bid was rejected as he wanted all the work done, with the refuse being delivered to his farm. There had been some previous attempts at public sanitation as, in November 1881, 'It was resolved to erect a Necessary on the south side of the Brae.'

In the 1880s, there was considerable controversy as to what body should rule the village. The Town Council wanted to be the Local Authority for the whole parish but the land-owners objected, observing that, until the boundaries were established in law, the Police Act of 1862 could not be invoked to give the Council this responsibility.

Under the provisions of the Local Government (Scotland) Act, 1867, on 30th June 1881, it was ruled that 'the Parochial Board of St Monance shall be the Local Authority for the whole parish.' That body set their stamp of authority on the conduct of local affairs. The list of Fees issued in 1883 made some additional provision for sanitation. Charges were:

1. Nets drying on common – 1*s.* 6*d.* (7½p.) per fleet of nets.
2. Boats when hauled up – 1*s.* 6*d.*
3. Boats on the common – 1*s.* (5p.)
4. Erections on the common such as galluses (structures of poles on which nets were dried) and huts to be removed.
5. No heaps of manure etc. on common without permission.

In 1885, it was resolved to form the town into a special drainage area under the Public Health Act. Today's water is supplied from a reservoir at Gillingshill, north of Arncroach.

Still smarting at their lack of authority and deciding to use the same stratagem as had been deployed against them by the land-owners, the Town Council directed the Clerk to communicate with the Lord Advocate, pointing out that the boundaries had never been established. His reply was to adopt the aforementioned Police Act and resolve the matter with the County Council, whose local representative was Sir Ralph Anstruther, the principle landowner! The County sought the opinion of the Court of Sessions, as a result of which the Board of Supervisors reversed their decision on 2nd May 1890. However, the Town Council refused to take responsibility for sanitation and the County Council became the local authority! It issued a By-law in 1891 that 'no shells etc. be put put in buckets and there would be no barking [tanning] of nets in the street.'

The first proposals for gas lighting were mentioned as having been discussed with the Pittenweem Gas Light Company on 23rd October 1855. Piped from the Pittenweem works at the West Shore, gas for street lighting had been estimated originally at £3,957 19*s.* (£3,957.95p.), subsequently amended for contingencies to £4,000. In its account of the event, the *Fifeshire Journal* noted that: 'There is not doubt of the new light proving a great advantage and saving to the inhabitants of St Monans, who are so much employed during the evenings making preparations for their piscatorial pursuits.' It should be remembered that, although replacing candle and paraffin lamp, gas-lighting was by a simple jet, the incandescent lamp or 'mantle', complete with protective glass globe, not being introduced for some years.

A great deal of refuse was dumped or flushed into the sea, with no regard for pollution. Sanitation in each house was primitive. A mains drainage system was not introduced until 1900. In 1934, electric lighting was introduced, the first installations being in the new housing scheme at Gourlay Crescent.

The *New Account* was happy to relate that: 'There are no blind, deaf or dumb in the parish although two male parishioners were boarded in the Dundee Lunatic Asylum.' Statistics observed by the Reverend Swann in that era were: 'I do not know more than one bachelor above fifty years old in the parish, but there are at least twelve widowers of that age and there are nineteen unmarried females above forty-five.' Although there was much illness, there were many inhabitants in their eighties and nineties. Again, despite the pace of modern living and the radical changes that technology has brought to eating habits, from the old days of 'tatties an' saut herrin', many St Monans inhabitants enjoy long and healthy lives.

The earliest known entry in a parochial register is the record for settling an account on 16th April 1597. The first trace of a marriage register is in 1684 and there are only three entries of births and baptisms before 1707. From that period, there is a more regular register of marriages, baptisms and burials.

At the beginning of the nineteenth century, the whole parish belonged to just two land owners, both Anstruthers, Sir Robert of Abercrombie and Sir John of Newark.

Census figures show that the population rose gradually from

780 in 1775 to a maximum of 2,054 in 1881, falling back to 1,370 by 1981. Typically, in 1831, there were 30 families in agriculture and 19 in trades, manufacturing, fishing, handicrafts and quarries.

St Monans Population Census	
1801	852
1811	849
1821	912
1831	1,110
1841	1,157
1861	1,498
1871	1,761
1881	2,054
1891	2,054
1931	1,819
1951	1,618
1981	1,370
1991	1,385
1996	1,580*

* *Estimate by North-East Fife County Council.*

Crime and the Law

In early Scotland, such criminal code as existed was little respected as there was no real law enforcement agency. Assassinations were perpetrated with impunity and property was unsafe from vandalism and theft. Each man revenged himself, when it was in his power to do so, and the nobility banded together in the commission of murder and rapine. Witchcraft was not a crime that escaped the royal eye or the wrath of church or populace, if detected. The fancied enormity of having intercourse with the Devil was punished by imprisonment, torture and death.

As in the history of St Monans, fact and legend are often inextricably entwined, witchcraft is the subject of a later chapter.

In the sixteenth century, a truly heinous crime was committed at a local landmark, known as the Boiling Cauldron. This is a deep cavity, worn by the tides and situated by a rock formation, known as the Sphinx, just below the Auld Kirk. As the water surges shorewards, it is trapped in the recess and 'boils' over the adjacent rocks, in a great fountain of spray. The formation lost its sphinx-like appearance when the upper portion broke off in a storm in August 1921.

Tradition has it that a young man, called Guilemus or William, the son of a neighbouring landowner, had been considered to be paying too much attention to Baron Newark's only daughter, Amica. Her father banned the lad from seeing her but it was his wont to sit on a nearby rock, hoping to espy her on the castle battlements. On one occasion, being seen by three of the Baron's retainers, he was attacked, severely beaten and thrown into the Boiling Cauldron for dead. Unbeknown to his assailants, he swam out to sea, where he was fortunately rescued by a boat bound for Leith. Some ten years later, a spaeman predicted that a stranger would appear and assume command of the castle. In twelve months' time, the victim returned, wooed and married his sweetheart and became the Sir William Sandilands, who gave the village its Charter.

Many misdemeanours were brought for judgement and discipline before the kirk session, rather than before any police or magisterial jurisdiction. The power of the church in those days was literally that of life and death, the ministers and elders, the lowest form of ecclesiastical court, being vigilantes, long before the citizens' justice of America's Wild West.

The earliest Session Book and Accounts of St Monan's Kirk, extant in the archives of the library of the University of St Andrews, are dated 15th May 1598. From that time into the early twentieth century, these records show an almost total preoccupation with sin and 'carnal dealing' or 'houghmagandie', as it was known. In 1705, there was much evidence of the elders' inquisitorial reign and harsh treatment of the so-called 'dolated' or misfortunate women, who had indulged their passions in 'ante-nuptial ffornication'. Even those who had subsequently married were 'compeared', that is, summoned, before a court to answer a citation, the crucial test period being that between the dates of marriage and the birth of a child. The agenda was always identical, opening with a prayer and then the minister enquiring as to what 'disorders' had been reported since the last meeting. There were even different categories of this particular sin; pre- or ante-nuptial, casual, adultery and disputed paternity. Occasionally, a meeting would simply be opened with prayer and immediately closed with prayer, there being 'no scandalous information to hand'.

On 19th January 1718, the 'ffornicatrix, Isaboll Nickle', was rebuked before the congregation; the male offender, Alexander Parker, was not even present. On 2nd February, she was again subjected to a tirade of venom from the pulpit. At the meeting on 23rd March, the minister reported that she was now serving at sea on a man-of-war and 'had brought forth a child'.

By the next meeting, Catherine Lumsdaine and Elspeth Thomson were the victims, the latter for being pregnant by 'a man from the North', unnamed but already married. Within a week, they were followed by Margaret Poustin, being found 'guilty of fornication with James Cockburn, a bombadier in Captain Pringle's troop'. The elders who passed judgment on that occasion were 'Messrs Duncan, Miln, Wilkie, Stevenson, Steedman, Mathison, Strachan, Webster, Leitch, Hay, Paxton, Morrice and Syme'.

The kirk session had a veritable army of 'famas', 'clypes' or tell-tales throughout the village. On 23rd December 1735, the session heard evidence of fornication from the girl, who had been lying in bed with the offenders! On 21st January 1759, Helen Harvie was interrogated on the grounds of a *fama clamosa*, a legal term for any notorious rumour, ascribing immoral conduct to a minister or office-bearer in a church. She was pregnant and was found guilty of fornication. The offending male, who could only have been the minister, an elder or the beadle, was never mentioned!

A famous exception was the case of the girl who was accused, but claimed that she had been raped. She refused to sit on the penitential stool as she was sinless. So strong was her defence of her honour that she was just 'exhorted to be of a better mind', and let off. The penitential stool or 'cutty' was a crudely constructed bench, with arms like an easy chair. Elevated above the pews so that the accused was in full view of the congregation, such chairs were indispensable furniture in every parish church in Scotland at that period. The sermon consisted of the unfortunate subject of humiliation sitting, while the minister harangued her for her sinful wickedness. Few men ever occupied the chair, although Robert Burns was known to have endured commitment on his local cutty.

The Elders could even order a woman to 'stop haunting men's company'. In 1823, William Forgan, a sailor, was accused of ante-nuptial fornication with Elspeth Fyall. They were rebuked before the congregation and then had their child baptised, having been married for nearly nine months!

The incidence of fornication in the village was so high that, in 1766, the subject was referred for discussion to the St Andrews Presbytery. The records of the kirk session for 17th March 1906 noted the end of trial by committee. The minister was delegated to deal with all Cases of Discipline and record the same in a separate book, to be submitted to the elders when asked.

Even lesser offences were tried. Tam Aitone, 'a wild lad', and Beatrice Youlles, 'a gey lass', were conducting a clandestine affair. In 1648, Tam was summoned before 'the august Sanhedrim', the kirk session, for 'drinkin' an bydin' in that ledy's hous in time o' sermon'. He was fined and admonished but to no avail. The kirk records witness 'he went by the kirk door on the Lord's Day at the minister's going to the pulpitt, blowin' an blastin' tobacco and cam not tae the kirk.'

Again, in the seventeenth century, taken to task and fined by the elders were 'ane Willie Robertson and ane Peter Fyall for smokin' an swearin' an spittin' in front o the kirk on the Sabbath.' Should a minister be found guilty of swearing or blaspheming, he could be fined one fifth of his stipend. Quarrels between neighbours and ownership of properties and goods were settled by the kirk, some cases going on for months or years. They also consigned people to the Lunatic Asylum, without seeking medical opinion or certification.

Occasionally, the records deal with more mundane topics. In 1722, it is noted that Alex Mill should be paid twelve shillings in the year for keeping the kirk door. The same account lists 'Nine Pounds for Wine', and 'Four Pounds to poor strangers'. There was no evidence of receipts for the transactions, nor were the recipients named. A later entry gives 'To a woman in needy circumstances £1'; 'to another woman in needy circumstances £1.'

Non-observance of the Sabbath was also high on the kirk's list of 'crimes'. The minutes for 1726 record 'Megg Mill, spouse to Thomas Wilson, had been found carrying water on the Lord's Day before public worship.' Again, in 1730, 'on 3rd May, being Sabbath, James Bruce carried a barrel of ale on a sledge for which he was rebuked in public.' In 1852, the session sat under the Moderator, the Reverend D.L. Foggo. The minutes state:

> The Moderator called the attention of the Session to the approach of the Herring Fishery Season, in which, for several years past, there has been a grievous amount of Sabbath Desecration, both by the Foreign Ships lying off the coast, and by the Fishermen in this and the neighbouring Parishes – He also intimated that he had had interviews on the subject with the French and Belgian Consuls, and with the Secretary of the Board of Herring Fisheries, that all these Gentlemen had entered warmly into his views, and had requested him to state at length the nature of the Sabbath Desecration, and the mode in which he proposed to put a stop to it. The Moderator therefore submitted drafts of the Memorials he had prepared for these parties, and also one for the Sheriff of the County – The Memorials respecting the Sabbath Desecration by the Foreign Ships to be forwarded by the French and Belgian Consuls to their respective Governments, and those which respect the Sabbath Desecration by the Fishermen in this Parish and neighbourhood to be forwarded to the Secretary of the Board of Fisheries and to the Sheriff of the County, calling upon these Gentlemen to use their legal powers in putting an end to this increasing evil. The Session having considered the conduct of the Moderator in this Matter, approve of the steps he has taken and the Memorials he has prepared, agreed that each member of the Session should sign them, and that the Moderator be requested to obtain Clergymen and Elders in the neighbouring Parishes to attest the truth of, and their concurrence in, said Memorials.

In 1864, there occurred 'a lamentable desecration of the Lord's Day', when 'kirk members carted nets to boats and twenty boats went to sea on Sunday.' The punishment for both fishers and carters was to be suspended from church privileges for a whole year, being restored to Communion only after public confession of penitence and the promise of due observance of the Sabbath and of the yearly Feast Day in future. On 4th December of that year, the Session Clerk sent a memo to the Manager of the North British Railway Company, adjuring him to stop running trains on Sundays. In 1856, they had petitioned both Houses of Parliament against 'the threatened infringement of the rest from labour afforded by the Sabbath, as specified in the Ten Commandments, by opening the British Museum, the National Gallery and the Crystal Palace on the Lord's Day.'

In 1873, Sir Robert Anstruther, the local Member of Parliament, presented a petition in the House of Commons that St Monans was in favour of the suppression of all licences for the sale of intoxicating drink.

Nor did the Session refrain from interfering in national politics. In 1851, they wrote to Parliament urging them to take drastic measures against Papal Aggression and to oppose Lord Melgund's Educational Bill!

The Charter of St Monans acknowledged the need for civil obedience and compliance with the law; in 1840, the council consisted of three baillies, a treasurer and fifteen councillors, although, originally, the baillies could nominate an indefinite number of townsfolk to assist deliberations. As stipulated in the Charter, the Superior signed all minutes.

Such a practice persisted up to the establishment of a Police Burgh in 1933. At election time each year, a list of proposed magistrates, baillies and treasurer had to be prepared for the Superior. The kirk records for 1852 note that 'the petition was left in the lock hole of the most patent [available] door of the mansion [Elie House].' Alternatively, it could be left with a servant. If no reply had been received, and indeed it never appeared to be, by noon the following day, the Superior's silence was taken as acquiescence in the selection and the feuars then proceeded to the polling booths.

Favouritism and downright nepotism were rife and in 1823, David Davidson and John Reekie pursued a law suit in the Court of Sessions in Edinburgh against the appointment of the two baillies, James Scott and Alexander Davidson, together with James Dickson as factor or treasurer.

Their Lordships' judgment read, 'Who was it that nominated and appointed these men? The answer is plain; their friend, the Town Clerk was the only officer who had a political existence and, to him alone, they owe their dignities and state, which, like the power that created them, is likely to be of a very short duration!' They were accordingly sentenced to be 'Reduced, Retreated, Rescinded, Cassed [made nought], Annulled, Decerned and Declared' by our Lords as 'null and void'. The Town Clerk was fined £500 sterling at Edinburgh on 4th June 1824.

There were twelve special constables, chosen annually from the populace for the preservation of peace. Leyton stated that there was a room in the Tolbooth or Town Hall, used as a prison, but no-one was kept there for more than one night. However, the Reverend Robert Swann, writing in 1837 noted:

> There are two prisons in St Monan's, under one roof, one on the upper floor of the town-house, and one on the ground floor. They are equally well secured; the lower by much the more dismal of the two. Persons are committed to one or the other according to their pre-eminence in delinquency, debtors upstairs and criminals downstairs. The magistrates imprison as sudden emergency calls for it; but they do not impose fines, except with the formalities of a regularly constituted court. So far as I have occasion to hear, imprisonment is a rare occurrence.

As the local minister, his account is likely to be more reliable than Leyton's, which encompassed the whole of Fife. The location of the Tolbooth appears to have been in the little cul-de-sac in East Street, known locally as 'the Bricks'.

With three breweries and no fewer than twelve spirit-and-ale houses in the parish, drunken quarrels, brawls and even riots were common. In the eighteen thirties, the bad behaviour of 'the Simmininsers' was proverbial in the surrounding districts. To quote one historian on ale-houses, 'the unhappy effects of the keepers of which, by their craft to decoy, are, with regret, seen upon the health and morals of the young and inconsiderate.' Again, from the Reverend Swann, 'As this place is no thoroughfare, there can hardly be said to be in it, one traveller's inn, where there is regular stabling or posting ... But there are too many ale-houses and their effect upon the morals is highly unfavourable.'

However, the Statistics for the Parish of Abercrombie in 1854 reveal that the number of public houses had fallen to ten, having been sixteen in 1844, and twelve in 1850. Convictions for criminal offences showed a similar trend, being ten in 1848–9, nil in 1850–1 and three in 1853–4.

Such was the demand of the brewers, that a Mistress Mackie had a malt barn built in Johnstone's Close (now the Maltings). In the 1930s, it housed a carpenter's business (Alexander Anderson) and a sailmaker's loft (James Main). In the Second World War, it was used as a factory for camouflage nets. The hillside there, between Braehead and West Street, is known locally as the Pleruck, but was recorded in 1862 as the Plattock. One of Mistress Mackie's tenants, a brewer by the name of Bonthrone, connected two premises on either side of the East Backgate by an overhead bridge. On 29th May 1875, she had strict instructions from the Parish Council to remove it if it caused an inconvenience to traffic.

The great conviviality of weddings, too, could result in guests spending the night in the local jail. Despite the superstition that Friday was unlucky, as it was the supposed day of St Monan's death, most nuptials were conducted then, as the boats were in harbour for the weekend. They were known as 'Penny Weddings', each guest contributing one penny to help defray the costs.

On Market days, including that for Lintseed, and at the Fairs, held in March, July and September, the population was swollen by visitors from the neighbourhood and surrounding farms, with, at its mildest, the inevitable clash of personalities. These events were held on vacant ground on the South Street (the harbour front), between the Braid and Narrow Wynds.

Sentencing was often harsh. In January 1870, at Cupar Sheriff Court, Thomas Small was arraigned for wife-beating, having assaulted his wife, Isabella Summers by kicking, punching and hitting her with an iron bread-toaster! He was found guilty on seven charges and sentenced to eight days, seven days, thirty days, three months, five months, six months and eight months. Having then been told of seven previous convictions, the Sheriff added another nine months, all to be served *consecutively*! Every period carried hard labour! The previous April, Leishman Brand, a lad of thirteen, was sentenced to ten stripes of the birch rod for 'malicious mischief'. Nor were women exempt. In 1876, Agnes Bain was given sixty days with hard labour, for her assault on a police constable. The following month, William Ireland and David Duncan received the same sentence, with the promise of a further six months, if the offence was repeated. Their crime was to have had in their possession equipment (nets) for the taking of game, and for unlawfully taking a hare at Balniel Farm on the estate of the Earl of Crawford and Balcarres.

Although from 1833, various Acts of Parliament regulated the establishment of regular police forces within major burghs, smaller towns and villages were policed by the County Force. Between 1833 and 1900, police commissioners, often the same as the town councillors, administered policy. After 1900, the Town Council was the Police Authority.

The year 1933 was an eventful one for St Monans, being then awarded the status of a Police Burgh. The election of the Town Council saw James W.M. Gourlay, the local schoolmaster, become Provost, with the senior and junior baillies being Henry Guthrie and William P. Miller respectively. One of the first items on the agenda of the new council was to debate the age-old controversy of 'St Monans' or 'St Monance', the latter being adopted, with no consultation or polling of the rate-payers! Street names were also 'modernised'; the Backgates, East and West, being re-labelled as Streets, the Wynds, Coal and Broad, becoming Forth Street and Station Road. This change of status had not been without controversy and, for some three years earlier, the local paper, the *East Fife Observer*, carried some fairly aggressive correspondence, criticising 'the appalling condition of St Monance'. The main antagonist, signing his letters as J.R., later as Argus, declaimed the state of the roads, particularly George Terrace. In February 1931, he wrote: 'if Sir William Sandilands of Newark, the gentleman who elected St Monance as a Burgh of Barony in 1633, were to look back, he could not but be pleased with the present municipal authorities for keeping the village in exactly the same manner as he left it, three hundred years ago:- no roads, no streets, dilapidation and mud all over.' The next week, Andrew Allan, for many years the Registrar of Births, Marriages and Deaths, weighed in with the comments, 'the Common was left solely for Fail, Divot and Grazing. ('Fail' was sward for building turf dykes). It is not so easy to understand what the Divot was for, except perhaps for the same purpose as it is used today, namely to fire at the Town Council.'

The burgh had 'gone dry' in 1900 and no liquor was sold until 1947, two plebiscites, held in 1920 and 1934 to repeal the ban, being unsuccessful. Today, there is one hotel, the Mayview in Station Road, and the Cabin Bar in the West End.

Religious Groups

To bring the people closer to their God, warding off the evils of strong drink and attempting to suppress unseemly behaviour, the kirk was supported by such organisations as the Temperance Movement, the Good Templars and by the Blue Riband, a women's group fostered by the church. St Monans has even been a fruitful recruiting ground for religious factions as alternatives to the Established Church. Indeed, an epithet for the village, still lingering in the East Neuk, is the 'Holy City'.

At the end of the eighteenth century, a small body of Seceders united and built a magnificent Secession chapel, adorned with two splendid Gothic stained glass windows. Unfortunately, the chosen site was a piece of waste ground above a disused coal working and the whole edifice collapsed! Undaunted, they rebuilt it. The blame for the calamity had been fixed on an old woman, of supposed evil influence. To avoid any possible repetition of the disaster, they gave her a half-a-crown (12½p.) and asked her to bless the new building!

The middle of the next century saw them joined with two Burgher groups, styled the Relief and the Anti-relief. Details were not given as to how two apparently diametrically opposed factions could unite, as there was much interdenominational rivalry in the village. The Reverend Gillies, observing that 'The King is Patron of the Parish,' was vexed at the increase of the different sects of Seceder in this part of the country '. . . whose teachers and managers craftily draw off the ignorant and the unwary of the Established Church.'

The Revival Movement, which was sweeping the whole of Scotland, was strong in St Monans. The *East of Fife Record* of 1869 reported:

> Three line boats, belonging to John Reekie, David Allan and David Easson had left the harbour, when the wind fell off. The crews warped the three boats together, allowing them to drop down the Firth with the tide. A religious meeting was extemporised and, for two hours, the men engaged in singing from Richard Weaver's hymns. When the wind freshened, each had again to take to his own boat.

The Revival was a source of some concern to the kirk and the *Record* reported in 1870 that 'the absence of fishermen on the coast of England had created an unsettled state of the religious community, owing to sectarian movements.' In an attempt to come in line with this competition, the Fast Day, usually observed in November, had been abandoned.

At the foot of King David Street, with a commanding view of the Forth, stands the Braehead Evangelical Church. It was originally built as the Free Church, being formally opened on 20th September 1870. Its creation was initiated by the Reverend Walter Wood who was, for thirty-seven years, minister of the United Free Church in Elie, now the Wood Memorial. He established, with much success, such a presence of his chosen form of religion in St Monans that, in due time, village residents were appointed elders to the Elie Kirk Session. David Thompson, in his excellent book, *Elie Kirk*, tells of the development of the St Monans Congregation, which

> had grown to such an extent that it had to be subject to a scheme of division into four areas for ease of administration as follows:

1. Eastern, extending from the east end of the town to the Square and including the Square.
2. Middle-east, extending from the Square to the Broad Wynd.
3. Middle-west, extending from the Broad Wynd to the Narrow Wynd, including the Narrow Wynd.
4. Western, extending from the Narrow Wynd to the West End of the town and including Newark Farm.

All this organisation sprang from a decision taken by the Kirk Session in Elie in 1869 in response to 'a remarkable interest in divine things, manifested in St Monance and ... the absence of any regular labourer there of any denomination.'

In 1868 and 1869, prayer meetings and the Sabbath service had been held in the old schoolroom, but the congregation, anxious to have better accommodation, resolved to raise funds to build a church. A meeting, chaired by the Reverend Wood, was held at Elie on 17th September 1869. The committee consisted of Mr A. Adams, baker, Mr John Robertson, boat-builder, Mr Thomas Murray, fish curer and Mr John Lockie, missionary. With the exception of the last named, who had been engaged at a stipend of £60 per annum, all were from St Monans. The estimated cost was £694 17*s.* 6*d.* (£694.87½p.), plus a contingency of £200, including £72 for the site. The final payment was £1,006, including £311 for extra work.

Built on land to the west of the curing premises of Provost Todd of Anstruther, in the Early English Style of architecture, it has large stained glass windows in the North and South gables and a neat, tiled spire. There was seating for four hundred in the church and for one hundred in the adjoining hall.

The project had not been without its critics. Writing in the *East of Fife Record* in 1869, Nemo, a pseudonym, whose identity was never revealed, accused the Reverend Wood of forcing the decision, asserting that, with only four Free Church families in the parish, it was impossible to constitute a viable church. The writer further alleged that, in a previous letter to the paper, Wood had 'reviled the Morrisonians' (the Evangelical Union Church) and 'laid false claims against them'. Again 'Mr Wood is setting forth in the article, the splendid deliverance, which his own right arm achieved for the people of St Monance.' It is somewhat ironical that the church now bears the title 'Evangelical' of the Morrisonians, who initially opposed its creation!

The funds were raised in fifteen months, between June 1869 and September 1870, a truly remarkable achievement considering the very poor fishing at that time. The village raised £142 11*s.* (£142.55p.), and the minister's wife, Mrs Wood, an incredible £702.

The Reverend Wood's opening sermon was taken from the Old Testament, the book of Haggai, chapter 2, verse 7: 'And I will fill this house with glory, saith the Lord of Hosts.' An address by the Reverend W. Arnot of Edinburgh included the anecdote of the fisherman who swore a lot. Trying to dissuade him from this bad habit, his minister pointed out that the Apostles were fishermen on the Sea of Galilee but never found it necessary to utter an oath. Back came the salt's reply, 'Och ay, it wis aisy fur thaim tae be guid; the Lord gae thaim great taks o' fish!' The Reverend Keay of Crail remarked on the speed with which the church had been raised, observing that it had taken his congregation twenty years to achieve the finances for their building.

The swearing-in of the Deacons required them to declare: 'I am persuaded that the Civil Magistrate has no jurisdiction or authoritative control over the regulation of the affairs of Christ's Church.'

David Thompson records, in the June of the following year, that it was agreed that the kirk session should meet at St Monans, once a month, as business required. By 1874, for financial and operational reasons, the Presbytery had approved of St Monans being treated as a station, responsible for all its outgoings, but still under the supervision of Elie Kirk Session. In that year, a Presbyterial Committee, appointed for the purpose, found that 'there is at St Monance a congregation of nearly two hundred communicants, four elders beside Mr Lockie, the missionary and a regular staff of Sunday School teachers etc. They possess new and suitable buildings, consisting of a church and vestry and a hall, which are almost entirely free of debt. For this gratifying state of affairs the credit is primarily, and chiefly, due to the Reverend Walter Wood of Elie, who first began the work at St

Monance and, at considerable trouble and expense to himself, has supervised it ever since.'

The Session Records for the first few years are relatively uneventful but, by 1876, the elders were seen to be following the tyrannical tradition of the Auld Kirk, with the first recorded charge of ante-nuptial fornication.

By 1877, there was dissension in the congregation, with John Lockie, the preacher, encouraging members to form another church. Three elders, Thomas Fyall, Robert Smith and Robert Allan, threatened to resign and did so, to be followed by William Aitken. December 1877 saw the opening of the first Congregational chapel.

The Free Church later became the United Church and in 1929, on rejoining the Church of Scotland, was renamed Braehead Parish Church. Its elders then were Alexander Innes, Thomas Aitken, John Howie, Andrew Fyall (the author's grand-father), James Steele and Alexander Smith.

However, changing circumstances of the population meant that the village could not support two major congregations, so, despite protests from both sides, union with the Auld Kirk was effected. Previously, the churches had virtually coalesced during the Great War. The *East Fife Observer* of 1st April 1917 noted joint services in the Parish Church and the United Free Church. The Reverend Hall, minister of the latter, had gone to the Front on duties for the Young Men's Christian Association. At that time, the Sunday collections were donated to the Scottish Churches' Huts venture in France. The manse on the Elie Road, which had stood empty since the departure of the last United Church minister, the Reverend John Anderson, then became the residence of the minister of the Parish Church; the original Auld Kirk manse was situated in Abercrombie.

For many years, the Congregational Church had occupied a substantial building in Station Road, built in 1846 by Sir Ralph Anstruther of Balcaskie as an infant and female school, 'to relieve the parish schoolmaster of his arduous duties'. The Congregationalists bought the Braehead premises in 1946, the first service being conducted on 4th December of that year. The breakaway group of 1877 had returned to their origins! Among the elders and deacons at that juncture were Tom Adam, Henry, David and James Anderson, Tom Davidson, John Hutt, Humphrey Tilbrook and Tom Wood.

In 1993, under the leadership of the Reverend Jack Anderson, the church formed a new constitution and adopted the present title of the Braehead Evangelical Church, St Monans, albeit the affectionate local name of 'the Cong' persists.

The anti-drink organisation, the Good Templars, attracted considerable local support. On 31st March 1871, the St Monans Lifeboat Lodge, with some one hundred and thirty-odd members, which had been formed only a few weeks previously, paraded through the streets, wearing the badge of the Order and with banners flying. In the evening, a concert was held in the Union Hall. After the speeches, the entertainment included renderings by Robert Morris on violin and James Butters on accordion.

By March the following year, membership was in excess of three hundred. Joint functions were held with neighbouring lodges, the Guiding Star of Cellardyke, the Rising Sun of Pittenweem and the Star of the East of Crail.

On one occasion, the Lodge marched to Elie to join the Brothers

47. Harvest of the Sea and Land. Braehead Evangelical Church. Rev. George Murray and Elder Humphrey Tilbrook.

and Sisters of the Beacon Lodge, a flute band 'playing lively airs'. United, they marched back to the Union Hall for a soirée, Brother William Leslie presiding. A local fish buyer, Brother Trainer, addressed the assembly on 'the evil consequences that flow from drunkenness' and Brother Fyall on 'the Beauty of Templarism'. After refreshment, music and recitations, they sang the closing ode – 'Brother, life has glorious heights', a somewhat chauvinistic choice with so many Sisters present! By 1872, the Lifeboat Lodge boasted a brass band, practising three times a week under their first appointed leader, James Christie. Like many other voluntary organisations, the date of the demise of such a strong group in the village was apparently never reported.

The *Third Statistical Account* of 1951 confirmed the 'Holy City' label by listing the Parish and Congregational Churches, the Salvation Army and four other religious sects. These show some changes from the Parish of Abercrombie lists of 1854, which give membership numbers as follows: Established Church 988, United Presbyterians 162, Free Church 2, Independents 16, Wesleyans 1 and Mormonites 2. The last is remarkable considering that Joseph Smith had only founded 'The Church of Jesus Christ of Latter-Day Saints' in 1830, in the United States of America; a small far-off village already had members.

For many years, the Convention of Pilgrims attracted large number of adherents each summer, with mass baptisms being performed at the now defunct bathing pool on the East Braes.

The individuality of religious persuasion which has characterised village life over the centuries, leading to the creation and continued support of the different groups, is well illustrated by reference to 'the Brethren', as they are known locally. There are two distinct groups, called, in the 1940s and 50s, 'Duff's Brethren', whose leaders were the Duff family from Pittenweem and 'Jimmy Ferguson's Brethren'.

The latter are more properly known as 'The Assembly' and their origins, rise and stability epitomise this sturdy independence of religious thought and practice.

During the Great War of 1914–18, a local fisherman, John Smith was skipper of a minesweeper in the Firth of Clyde. He had been baptised during a summer fishing season in Fraserburgh and then, by chance, was invited to the local assembly in Ardrossan. His experience there stimulated him to try to bring this particular form of worship to St Monans. The nearest meeting was held at St Andrews and, in the early part of 1924, John and two other brethren cycled the twelve hilly miles there and back to attend meetings. Visits to St Monans, at John's behest, by two evangelists, Arthur Gilmour and Jack Roberts, brought more converts. Roberts pitched a tent on the Mair and, as well as preaching, taught the elements of baptism, separation and church principles. During his crusade, he was invited to stay at the home of Mr and Mrs James Ferguson, who owned and ran their bakery at the Hope Place end of Miller Terrace. In 1924, Jimmy was to help form a scripturally-based assembly, whose members were mostly recruited from the local Congregational Church. Initially, meetings were held in the Ferguson's front room and even in the flour loft above the bakery. A sectional wooden hut, a relic of the war, was then acquired and erected by voluntary help in George Terrace on the Doocot Hill. By the time the now-named Gospel Hall was ready, the Yarmouth fishing had claimed many of the new adherents and only six members celebrated the first Communion.

In 1956, the present fine building was erected on the 'Maister's Walk', curiously just across the road from Barron Hall, built in the nineteenth century, the old home of John Smith, the founder, where the first meetings had been held.

For many years, a Salvation Army Officer was stationed permanently at St Monans, with headquarters in the Citadel in West Backgate. Apart from its staunch adherents, many members of the churches supported the branch, particularly its Home League for women and, in the 1930s and 40s, a thriving youth club. A life-long member was local dressmaker, Maggie Fyall, who never missed a meeting. A good Samaritan, she made trousers and skirts for the children, at no cost, when times were hard. At that time, the Sergeant-Major was Willie Davidson, a fisherman, much respected in the community for his profound Christian beliefs and practices. Both of his family, Robert and Catherine, became full-time officers. Robert was brutally executed for his faith by the Japanese Army in the infamous Changi Jail in Singapore.

Another Salvationist was Brigadier Martha Fyall. After school,

48. Brigadier Martha Fyall, Salvation Army, chats with Anne, Princess Royal.

she worked in an oilskin factory in Anstruther, but in 1936, then in her mid-twenties, left to attend the Salvation Army Training College. Commissioned on 11th May 1936, her first posting was to the Vennel in Edinburgh. She spent the war years, 1939–45, at Hope House in Glasgow and in 1953 moved to the Hostel in Dundee, where she served for ten years. Returning to Glasgow in 1963, she spent two years as Assistant Warden at Baldorran, before being promoted to Warden at the Vennel. After twelve years, she retired from active service at the age of sixty-five, but remained in her appointment until early 1977. Brigadier Fyall was very much part of the life of the Edinburgh Congress Hall, later to be known as the Edinburgh City Corps. To quote from the tribute at her funeral, 'many people have been grateful for her spiritual maturity and experience, which she had been able to share with them' and again, 'she leaves an influence, which will live in the hearts and minds of those she has touched.'

The Church Hall in Station Road was built in 1913 by the architect Robert Lorimer. The Feu Charter, granted to Trustees for members of the Parish Church, stipulated, *inter alia,* that it must not be let to professional or theatrical companies (the author recalls a travelling repertory theatre performing there in the 1930s) 'nor shall it be let for any public ball or promiscuous dancing'! Dancing at private parties and weddings was permitted. The penalty for infraction of the rules would be to render the Feu Charter null and void. The Charter, as ever, 'Reserved, to the heirs of entail, all coal, limestone, ironstone and every other kind of mineral and metal' with 'full power and liberty to work, win, calcine and carry away.' The condition being enforced by February 1921 had avoided the mention of 'promiscuous dancing' but limited numbers.

The first meeting of the Parish Hall Committee, on 15th August 1914, set the following scale of charges:

Bazaar – whole hall	£2 + 5*s.* (25p.) to caretaker
Religious Service	7*s.* 6*d.* (37½p.)
Political meeting	£1 1*s.* (£1.5p.)
Marriage: ceremony only:	nil + 1*s.* 6*d.* (7½p.) to caretaker
supper:	£1 10*s.* + 7*s.* 6*d.* (37½p.) to caretaker
Lecture	10*s.* (50p.)
Concert	£1 5*s.* (£1.25p.)
Soirée	£1 1*s.* (£1.5p.)

Gas was extra in each case.

Later charges allowed 'Camping Parties @ £2 10*s.* (£2.50p.) per week.' On 28th January 1944, it was agreed that the local company, troop and pack of Girl Guides, Boy Scouts and Wolf Cubs could have free use, but would make a contribution to light and heat. During the 1939-45 conflict, there was a proposal that the hall be let for the purpose of making camouflage nets for the Forces at a rent of ten pounds per month. This venture was eventually located in the Malt Barns off West Street. The hall was requisitioned in 1940 by the Home Guard, who paid half the costs of installation of electricity in the main hall – some £24 9*s.* (£24.45p.).

The Masonic Lodge is St Monan, Number 1348 in the Register

of the Grand Lodge of Scotland. As many local men were members of nearby lodges, principally Lodge St Ayle, No. 95, Anstruther; Lodge St Adrian, No. 185, Pittenweem; and Lodge Balcarres, No. 1240, Colinsburgh, Brother William Dunn proposed that a lodge should be founded in the village. The Temple, originally the Union Hall, was bought for the sum of £411. The lodge was consecrated and erected on 11th August 1926, by the Right Worshipful Provincial Grand Master of Fife and Kinross, the Right Honourable Edward James Bruce, 10th Earl of Elgin and 14th Earl of Kincardine. The first master was the Reverend John Hart, the elected officers being: William Sommers, Depute Master; Walter Reekie, Substitute Master; James Allan, Senior Warden; Andrew Allan, Junior Warden; Andrew Paxton, Secretary; David Bremner, Treasurer; Gerrard Reekie, Senior Deacon; William Anderson, Junior Deacon; William Dunn, Inner Guard; and William Ferguson, Tyler. Most of these were local businessmen, shipbuilders and other artisans, as the sea-faring members could not guarantee regular attendance. There were also twenty-four founder members, including the author's grandfather, Andrew Fyall, already a member of Lodge St Adrian.

In his fine history of the Lodge, Alex McDonald, a Past Master, observes that the Lodge became an integral part of village life, being, apart from its primary purpose, the venue for soirees, socials, whist drives, weddings and receptions, particularly after the closure of the Hut.

The author, a Life Member of Lodge St Monan, then Provincial Senior Grand Warden of Hampshire and the Isle of Wight in the English Constitution, was privileged to take part in the Golden Jubilee celebrations in 1976, when the ceremony of re-dedication was performed by the Provincial Grand Master, the Right Honourable, the Earl of Elgin and Kincardine, son of the original consecrating officer. Brother Harry Montador, Right Worshipful Master, took the chair, presiding over a large assembly of Freemasons from lodges from many parts. The Director of Ceremonies was Brother Alex McDonald.

As happens in a small community, members are scattered all over the world, many having reached senior ranks in other masonic bodies. It is appropriate to note the selfless dedication of Past

Master David I. Black, who received his Parchment for Services to Scottish Masonry from Grand Lodge, and of Past Master Alexander Ovenstone, Past Provincial Senior Grand Warden, for many years the corner-stone of the Lodge.

Today, the Lodge also runs a very popular Social Club, which welcomes many visiting brethren, particularly over the summer months.

Past Masters Lodge St Monan No 1348	
1926/27	Rev. John Hart
1927/28	Andrew G. Paxton
1928/29	James Allan
1929/33	Andrew Allan
1933/34	Gerrard Reekie
1934/36	Robt A. Brown
1936/38	Rev. Walter R. Gordon
1938/40	John Gowans
1940/42	George Miller
1942/45	Thomas E. Allan
1945/46	James N. Miller
1946/47	William Mathers
1947/49	William Reekie
1949/53	David I. Black
1953/55	Alexander Ovenstone
1955/59	Samuel McGregor
1959/60	John Cunningham
1960/62	John C. Gerrard
1962/65	Wm. R. Kinnear
1965/76	David Kinnear
1967/69	Alexander W. McDonald
1969/70	David Kinnear (2nd time)
1970/72	Henry Barclay

1972/74	Eric Brown
1974/76	Harry Montador
1976/78	John G. Ovenstone
1978/80	David Brisland
1980/82	Peter McFarlane
1982/84	Robert N. Legg
1984/86	David Legg
1986/88	Charles Howie
1988/90	William E. Hill
1990/92	Andrew M. Dorward
1992/96	William E. Hill (2nd time)
1996/97	Alex. McDonald (2nd time)
1997–	Robert C. Winton

Hard Times

A prime objective of the Kirk Session was claimed to be the succour of the poor, funds coming principally from the weekly collection at the church door. However the Session was effectively, for many years, the village banker, the local Treasury. They might help out on the purchase of property but if the borrower defaulted, the assets were seized and rouped publicly, the proceeds going to church funds. Accounts were often very vague with the identity of those relieved being anonymous, as in 'To a man taken by the French £1'! However, in 1704, they did grant £1 4*s.* (£1.20p.) to Helen Robertson and Agnes Armstrong to buy shoes. They often paid for a pauper's burial, coffin, grave and mort-cloth or shroud. Occasionally, conditions were attached to grants as recorded in 1758: 'To a Member of the Session in Straits by long continuance of affliction, which if Providence bring him in circumstances and ability to pay, it shall be demanded again, – £6.'

However, in 1799, the Reverend Gillies observed that 'owing to the increase in the numbers of members of the Established Church drifting into the various other sects, there has been considerable loss of revenue.' The Kirk Session warned all who left that, should they require financial assistance, they could not expect it if they had made no contributions. There were 'three persons and two orphans' on the Poor List that year. None was allowed to beg publicly despite the view that 'the parish is much infested by beggars from towns at a distance.' The Reverend Swann relates that, for the year ending December 1836, the number on the Poor Roll was nineteen, receiving an average of 3*s.* 2*d.* (16p.) each month.

On 18th February 1843, the death was recorded of Bina Fial, a pauper who had been supported by the church. The expenses for her funeral were £2 7*s.* 5*d.* (£2.37p.); the roup of her meagre effects raised £3 4*s.* 9*d.* (£3.24p.), so the kirk was in balance.

Parish accounts for 1849 detail the running of a kitchen for the poor. In four months, soup had been supplied on thirty occasions, feeding fifty mouths each time. The bill reads: Coals 8*s.* 3*d.* (41p.), Beef £5 15*s.*, (£5.75p.), Barley, Rice, Candles £2 7*s.* 4½*d.* (£2.37p.), a grand total of £8 10*s.* 7½d. (£8.53p.); that is just over one-halfpenny per helping in today's currency. That year, a Session House, a defaulted property at Burnside, was acquired by the kirk for the sheltering of paupers, 'who shall be all aged, respectable persons.'

The Poor Rate on the Accounts of the Parochial Board for 1875 lists twenty paupers. Typical payments were: a weekly allowance of half-a-crown (12½p.) for Ann Duncan and Robert Hutt; a florin (10p.) for Janet Gowans, Betty Fyall and Agnes Meldrum; half-a-ton of coal per annum for David Scott and Margaret Lowrie, with Elspeth Fyall being supported in the Asylum with a yearly grant of £26.

With none of the advantages of a Department of Social Security, the seamen and other professions had their own Friendly Societies, paying small, regular subscriptions into so-called 'Boxes', as insurance against loss of employment and deprivation. The Sea-Box Society was reportedly instituted at the Union of the Crowns of Scotland and England in 1603; it was still flourishing in 1845. While sea-faring folk constituted a clear majority of members, it was also open to other occupations. The Society became defunct in 1876 but the *East of Fife Observer* of 5th November 1936 noted that £25 of the monies had been on deposit with the National

Bank of Scotland since 2nd November 1875! It may only be surmised that the local bank manager was not a share-holder in the Society!

A Brotherly Society was formed in July 1821, the weekly deposits amounting to about two pounds in total. The Laws and Regulations of 1834 list the following office bearers: James Adam, Preses; Thomas Lindsay, Treasurer; Robert Lindsay, Clerk; Alexander Elder and Collin Adamson, key keepers; John Robertson, Alexander Meldrum, Alexander Simpson, Alexander Fulton and James Peattie.

There were two savings banks, a very old one and another opened in December 1835. A curiosity was the establishment of a 'female savings bank'; no details are given other than it appeared to be doing well. This may be identified with such a bank which only closed in Scotland in 1997. There was also the Penny Savings Bank noted in the 24th May 1878 issue of the *East of Fife Record.* The half-year deposit was just £270, at a time when two-storey houses were selling for £250 to £300 each.

The all-night vigils over newly-completed graves to foil the theft of corpses for medical research, as has been mentioned in connection with Abercrombie Kirk, were replaced by a more permanent safeguard, an iron cage. A Mortsafe Society was founded in 1831, with the heads of one hundred and fifty families paying between sixpence and ninepence (2½–3½p.), per year for the upkeep of the cages, which could be installed for 5*s.* 6*d.* (27½p.).

In an effort to reduce the price of bread, there was a proposal in 1871 to start a Cooperative Baking Society. It met with little success and, by 1875, was bankrupt and being sued for the non-payment of flour supplies.

Building Restoration

In the early 1960s, the National Trust for Scotland instituted its 'Little Houses' initiative, aimed at buying, restoring and re-selling private residences considered worthy of preservation.

The Trust's first project at St Monans was in 1967, at Number 4, West Shore, with W. Murray Jack as architect. A much larger scheme, supported by the Town Council, under Provost James

Braid, was then launched by the Trust on a number of properties. Mainly in the harbour, Virgin Square, Station Road and Forth Street areas, these restored dwellings have much enhanced the appearance of the village.

Distinctive features, typical of domestic Scottish architecture associated with the East Neuk, are harled walls, dormer windows, stone guttering, pantiled roofs and crow-stepped gables. The pantiles, with their characteristic cross-section of an ogee or S section curve, are not nailed down, so the gable walls are continued above roof level to prevent the wind from lifting them. They were brought to Fife by Dutch trading ships as ballast. Up until the 1930s, Netherlands vessels shipped potatoes from St Monans harbour. Sandstone, the basic building material of the era, is difficult to cut on the diagonal, so the gables are topped off with the attractive 'crow-steps'. A feature of the restored houses is a noticeable lack of wood, occasioned by high prices, when building in the early eighteenth century.

As multiple tenancy was common, many two-storied homes had a forestair, an independent entrance to the upper level. A wealthy family would occupy the whole house, utilising the downstairs to store gear. Few such homes survived modernisation. The post-war demise of the fishing industry could never have been anticipated, when the major new housing scheme at Gourlay Crescent was built in the mid 1930s. Following local custom, every house had a loft or attic to store nets and other gear, the materials being hoisted through a window in the gable end or rear of the house, by a block and tackle, suspended from a built-in cat-head or wooden beam. Jenny MacDonald tells an amusing story of earlier building. Her grandfather built Number 1 Miller Terrace; granny refused to move so he sold it and built Number 2, but again, refusal. By the time he had built most of the houses on the seaward side, he was convinced that there would be no change of mind, so gave up!

The village has always attracted many artists and the summer months see school and club groups committing such features as the Auld Kirk and the harbour to canvas. Five of the most important artists who depicted St Monan's scenes were Sam Bough, Robert Kilpatrick, William Wilson, Anton Dekker and John

49. James Braid OBE, JP, Freeman of the Burgh – St Andrew's Day, 1974.

McGhie. The first, who was born in Carlisle in 1822, was a gifted landscape painter, being elected to the Scottish Royal Academy in 1875. He died in 1878; unfortunately most of his works, including a magnificent view of the Auld Kirk, are now in private collections, although the Crawford Art Gallery in St Andrews has staged a public exhibition. Kilpatrick, who rented a studio every summer,

50. "E's makin a braw job o't.'

at Kirklatch, Pittenweem, executed powerful seascapes and is now very collectable. William Wilson, RSA, was an important print-maker in the thirties, working with Bartholomew's, the map-printers. He did many drawings and engravings of St Monans, most of which are in the National Gallery of Scotland in Edinburgh. Dekker was a German citizen, who was deported at the beginning of the First World War. McGhie, who was the President of the Glasgow Society of Etchers, is best known in the East Neuk for his portraits of the Pittenweem Fisher Lass.

Archaeological Finds

The advent of modern technology in the form of the metal detector has enhanced considerably the capabilities of both the serious archaeologist and the amateur enthusiast seeking treasure trove.

Such activities in and around St Monans are described in a fascinating research paper by Adrian Cox and Michael King. The following details are quoted almost verbatim from their publication in the *Tayside and Fife Archaeological Journal.*

> Metal detecting and organised field-walking by the Tayside and Fife Archaeological Committee have produced finds from

two fields to the west of St Monans. Few metal or pottery finds have been made in the field directly to the north of St Monans Church, except for a few shards of White Gritty pottery, probably spread with midden material. However, finds in the field to the west of St Monans Manse, and within the mediaeval parish of Abercrombie, have been particularly notable.

Metal finds from this field include a silver Fede ring, a lead-alloy papal bulla of Pope Alexander IV dating to 1254–61 and a pilgrim's badge.

The bulla may possibly relate to the granting of papal permission for the construction of an earlier chapel on the site of that 'founded anew' by David II in about 1362. The bulla may equally relate to Abercrombie, the parish church of St Monans in the mediaeval period, or indeed it could have been dropped or displaced some distance from its original or intended destination.

Numismatic finds from this field have also been numerous. These include i) a Long Cross silver penny of Henry III, London mint, moneyer Henri (1248–50), ii) a silver farthing of Edward I, London mint (c 1279–81), iii) a Scottish billon plack of James IV (c 1500–10), iv) a Scottish billon plack of James V (1513–26), v) a Scottish billon half bawbee of James V (1539–42) and vi) a French copper double tournois of the type current from the reign of Henri III to that of Louis XIII (1577–1643). A plack was an old Scottish coin, worth a third of an English penny of the same period.

Field-walking was carried out using 20 metre squares in a sample north-south transect, 40 metres wide across the centre of the same field in March 1997. Large amounts of White Gritty pottery dating from the twelfth-fifteenth centuries were collected in 16 squares, averaging 22 shards per 20 metre square.

The author has suggested that more rewarding areas for the metal detectorists may be the Mair, scene of the battle with the English in 1549, the 'meeneral', visited by thousands of pilgrims, the Hermit's cave by Burnside, Abercombie kirk and Newark Castle. He also suggested the fields of Newark

Farm, where the materials from under the kirk floor were scattered as fertilisers at the time of the kirk's restoration.

Fede rings were often worn as betrothal or engagements symbols, but sometimes merely as tokens of affection. The term 'fede', as applied to a ring with a representation of clasped hands, is derived from the Italian *mani in fede* (literally 'hands in faith/trust'). This type of ring has a long currency: examples of Roman date are known, such as those in the collections of the Victoria and Albert Museum, and the type enjoyed an unbroken popularity until the nineteenth century.

The description of the ring is as follows: 'Original maximum external diameter about 24mm; maximum internal diameter about 21mm; width of bezel 4mm. Silver. Fede ring with clasped hands at the apex, the detail of this design almost entirely worn away. Several indentations around the outer edge of the hoop may represent remains of a design or inscription. The object has been distorted and is corroded. Found by J. Gosk, 1996. Pending Treasure Trove decision.'

From the Latin, Papal bullae are circular, leaden seals, bearing on one side a representation of Saint Paul and Saint Peter and, on the other, the name of the reigning pope. A bulla was attached to a document by a cord, of silk if a 'Bull of Grace' and of hemp if a 'Bull of Justice', and gave authenticity to it. The description is as follows: Diameter 37mm; thickness 4mm. Lead alloy. Papal bulla of Alexander IV (1254–61). Approximately circular, with perforations through the edge, at the top and bottom of the object, which would have accommodated a cord. Both faces are decorated in relief and both are slightly damaged. The obverse face bears the legend ALEXANDER. PP. IIII. The reverse face bears the legend S. PA S. PE above facing heads representing those of Saint Paul and Saint Peter with a cross *pattée* between them. Found by J. Gosk, 1995.

Also found near St Monans was a badge, moulded from lead alloy to the form of a scallop shell. The find can be interpreted as representing a pilgrim's badge, (usually worn on the side of the hat), perhaps lost by a traveller who had made the journey to Santiago de Compostela in north-western

Spain. The scallop-shell emblem is associated with Santiago de Compostela and with St James, the apostle, whose remains are reputed to be interred in a tomb there, having supposedly been discovered at the site in the 9th century, after being carried from the Holy Land. Santiago de Compostela subsequently emerged as a principal site of pilgrimage during the Middle Ages, and, after Jerusalem and Rome, it is still the third most important centre of pilgrimage of Christendom, its badge being the scallop shell.

Local connection with the Crusades was mentioned in the story of Abercrombie Kirk (Chapter 5).

Badge. Length 34mm; width 34mm; thickness 5mm. Lead alloy. Moulded badge in the form of a scallop shell, with traces of possible gilding near the apex. A pin for securing the badge to clothing, probably made from copper-alloy wire, is attached to the undecorated rear face. This pin is broken and distorted. Also on the rear face, near the apex, is a small projection which may represent another component of the fastening device. Found by B. Watson, 1996, near Ardross (NGR NO 5120 0130). Pending Treasure Trove decision.

The scallop is also used symbolically in the Masonic Order of the Knights Templar.

Chapter 22

Writers

Thomas Mathers, The Fisher Poet – 1794–1851

IT IS NOT ONLY AMONGST THOSE with the privileges of position and education that talent is found. Albeit not so famous as Robert Burns, St Monans had its own poet. Born just two years before the Bard's death in 1796, Thomas Mathers was the son of a poor Cornish miner, one of the hundred men employed at that time in the coal pits in Pittenweem. The rigours of his task and the Black Death cut the unfortunate collier off in the prime of his life. His dying words to his wife, Jean Allan, were: 'I hae this consolation, lassie. I ken ye'll be guid tae the bairns.' And good she was, toiling all hours, in service at Balcaskie and Lathallan, to support her three orphan boys. William and Jean had been irregularly and clandestinely married in Edinburgh on 16th April 1783.

Thomas was an almost totally self-taught man. He had started school with the old master, Dominie Davidson, but had made little progress with his only book, the Proverbs of Solomon. However, he was feed as a herd laddie to the tenant of Easter Kellie farm. With a child-like faith in Providence, he wrote: 'I was cowering at the foot of a bush, intent on an old volume of the *Spectator* magazine, when the master's son, just home from college, spoke to me about books, and from that day, by his kindness, I was never without one in my bosom.' A young local tailor, Robert Lindsay, shared his taste in literature and had one day acquired a copy of the *Iliad*. He read it avidly and then offered it to his friend. 'What a glorious book, Tam; it maist took my breathe awa' – it's Homer!' The reply came swiftly. 'Hoots, Rab, I read that when I was a bit loon, herding Andrew Peat's kye at the fit o' Kellie Law.' His real love was the sea and he sailed as an apprentice to Greenland on the *Eastridge*, out of Dunbar. Service over in the Arctic, he came home to learn navigation. For a time, he was chief mate on the little brig, the *Pilot*, out of Elie and then on the *Gem* of Inverkeithing. When the latter berthed in the port of Venice, he was hailed by an English tourist. In the discussion that followed, he felt thrilled by the magic and magnetism of the stranger's eyes and voice. 'He pressed my hand as we parted,' he told friends with enthusiasm to his dying day. 'It was Byron; yes, I never saw a king but once and it was he.' George Gordon, Lord Byron inspired him for the rest of his life. His critics maintained that he boasted of this famous meeting at every opportunity, but his closest friends had no doubt of his sincerity. He left the sailing, married his first love, Maggie Thompson, on St Valentine's Day 1828, and then took to net and line in St Monans. It was often the rule, rather than the exception, in any fishing village, to return from a long trip in debt. After such a season on the stormy coasts of Wick and Peterhead, Thomas made light of their misfortune.

Vow, Maggie, what ails ye, ye're in sic a tune,
Aboot starvin weanies for cleadin and shoon,
Tis nae fairly winter, an' tent me, guid wife,
We're as sure o' our cleadin' as we are o' our life.

He was the poet laureate of the Temperance Cause in Fife, especially at their meetings in Anstruther, with such espousers of the Anti-Drink Movement as James Clark, the Poet Gardner of Elie, and his old friend, Robert Lindsay.

In his poem 'Let Merry Topers', he gives a warning about hangovers!

Let moderation pree an' sip,
Wi' stinted draps to weet his lip,
The wary chiel at times will dip,
Ower deep in dissipation.

Then a' neist day, wi' drowsy e'e,
An barley fever like to dee,
The ne'er a morsel he can pree
For a' his moderation.

His solution was simple:

Then gi'e to me the cauler spring,
I'll cheery as a lintie [linnet] sing,
An' never feel the bitter sting
O' reckless dissipation.

His verse portrayed events from the everyday life of his times; 'Scene in a Sheriff Court', 'Lines on the loss of two fishermen from their yawl on 26th April 1848', comments on epidemics of cholera, influenza and smallpox and epistles to fellow rhymsters whose works he enjoyed, like Captain Charles Rey RM, who wrote *Lays and Lyrics*, and William Thom of Inverury for his *Blind Boy's Pranks*.

He wrote beautiful hymns, which were sung in the Auld Kirk, in which he was ordained as an elder. Although not as pre-eminent as Lord Newark, he served his church as faithfully and as assiduously as the General.

Contributing to local and national newspapers, he often turned his talent to semi-humorous verse. His ditty, 'My auld auntie Lizzie was famed for a spinner' was popular at village soirées. An avid Burns fan, he wrote a poem for the 'Fifth Anniversary of the St Andrews Burns Club' in 1851. Like the Bard, he wrote on natural phenomena: the Bass Rock, the Swallows, the Seasons, on the Drave, and Patriotism. A keen conservationist, his song 'St Monans', starting,

O this is no our ain moor,
I ken by the diggin o't,

lamented its cultivation and the loss of the beauties of Nature, such as the whins and the thistles! This event in village life, so recorded, may give an explanation as to why there were no relics of the battlefield of 1548 found subsequently.

In 1851, he realised a life's ambition with the printing of a neat Duodecimo volume of 168 pages, entitled *Musings by Sea and Shore*. In its publication, he had been aided financially by his friends, including Lady Anstruther, afterwards Mrs Crosby of Ardfert Abbey. To her, he dedicated his book 'for her unwearied benevolence in prompting the temporal and spiritual welfare of the young and poor of St Monan's.' He told the bookseller proudly, 'If it's no bread, it'll be kitchen tae me a' ma days, Andrew.' Unhappily, the sheets had hardly left the press when he contracted jaundice. He died on Thursday 25th September 1851 and was buried by the pulpit window of the Kirk. Like many another unsung pillar of the community, neither headstone nor plaque marks his grave. This is a significant omission from the history of the village, which should be rectified for posterity.

William Cowper – 1731–1800

Albeit he was not a native, the author and poet, William Cowper is associated with St Monans. For over 350 years, Stenton Farm on the Balcaskie Estate had as its tenants, the Cowpers or Coopers. Coming from an English branch of the family, William, who lived in Norfolk, often visited Stenton. It is claimed that his acquaintance with the East Neuk led him to write the poem beginning:

I am monarch of all I survey,
My right there is none to dispute,
From the centre all round to the sea,
I am Lord of the fowl and the brute.
O, Solitude! Where are the charms,
That sages have seen in thy face?
Better dwell in the midst of alarms,
Than reign in this horrible place!

He attributed the words to Alexander Selkirk, describing his being marooned on the Isle of Juan Fernandez, from 1704 to 1709. Selkirk, who lived from 1676 to 1721, was a native of nearby Lower Largo. However, another view is that Cowper was influenced by reading of Selkirk's adventures in Daniel Defoe's *Robinson Crusoe,* published in 1719. Cowper is best remembered for the writing of such hymns as 'O, for a closer walk with God'.

A Stenton relative enjoyed longevity as the *New Account* records. 'In 1828, there died in the parish, in full vigour of body and mind, a respectable farmer John Cowper, in his 92nd year.'

A letter from the Napoleonic Wars

The Napoleonic Wars of 1805 to 1815 had an impact on village life as Army recruiting sergeants, offering the King's shilling, and Navy press gangs, claimed many a youth. The plight of one lad is described in the following letter to his mother.

> Dear Muther am in french prizen and this cum to lat you no that am well hopin to find you in the saim – folk will think am ded but thats no tru dont think I will tell you a ly and tho any wan say am dead nevir belivie wan word ont till you heer from mysell for the deels ay bizzy but am yours till ded Andrew Duncan.

Later, the Reverend Robert Swan had news of Andrew's death. However, Elspeth, who could neither read nor write, had her son's letter read over to her and refused to believe the news, claiming that 'the minister wis on a gouk's [fool's] errant frae the Deil'. She lived and died believing that her son was still alive. Indeed, from her meagre earnings, she made half-a-dozen 'superior' shirts for his homecoming.

John Jack

The only published history of St Monans came from the pen of John Jack, a private schoolmaster. Born in Pittenweem in 1796, he chose to go to sea but his ambitions were thwarted by poor eyesight. Settling in St Monans, he established a private, so-called adventure school in his house. Serving on the local council from 1827 until his death, he was a baillie for six years.

He was not altogether popular, being accused of using his position on the council to obtain personal advantage. In 1841, there was much opposition by herring curers and local householders to his acquisition, by council consent, of a piece of land adjoining his property. It was to be used for fish-curing, but the standard practice of rouping the stand had not been followed.

In 1844, he had produced at Cupar by G. Tullis, publisher, *An Historical Account of St Monance, Fifeshire, Ancient and Modern, interspersed with a variety of Tales Incidental, Legendary and Traditional.* He contributed articles to newspapers and wrote another book on *The History of the Isle of May.*

Christopher Rush

In more recent years, the only significant contribution to literature from St Monans has been made by Christopher Rush. A descendant from the Scott family from the East Backgate, he is a teacher of English at George Watson's College, Edinburgh.

His fine writings in prose and poetry have much specific reference to the history and anecdotal past of the village. His is a rare talent that can perhaps best be described as fiction with a factual background, often with autobiographical overtones. He is also the author of the screen play of the very successful film *Venus Peter.*

Chapter 23

Superstition and Witchcraft

And twenty ghosts, in winding sheets as white as snow, sat cocking on St Monan's steeple

General

LIKE MOST CIVILISATIONS in their early development, Scotland had its own share of superstition and mysticism. This was particularly evidenced amongst the rural and seafaring communities, whose daily encounter with the elements of nature, coupled with a general lack of education and heightened by a Celtic heritage of fear of the supernatural, made them easy prey to 'auld wive's tales'. Ancient Fife can vie with the legendary occult history of the Western Highlands for weird and outlandish stories.

Witchcraft and necromancy in the Kingdom were dominated by the Great Seer himself, Sir Michael Scott of Balwearie, near Kirkcaldy, immortalised in the 'Lay of the Last Minstrel' by his namesake, Sir Walter, as the Wizard of the North. Linguist, astrologer and chemist, hypnotist and chiromancer, mathematician, theologian and philosopher, seer and traveller, Sir Michael studied the 'Black Art' in the role of the wealthy academic, journeying to royal courts and universities, the length and breadth of Europe.

There were, however, many of his countrymen and women of far humbler origin or schooling, who nevertheless became deeply involved with the machinations of His Satanic Majesty and, throughout the county, covens and witches' squadrons thrived. A coven consisted of thirteen; the Devil, who was the leader, the Devil's Registrar, a maiden and ten other witches and warlocks.

When King James VI was to marry Anne of Denmark, the Scottish fleet sent to collect her was driven back to Norway by a violent tempest. As a result, the King had to sail to Denmark and marry her there. Witchcraft was suspected and the Fife sorceress, Agnes, was duly brought before the King and his Council. She confessed that she, with two hundred of her 'sisters', went to sea in sieves and riddles and landed at North Berwick kirk, where the Devil christened a black cat, causing adverse winds to blow against the bride's ship. Agnes and many other Fife women were tortured and put to death on the basis of such absurd statements.

Robert Baillie, one of the most respected of Presbyterian ministers and Principal of the University of Glasgow, wrote in 1643, 'upon the regret of the extraordinary multiplying of witches, above thertie being burnt in Fife in a few months, a committee was appointed to search and cure it.' His strict dictum was, 'Thou shalt not suffer a witch to live.'

Long before Burns wrote in 'Tam o' Shanter' of 'warlocks and witches in a dance' in 'Alloway's auld haunted kirk', St Monans had its own visitations by such creatures. In his history of the village, Jack records that the Calliard Hill, just above Ardross Farm on the road to Elie, was, traditionally, the principal arena where kelpies and other imaginary beings held their midnight revels and carried out their incantations. Even in the nineteenth century, a man was taken from that enchanted eminence and carried nine times round Kilconquhar Loch – or so the spellbound individual himself declared!

Over the door of nearly every house in the village was hung the traditional horse-shoe, not as a symbol of good luck, but as a defence against evil spirits. Another safeguard or talisman, believed infallible, was to incorporate a scarlet thread into every hand-woven cloth or knitted garment.

In those far-off days, St Monans was divided into two distinct sections. The one situated between the Braehead and the main Pittenweem-to-Elie road was called the Uppertoun or Overtoun; the other lay at the foot of the hill bordering the shore-line of the Forth, and was known as the Nethertoun. The landward inhabitants were peasants and farmers and followed a totally rural calling, trading from their small-holdings in milk, butter, potatoes and, of course, bacon. In the Nethertoun were the fisher folk who, despite their fearless pursuit of so dangerous a calling, lived in constant torment from the superstitious dread that they might lose their souls.

Cauld Iron

In particular, the sea-faring community had a totally paranoid hatred of the simple farmyard pig, believing that it cast evil spells. Deliberately avoiding its generic name, they called it the beast, the brute, curly-tail or the grunter. The spell under which they fell immediately, at the mere sight or contact with the animal, could only be broken by touching metal and calling out, 'Cauld iron.' There was an alternative, namely to grasp the latch of the kirk style and thrice call out the name of Holy St Monan. Every seaman knew that in a pig's trotter could be seen the hole whence the malevolent spirits flew out.

They had no trade union to stage an official or even a wild-cat strike, but any sighting of a curly-tail by a fisherman as he made his way to the pier, suspended all sailings until an ebb and flow of the tide had washed away the curse. Angered by the loss of livelihood occasioned by the presence of the sties in the Overtoun, the 'doon-the-touners', as they are still known today, waged a virulent vendetta against the pig breeders. This culminated in the mariners, armed with boat-hooks and their three-pronged leisters or fish-forks, marching up the brae to assail the cottars. Cunningly, the yeomen simply opened the pens and drove their stock headlong into the approaching horde, precipitating a total rout.

Perhaps the best-known tale of this fear concerns the induction to the parochial charge of a new minister to the Auld Kirk in the seventeenth century. As 'a new besom sweeps clean', multitudes were drawn to the service, more out of irresistible curiosity than religious fervour. Unfortunately, the poor man killed any possible popularity on the very threshold of his ecclesiastical career. Having selected from the 15th chapter of the Gospel according to St Luke, the Parable of the Prodigal Son, he launched into his sermon with the well-known words, 'And he sent him into his field to feed swine.' At this, 'cauld iron' was whispered simultaneously from every throat, accompanied by a desperate stretching of necks and arms to discover nail-heads in the pews on which they might place their fingers. The parson paused, unable to fathom this outburst. At length, he conjectured that it might be a local way of saying 'Amen', so he reiterated the sentence, whereupon 'Cauld iron' now rang through vaulted nave and aisles in wide-mouthed, united clamour. The bewildered cleric then surmised that, as the kirk had already withstood the ravages of three centuries, perhaps it was part of the fabric giving way which had produced such an uproar. However, observing no apparent damage in the form of crumbling or falling masonry, he pressed on, pronouncing in ringing tones, 'And he would fain have filled his belly with the husks that the swine did eat', whereupon his flock rose as a man, bolted from the pews, leapt from the galleries and, with torn 'Sunday best' and bruised *cuits* (ankles), emptied the kirk. Such was the animosity and enmity, that the Lord of Newark banned the keeping of pigs, and none was seen in St Monans for more than a century.

On the accession of Sir James Sandilands to the Barony of Newark, he exercised his lordly privilege and granted leave for the pigs to be reintroduced. However, he made the stipulation that they should always be moved from one site to another in a poke or sack. On one occasion, the beast gnawed a hole in the bag, escaped and chased a passing fisherman. Such was his terror that he committed suicide by leaping off the end of the pier and drowning. His poor wife had witnessed the chase and succumbed to nervous convulsions and premature labour. Her husband was denied a Christian burial, but was interred 'betwixt three lairds' lands', with a large wooden stake driven through his heart to hold him down securely, otherwise, 'that the suicide, after having been twa an' forty haill days i' the yird would emerge and continue his nocturnal wanderings aboot the neighbourhood, where the deed was perpetrated.' Peter Rolly, owner of the offending pig, was summoned by Thomas Binning, chief magistrate, who sentenced the animal to be burned alive at midnight on the Calliard Hill. Rolly appealed to the Baron, but the Court, convened at Newark Castle, approved the punishment. However, the Baron, noting Binning's complacent grin, added the rider, 'The sentence shall be carried out by our chief magistrate.' The terrified Binning then pleaded for mercy for Rolly, and implored Newark to reverse the decision, postulating that no law had been broken, the release of the grunter had been a regrettable accident and that the decision had been wrongly based on superstitious prejudice! A stay of execution was granted but the baillie was sternly warned that, in future, he must discharge his duties in a more responsible manner.

Fish

Other superstitions concern the fish themselves. To this day in St Monans, a seaman will never call a salmon anything other than a 'red fish'.

Again, at the drave fishing, when the herring shoals were in the Firth of Forth, the solid brass bell, hung on a tree in the graveyard and rung to summon the faithful to worship, would have its clapper, or tongue, tied to avoid frightening away the fish. On one occasion, the beadle forgot and started to ring. The congregation tossed him unceremoniously over the kirkyard wall, felled the tree and smashed the bell. Nor was the sighting of the minister considered a good omen, should he be met by a fisherman on his way to his boat. Superstitious tradition demanded that the sailor return home, remove his cap and sit down. If, unfortunately, the clergyman was still in the vicinity when the poor man again left his house, the voodoo-breaking exercise had to be repeated.

Friday was always considered unlucky in the village, not, as in the rest of the world, because of the Crucifixion, but by reason of the belief that, on that day, St Monan passed into the life beyond the grave, after a final, unavailing conflict with demoniacal foes.

The Burning of Maggie Morgan

Inhabitants of the East Neuk today may know of the visit of King Charles II to the Royal Burgh of Pittenweem in the seventeenth century. Few, however, may realise the weird on-goings which coincided with this historic event.

News having reached St Monans that His Majesty had entered Pittenweem, almost the entire population flocked there to ascertain just what a king looked like. With neither television nor radio and few newspapers, they had very romantic notions of such an august and powerful personage and there was naturally a good deal of excitement at the prospect of seeing the Merry Monarch in the flesh. He had been proclaimed king in Edinburgh, following the execution of his father, Charles I, in Whitehall in 1649, and was then crowned at Scone Palace on New Year's Day, 1651.

The Fifers were, of course, denied the pleasure of meeting Nell Gwynn, the orange-seller, who was but a babe-in-arms at this time and who did not enter the monarch's life until after the Restoration. However, he brought a lively Court as his entourage for the visit to Fife and the whole district was agog with expectation.

Even the parson was infected by the occasion and dashed off to the 'scuil' to persuade his bosom pal, the master, to make the pilgrimage. The worthy pedagogue was, at that moment, regaling his pupils with a portion of Holy Writ. As the minister burst into the classroom, he heard, 'Behold, the King cometh,' whereupon he exclaimed in his impatience, 'Weel, come on then, let's go and see him!' The dominie, needing little persuasion, hung up his tawse and gave the pupils a holiday. The two portly carles, puffing and blowing, set off on the Coal Farm Road, leaving their wives, two sisters, to bring up the rear.

The royal visit was chronicled in the Pittenweem Council minutes of 14th February 1651:

> The Baillies and Council being convened, and having received information that his Majesty was to be in progress with his Court tomorrow, and to stay at Anstruther House that night, have thought it expedient according to their bounden duty, with all their reverence and due respect, and with all the solemnity they can, to wait upon his Majesty as he comes through this, his Majesty's burgh and invite his Majesty to eat and drink as he passes; and for that effect hath ordered that the morn afternoon the Town's colours be put upon the bartisan of the steeple, and that at three o'clock the bells begin to ring, and ring on still, until his Majesty come hither and be past to Anstruther; and sick-like.
>
> That the minister be spoken to, to be with the Baillies and Council, who are to be in their best apparel, and with them a guard of twenty-four of the ablest men with partizans [long-handled spears], and another twenty-four with musquets, all

in their best apparel – William Sutherland commanding as captain of the guard – are to wait on his Majesty and receive his Highness at the West Port, bringing his Majesty and Court through the town until they come to Robert Smith's yeat, where a table is to be covered with one of my Lord's best carpets; and that George Hedderwick have in readiness of fine flour some great bunns, and other wheat bread of the best order, baken with sugar, carvell, and other spices fitting; and James Richardson and Walter Airth have care to have ready eight or ten gallons of good strong ale, with Canary, sack, Rhenish wine, tent, white and claret wines, that all his Majesty and his court may eat and drink.

That, in the mean-time, while his Majesty is present, the guard do diligently attend about the Court; and, as soon as his Majesty is to go away, that a sign be made to Andrew Tod who is appointed to attend the colours on the steeple head, to the effect he may give signal, to those that attend the cannon, of his Majesty's departure and then the hail thretty-six cannon to be all shot at once.

It is thought best fitting that the minister and James Richardson, the oldest Baillie, when his Majesty comes to the table, show the great joy and sense this burgh has of his Majesty's condescendencie to visit the same, with some other expressions of loyalty – which was acted.

The King having departed, the inhabitants of St Monans trudged back to their work, disillusioned that the head of their realm was but a mere mortal. Their feelings were summarised in the observations of a local worthy. 'Gosh, thae Pittenweem fouks mak a din aboot naething. A king's jist like ony ither weel-dressed man; an' gif I had lang tails to ma Sabbath-day jecket, I micht be a king masel!'

However, the worthy pair of the story, the minister and the dominie, intent on making a day out of it, retired with their spouses to Peter Bizzie's inn. There, they became kings themselves and, having elevated that jolly publican to the peerage, then conferred upon him the dignity of Prime Minister. When midnight struck summoning their departure, the hostess, from her private room, produced the ladies, as royal as their lords.

Now, by coincidence, there was that night a witch review in Pittenweem's Witch Loan. Attending was Maggie Morgan, from the Overtoun of St Monans, for the purpose of receiving additional powers and being fully admitted into the black secrets of the dread fraternity by inscribing, as was traditional, the infernal oath in her own blood. Maggie, a pretty young girl of peasant stock, had caught the eye of one of the young noblemen from Elie House. Seduced by the flattery of this well-dressed and rich gallant, she became pregnant but soon found herself ruined and deserted. 'Poor thing, it's a pity, for she was a bonnie, lightsome lassie', was the verdict of the villagers, all powerless to question higher authority. After the birth of her child came inquisitorial visits from the parson, whose will was absolute in such matters. He also consulted a well-known 'clype' or gossip, who further embellished the smears on Maggie's character.

Alone, Maggie was arraigned before the Kirk Session. The night before her trial, the minister had been seen leaving the schoolmaster's house, in an advanced stage of intoxication. Daring to suggest that the infant was the progeny of a gentleman who was conspicuous by his absence, she was branded 'a harlot and a limmer' by the parson; the schoolmaster agreed, the other elders nodded assent and she was found guilty on all counts. Her punishment was to appear at the Auld Kirk on three successive Sundays. Clad in sackcloth, she had to stand in the vestibule during the pealing of the warning bell, repeating constantly, 'Fause tongue that lied.' Then, for the whole of the service, she was placed above the congregation on the penitential stool to suffer the preacher's prolonged and wrathful sermon.

Maggie swore revenge on her seducer and her persecutors but seem unlikely to achieve her aims against such important and powerful men. However, one night, at the height of a terrible storm, she was visited in her humble cot by a mysterious female. The stranger advised Maggie, that, if she wanted power, 'tae git yir ain back on the blaggards', she should attend the witches' coven, 'to be held on the Loan, on the fifth day of the week at ten hours o' the clock.' The coincidence of this date with the aftermath of the King's visit presented her with the perfect opportunity to strike, not only at the minister, but also at his aider and abettor, the dominie.

The night on which the mellow quartet bade farewell to their host, 'Sir' Peter Bizzie, and set their ruddy and glowing noses towards home, was black and starless, and filled with witches and wizards, ghosts and goblins, spells and spunkies, and all manner of fearsome apparitions. Perhaps such evil was more than enough to frighten ordinary mortals, unfortified by 'bold John Barleycorn', but the parson always had a shibboleth or test-word at his finger-tips for such occasions, while the dominie swore that the quotation of the theorem of Pythagoras was sufficient protection against any power that Auld Nick could launch against them.

However, not a quarter of a mile out of the town, Maggie cast a spell over them. Rooted to the spot, they stood quaking, as, in a dazzling flash of light, they were suddenly confronted by – a white rabbit! As they gazed spellbound, the creature loped around them seven times; this was none other than Maggie, bewitching her foes. By her wizardry, they were infused with new life, energy and laughter, and made to change partners! Now, the sound of merry music filled their ears and they were irresistibly drawn towards its source. Thus it was that they joined the revelry of the infernal coven in the Witch Loan. This piece of common lay to the north of the village and, before becoming unhallowed ground, had been the local arena for athletic games, military drilling and other public exhibitions. The witch squadron were incensed at this unwarranted intrusion into their secret society. History is significantly silent on the details of their terrible experiences at the hands of the warlocks but when the horrible confusion had ended, they had been mysteriously transported back to the very spot where they had first seen the rabbit. The women were 'denuded of their garments even to an infraction of the laws of decency' and the fine black coats of the men were transformed into fishermen's guernseys. But Maggie was not yet done with her victims and now they beheld Auld Hornie himself in hot pursuit. Each seizing the other's wife, for they were still on enchanted ground, they ran pell-mell down the road towards St Monans, but Clootie clicked their heels and up-ended them in a muddy ditch where, tired out by the exertions of the day's events, the exhaustion of their experiences, and befuddled with drink, they fell asleep.

There, they were found in the morning by four ploughmen on

their way to work, while browsing nearby was the Prince of Darkness himself, the parson's own cow, who had broken out of her byre and strayed off. It was a sorry-looking and bedraggled group who retraced their steps to Peter Bizzie's hostelry, where they tidied themselves up and sat down to ponder the consequences of their escapade. The tidings would most likely reach the long ears of the Presbytery and so, dreading excommunication or the loss of their posts, they resolved to seek a Royal Pardon for their waywardness.

Tramping through Pittenweem to Anstruther Place, at the junction of the Crail and St Andrews roads, where the King had stayed overnight, they craved an audience. Pathetically, they pledged undying loyalty and asked for the King's forgiveness. Granting their wish, Charles issued an edict in which, 'the King renders null and void, all libels or indictments of any judiciary, civil or ecclesiastical, that might be preferred against the parson and dominie of the town and parish of St Monance for alleged indecorum, fama or misdemeanour, purported to have been committed by them within twenty-four hours after the royal departure from Pittenweem, accordingly assoilzied [acquitted] by the judge and jury for every such charge as aforementioned by His Majesty's will and pleasure.' Thinking that their troubles were over at last, they joyfully took the road home. However, such was not their luck, for, on arriving at the spot where their misfortunes had all begun with the appearance of the white rabbit, they found their wives locked in desperate conflict. These good ladies, now disenchanted, had suddenly realised that each had spent the night, albeit sinlessly, in the arms of the other's husband and were blaming each the other for such outrageous impropriety. 'Desist!' shouted the schoolmaster, whereupon his wife screamed back, 'Embrace your concubine, ye rakish rooster.' This reply won her a very prompt 'dad on the lug' from her man, wherewith hostilities abruptly ceased. They made their separate ways home, never to speak to each other again. Tradition has it that the scene of such capers was thereby called the 'Daft Hill' or, as it is known today, the Taft Hill.

The evil of that night was not without consequence in St Monans. The large, gilded, metal image of a salmon, which had adorned the spire of the kirk, disappeared. Some claimed that it had been melted by lightning but the more superstitious that it had been stolen by the Picts, who were considered a fairy race. Felled too was the Town Cross. This 'emblem of dignity', as Jack called it, was situated in the centre of the market place. One complete stone monolith, twelve feet high, being based on a circular flight of steps, it was surmounted by a replica of crossed fish, with the Coat of Arms of the town underneath. It was set up again but was not seen after the middle of the eighteenth century.

Around 1750, a comet appeared and was said to be visible for four months; history records that Haley's comet was seen in 1757. Many abandoned the fishing, believing that the end of the world was nigh; some became house-bound and others even bed-ridden. Money was hidden away for security and, years later, coins of the reigns of James VI and the two Kings Charles were discovered in the Narrow Wynd.

Maggie, flushed with her triumph and newly-found powers, now targeted the real hate of her life, her former paramour from Elie House. One beautiful morning in June, she espied him with a new fiancée on his arm, on his way down to St Monans harbour. They were about to embark on a boat trip to the Island of May. Using her black art, Maggie flew to Pittenweem, where she consulted Brown of the Braes, a noted warlock and Commander-in-Chief or Devil of the flourishing local coven. He instructed her to find a secluded spot along the East Braes, with a good view of the harbour. There she was to float a wooden bowl in a tub of water. When the boat was a fair way from the harbour-mouth, she was to whirl the bowl seven times round and then 'cowp' it when her fatal design would be accomplished. Old Cowzie, as he was nick-named, bade his pupil, 'Deil speed' and she flew back to St Monans, prepared her spell and successfully sank the boat with the words, 'Here – mak yir bridal bed among the partans.' The crew swam ashore, but the young lovers were found drowned at low water next day.

Maggie's devilish work had not, however, gone unnoticed and the parson, who had suspected her hand in his own affair, worked hard to obtain evidence for her apprehension as a witch. In due time, she was arraigned again, under the grave charge of being in league with the Devil. Being now sated with revenge and regardless of life, she pleaded guilty and confessed all. After a brief trial, she was summarily convicted, with the inevitable sentence: 'That ane great pile of faggots be up-bigget on the Kirk Hill the morrow morning, after whilk she sall the morrow be brought forth and laid thereon where she sall suffer the pains of devouring fire in the face of the noon-tide sun of heaven, that all may tak warning, and avoid sic like affinity, league or compact wi' the wicked spirits of darkness.'

Two sergeants, petty Officers of Justice, appointed annually by the feuars to keep the peace, were detailed to watch her in order to prevent escape and sleep. Why deprive the condemned of slumber? Well, the whole district was familiar with the tradition concerning Witch Grizzel of the fifteenth century. Like Maggie, she too had been condemned to burn but was allowed to fall asleep, when she used her powers to transform herself into a bum-clock or flying beetle and make her escape. So it was that, for nearly twenty-four hours, while one sergeant blew a large horn in her ears, the other assiduously applied the witch-goad to test if she was still awake. This latter instrument was a wooden paddle, bristling with nails, and undoubtedly painful when administered by the strong arm of the law.

When her pyre was completed on the Kirk Hill, she was secured on top. The kirk's three main dignitaries sat in ancient elbow chairs, and the beadle, as was his duty, set a brand to the kindling, in view of the assembled population. So died Maggie Morgan, the last witch to be burned in St Monans. When the grisly execution was completed and the holiday crowd had dispersed, the beadle's final task was to scatter the ashes to the four cardinal winds of heaven and to collect the fragments of burned bones which remained. These he deposited, as was his wont, in the Brunt Laft of the Auld Kirk. This was a peculiar recess in the upper regions of the tower, accessible by the steeple stairs. It appears unlikely that it was constructed for such a ghastly purpose when the good King David had the church built. However, when witch burning became popular, the post of beadle included the title of chief executioner and he had the full agreement of the Session to deposit all such remains therein.

Buff Barefoot

Yet another eerie tale from the reign of Charles II links St Monans with the House of Grangemuir in Pittenweem, which has long since disappeared.

One moonless, winter's night, a tall figure, enveloped in a black cloak, was seen hurrying along the coastal path from Newark to St Monans. Knocking on the door of the tavern near the harbour, kept by Grizzle or Grizel Miller, the stranger deposited a basket on the doorstep and then vanished. In the seventeenth century, things supernatural were always lurking on the threshold, so Grizel, somewhat apprehensive, called to her niece who, noting the anxiety in her aunt's voice, came out carrying the open Bible. A shrill cry from the basket confirmed their worst fears. Despite there being no new-born child to steal in its stead, the fairies had left one of their imps. But this was no ugly hobgoblin. Lying in the finest blankets and linen was a beautiful baby girl, richly clad and, by her side, a bag of gold.

As the years passed, Grizel and her household came to love the foundling gift of the fairies. They took the precaution of making her wear a necklace of amber or 'lammer' beads, to ensure that she would not respond to her kindred calling her back to Elfin-land. The rhyme, well-known in Fife for dispelling evil spirits, was:

Black luggie, lammer bead,
Rowan tree and red threid
Put the witches to their speed.

A luggie was a wooden pail or dish, with a handle formed by the projection of one of the staves above the others.

The child grew into a lovely young woman. Conforming to the customs of the peasant class in which she was raised, she wore neither shoes nor stockings. Her Christian name, if she ever had one, was forgotten and she was known in the village as Buff Barefoot. She became very popular with the youths who frequented her adopted mother's tavern, and all was well until a relative of the family at Grangemuir, a Scott or a Ramsay, came to visit. A notorious Border freebooter, he was taken to pay his respects to the family at Newark. Through them, he met the mysterious lass, who had an undisclosed connection with the castle. The maid was, at that time, betrothed to a shipwrecked sailor who, having been rescued from the sea, had sailed abroad to seek his fortune. Now a captain, he was returning to claim his bride, but the Border raider intercepted their mail and discovered a message. Buff was to welcome back the exile in the moonlight beneath Queen Mary's tree on the Doocot Hill. She told Grizel that she must keep the tryst but soon the villagers were roused by cries for help and the sound of pistol shots. They found Buff Barefoot dying on the ground and sighted the fleeing figure of the sailor.

In his book *Bygone Fife*, Wilkie asserts that whatever happened that night was a matter of conjecture. Who was responsible for the cowardly murder? The sea captain was apprehended and incarcerated in one of the Castle's dungeons but the villain of the tale, the wild Borderer, was overcome with guilt and remorse and committed suicide.

From the moment of her death, the spirit of Buff Barefoot haunted Grangemuir. Every night, its occupants were kept awake by the slapping sound of bare feet, running through the rooms and passages. Some guests claimed to have seen her apparition and, for over a century, the old house was only used by those of strong enough character to be sceptical of the unknown. At the beginning of the nineteenth century, the mansion was demolished completely, and not one of its stones was used in building another, lest the spectre of Buff Barefoot should follow.

The location of her tryst with her sailor lover is open to speculation. There is the ancient doocot of Sir David Leslie at Newark; the visit of Mary, Queen of Scots, to the Castle could have been marked by the customary planting of a tree. However, it is more than likely that there would have been other pigeon lofts in the village. Within living memory, the brae between George Terrace and the back of East Street has always been identified as the Doocot Hill.

The Face at the Window

The sighting of an apparition is also recorded early in the twentieth century. The Auld Kirk being heated with solid fuel, it was the beadle's task to clear the ashes from the furnace. Late one evening, after the service, as he was tipping the rakings over the sea-wall, he was petrified by a face which appeared at a high window in the steeple, inaccessible except by ladder or scaffolding.

A few days later, his duties took him to the manse at Abercrombie. Now, there existed a fine portrait of General Sir David Leslie by the artist George Jameson (1588? to 1644), who was known as the Scottish Van Dyke. The minister, probably the Reverend Doctor John Turnbull, had been given a copy by a friend in Edinburgh, so he had it hung in the hallway of his manse. The beadle, seeing it as he came in the front door, nearly died of shock. It was the mysterious face that had appeared at the kirk window – and Leslie had been dead for two hundred and fifty years!

The Witchcraft Act of 1735 was invoked in 1944, at the Old Bailey, to prosecute and jail an Edinburgh woman, Helen Duncan, as she was said to foresee and announce war-time defence secrets in her séances. The then Premier, Winston Churchill, denounced the trial as an absolute travesty of justice. Today's witchcraft is still as feared by fundamentalist Christian groups as it was in the Dark Ages. Prosecution is now brought under the Fraudulent Mediums Act of 1951.

Chapter 24

The Charter of St Monans

William Sandilands
Sir James Sandilands of St Monance
to the Town of St Monance.

TO ALL AND SUNDRY PERSONS that shall hear or see this present Charter. William Sandilands of St Monance franctenements of the town and Lands of St Monance and tennandrie thereof with the parts and pertinents thereof and Sir James Sandilands of St Monance Knight Fiar thereof his eldest son and apparent heir and we both with one consent and assent Greeting in God everlasting. Foresomickle as our Sovereign Lord the King Majesty having respect to the common well of this his Highness realms and Leids thereof after the act of annexation of the Kirk Lands of the Crown, with his Highness Charter under the Great Seal Erected our port and Town of St Monance in an free Burgh of Barroney and the Port and Haven thereof in an free port and havening place which Charter after the restitution of the Bishops of this realm to their former place and Dignities is duly confirmed by the Archbishop of St Andrews now our immediate Superiors of the Town Lands and Tenandrie aforesaid with an clause de non dan and other Clauses Conservit in our favour and sensigne confirmed in Parliament and now considering and well advisedly foreseeing with ourselves after long and mature deliberation that the upbigging of our said haven and a sufficient Bulwark there untill is not only apparently and very liable to be profitable and helpful to our said Tenants fewars Baillies and present inhabitants of our said Town their heirs and successors But also is liable with progress of time to be commodious and very profitable to ourselves our heirs house and successors by the resort and Confluence of Honest Neighbours,

Countriemen and others whom may be able to resort and repair our said town and use traffic and make residence therein in time coming the said Haven Port and Bulwark therein being repaired bigged and made an sufficient harbour without great charges and expenses to be advanced and depursed upon the same and perceiving the goodwill and intention of our said Tenants the present Ballies fewars and inhabitants of our said Town by their bigging and Erecting of honest and sufficient houses in the same Town to the great Decorment thereof and their readings and good mind to the repairing of the Haven and Harbour thereof (where untill they have already made an good entrie and progress) and to make further police and bigging in the said town and willing to give them all good occasions and encouragements to continue the good proceedings and intentions and specially to the bigging and repairing of the said Haven and Bulwark therein. Wit ye as therefore the said William Sandilands of St Monance and Sir James Sandilands his Son and Apparent Heir both with one consent and assent in consideration of the premises and being most willing to give the said Baillies Council fewars and inhabitants of our said Town all good occasion possible to pass forward with their began work and also to the erection and upbrigging of ane Tolbooth and Common house in our said Town for the better administration of justice in time coming and also for seeing and perfectly understanding the well and profits of us our heirs and house to the yearly augmentation of our to the sum of ten pounds of this realm never paid at any time thertofore to us nor our predecessors for the piece of ground and Sward under written part of Muir having gaits wynds and vennills and common passage aftermentioned and for diverse and Sundry other profits Pleasures Gratitudes and good deeds and also for certain sums of Money paid and delivered paid to us by the present Baillies Council Fewars and inhabitants of our Said town of St Monance and hailly converted and applied to the well and profit of us and our heirs and whereof we hold us well contented and Completely paid and for our heirs Executors Successors and assigneys Exonerous quits Claims and discharges the said present Baillies Council Fewars and inhabitants of our said Town of St Monance their heirs Executors and successors of the same sums of money for now and ever by their presents to have granted Let and in few farm and heritage lett left in heritably by our present Charter confirmed and by the tenor hereof give grant lett and in few farm and heritage lett heritably and also by this our present Charter confirm to the said present Baillies Council Fewars and inhabitants of our said Town of St Monance and their Successors all and haill our foresaid haven and Harbour of St Monance with all and Sundry the Customs anchorage Profits Privileges Casualties and Commodities of the same our whatsomever pertaining or that may or can be known to appertain thereto with the haill custom of the fairs of the said Town and all and sundry the common lones gaits wynds vennils and common passages to and frae the Southmost part Muir and Commonity of St Monance to and frae the foresaid Town of St Monance and haven thereof as well within our said Town as without the same used and wont with free ish and entry and other Priveleges Liberties Easements and Commodoties of the same and that Southmost part and piece of Muir of St Monance lyand and bounded as follows viz Betwixt our Arable Lands called the Newlands upon the East and our other Lands and east and west on the Braehead until it come to the loan pass and from the said Town to the same piece Muir upon the South and other arable Lands also above the Braehead striking South and North upon the West, the common gaite coming from the old wind Milne Eastwards through the said Muir while it comes to our said Lands upon the north parts with free ish and entry together also with that part of the Sward earth and Braes lying upon the north part of the Yards of our said Town between the same Yards on the South and the Cornfield Lands above the Brae upon the north part of Robert Boyds Yards upon the West and north west Nuck of Thomas Brown Yards upon the East parts and sicklike all and haill ane Piece and part of Ground which is the house and Yard presently occupied by Grizell Miller relict of umqle William Bollo Smith never fewed off before lying within our said town and bounded as follows that is to say betwixt the tenement of James Binning and Andrew Dishington on the east the House of Annable Martine and the Yard of umqle David Stevenson on the north part with full power and license to be Baillies Council Fewers and inhabitants of our said Town present and to come to Erect Edifice and big up ane Tolbooth and Common house for administration of justice in our said town upon the aforesaid piece of ground bounded as said is with Cellars warding house and other Houses and easements necessar and requisite for ane Common Tolbooth as said is and the same being Edified as said is and bigged and completed joyse use and possess the same as an Common house as said is in few farm heritably in all time coming with all rights priveleges liberties profits and commodities of the same whatsomever all lying with their Tenandries of St Monance and Sheriffdom of Fife Reserving always the haill coal and coal hughs within the bounds above specified to us and our heirs to win by us our colliers or servants to our own proper use in time coming to be holden and to hold all and haill our foresaid Haven and Harbour of St Monance with All and Sundry the Customs anchorages and profits priveledges casualties and commodities of the same with the hail Customs of the free fairs of the said town and all and Sundry the common Lones, Gates, wynds vennils and common passage respective before specified with free ish and entry and sicklike all and haill the foresaid part and piece of St Monance Muir within all the bounds thereof Expire in it together also with the said piece of Sward earth and Braes sicklike before mentioned within all the bounds of the same and also all and hail the foresaid piece of Ground which is the house and Yard lying within the town of St Monance bounded as said is and the Tolbooth and Common house to be bigged thereupon in manner before rehearsed with free ish and entry and all and sundry yr. pentinents to the present Baillies fewars Council Community and inhabitants of our said Town of St Monance their heirs assigneys and Successors of me the Said William Sandilands during my lifetime and after my Decease of me the said Sir James Sandilands of St Monance Knight and heirs in few farm fee and Heritage forever by all their rights marches meiths and devices as the same lie in length and breadth with free ish and entry and all the sundry others the commodoties easements freedoms liberties and righteous pertinents thereof whatsomever pertaining or that may be known to appertain thereto in time coming freely quietly well and in peace But any revocation obstacle impediments or again calling whatsomever giving therefore yearly the said Baillies Council fewars and inhabitants of our said town of St Monance the heirs assignees and successors to me the said William Sandilands elder of St Monance during my Lifetime and after my Decease to me the said Sir James Sandiland and my heirs the aforesaid sum of Ten Pounds usual money of this realm of Scotland at two usual terms in the year of Whitsunday and Martimas by equal portions together with two hundred herring for ilk drave Boat that pays assize Herrings in our said Town of St Monance and that yearly at any one of the two Draves summer or winter labouring whatsomever and for ilk Boat passing to the Lenton great lines within the Scots firth ane Killing and ane Bannock fluck or any fish as good as ane Bannock fluck yearly in the same bees together conform to use and wont and also for Bark and Boat passing to the fishings to Peterhead Orkney or Zetland yearly one Dozen good sufficient Killing and as for every Bark Ship or Creer of our said that sails to the Isles in winter being above have loadned or within half loadned ane Barrel of sufficient well made Herring at their returning from the foresaid fishing in name of the few farm and also the said present Baillies Council fewars and inhabitants of our said Town of St Monance present and to come their heirs and successors giving their suits and presence yearly to our three head courts to be holden at our place of St Monance called the Newark and that but any warning thereto and also all other our courts to be holden at the place foresaid so oft as they shall be warned thereto and they no none of them Decline our judgment in the said Court betwixt Neighbour and Neighbour and sicklike the said Baillies Council Fewars and inhabitants of our said town of St Monance are and shall be in all time coming obliged and astricted to come with their hail malt corns as well growing upon our Grounds and bound as others Coft and inbrought by them within the same bounds and town to our Miln of St Monance to be Milned and Grind thereat and paying the mullure and duty used and wont therefore and at no other Miln in time coming and further the said Baillies Council Fewars and inhabitants of our said town of St Monance their heirs and successors shall be holden and restricted to repair beit and uphold the Kirk and Kirkyard Dykes of St Monance in timber Slait Lime and Glass sufficiently as Effeirs in all time coming and furder said Baillies Council fewars and inhabitants and their successors doing and observing the haill Clauses Conditions and provisions contained in their particular few charters made by me the Said William Sandilands of St Monance to them of their several tenements respective in all points providing always notwithstanding of the setting of the wynds loans venills gates and common passages foresaid in few farm and heritable as said is not the less that the same loans gates and common pasages shall be brucked in commonty as well to us and our heirs and tenants servants and Fewars of any part of the said town and yet to come as to the said present Baillies Council Fewars and inhabitants of our said town and their successors in time coming and also providing the persons who shall happen at any time thereafter to obtain and receive house tenants or roums the ground to big houses and Tenements upon in few and Heritage of us and our heirs within our said Town of St Monance and Territorie of the same shall be bruck joyse use and possess the priveledges liberties and freedoms of the said haven and Harbour of St Monance Tolbooth and Common house and part of Muir and Sward as writen Lones, Gates, wynds, vennils and common passages above Expremit as the present Baillies Council Fewars and iniahbitants of our said Town and successors by virtue of their present Infestments done or hereafter may do so and that with condition that all the same fewars which we or our heirs shall happen to receive hereafter shall first and before they be admitted to the freedoms aforesaid contend and pay to the said present Baillies Council fewars and inhabitants of our said town their heir successors and assigneys to the upholding of the said Haven and Common Ground of the said town sicklike and great composition at their entry as such persons admitted to sicklike priveledges and freedoms in the burghs of Crail Anstruther or Pittenweem pays presently or shall happen to pay for the freedom in the same burrows allenarally – Attour it is specially provided by this our present Charter that the Baillies and Council of the said Town shall be yearly chosen by special advice and consent of the said William Sandilands elder of St Monance and my heirs, and furder providing that our haill tenants and Cottars dwelling within said Lands and Territorie of St Monance be free from payment of any custom with the said town and harbour for whatsomever wairs they shall buy and transport within and from the same and all that our haill Tenants the town and Tennandrie of St Monance shall no ways be stopped by the said Baillies council and fewars of the said town from brewing and selling of vivers and others therein they keeping the statutes and ordinances within the Burgh and the contraveners paying for the town the unlatres so often as they contraveen and being submitted to their jurisdiction, and it is provided that the accompt of the Silver of the Seamen's Box which shall be collected by the Sailors of the Said Town shall be made yearly in presence of me the said William Sandiland of St Monance and my heirs with Baillies and councillors of Said Town and moreover we for us and our heir Will and Grant by their presents that ane only sasine to be tane by the said Baillies and council of the said Town or by any one of them in name or for the haill rest and remnant and their successors at the full Sea and Mouth of the said Haven and Ground thereof shall be sufficient sasinning for the same haill Haven Tolbooth wynds vennills gates common passages common part Muir before specified part of Ground and Sward Earth and Braes respective foresaid in all time coming with the foresaid Customs anchorage priveledges and pertinents as writen And we forsutch the said William Sandiland of St Monance Knight and our heirs shall warrant acquite and forever defend all and haill our said Haven and Port of St Monance gates vennills common passages respective foresaid and the foresaid part and piece of Muir as writen piece of Ground designed for building ane Tolbooth sward and others foresaid with their pertinents to the said present Baillies Council and inhabitants of our said town of St Monance and their heirs and successors in all by all things as is above specified and also from all rents, Liferents Dispositions straits sasinnings publick and private made to any other person or persons of the same or any part thereof and other perils and inconveniences whatsomever against all Deadly as Lawwile Reserving alwise to us and our foresaids the Coal under the Earth priveledge of wayfare and water passage working and winning there of upon provision contained in the particular Charter Granted by us to the foresaid inhabitants of the tenements within said town therefore we charge you Mr Robert Lermoth of Dairsie our Baillies in that part conjunctly and sevaraly specially constitute that incontinent their presents seen but delay you or any of your pass to the said Haven and Harbour of St Monance and full sea thereof and there is at the principle Manse give and deliver state and heritable Sasine and also corporall real and actual possession of all and haill our said Haven and port of St Monance with the Customs anchorage parts priveledges profits and pertinents of the same and custom of the free fairs as writen and also of the part and piece of the Sward Ground Braes and piece of Ground designed for the said Tolbooth and all their pertinents to the said present Baillies Council Fewars and inhabitants of the said Town or any one of them in name of the rest by giving and delivering of Earth and Stone of the Grounds of the said Haven at the full sea thereof as principle Manse foresaid Reserving always the hail coal and coal hughs within the bounds before specified to us and our heirs to be win us our colliers and servants to our own proper use in time coming conform to our Charter as written and after the form and tenor thereof in all points, and this in no ways ye leave undone the which to do I commit to you conjunctly and sevarally our full power in witness whereof to this present Charter and preceipt of Sasine written by David Richardson, son of David Richardson, Merchant Burgess of Edinbr. and subscribed with our hands, our seals thereto hung. At the said town of St Monance the twenty eight day of October in the year of God sixteen hundred and twenty two years before these witnesses. Mr Robert Lermonth Lawfull son to umquhile James Lermonth of Dairsie Andrew Stevenson Common Clerk of Pittenweem Arthur Kilmany School Master of St Monance Arthur Ray nottary and the David Richardson Younger Sic Sub William Sandilands of St Monance James Sandilands.

Mr Robert Learmonth, Witness, Andrew Stevenstone, Witness, Arthur Kilmanie, Witness, Andrew Ray, Witness.

Bibliography

Sir Robt. Sibbald, *History of the Sheriffdoms of Fife & Kinross* (Watson, 1710)

Statistical Account of Scotland Vol. X Fife (1799)

Sir James Sibbald, *History of Fife & Kinross* (R. Tullis, 1803)

Professor Wm. Tennant, *Anster Fair* (Oliver & Boyd, 1812)

John Leighton, *History of the County of Fife* (J. Swan, 1840)

John Jack, *An Historical Account of St Monance, Fifeshire, ancient & modern* (G. Tullis, 1844)

New Statistical Account of Scotland (1845)

Thomas Mathers, *Musings by Sea & Shore* (Private Printing, Ann Duncan, St Monans, from the original of 1851)

Wm. Ballingall, *The Shores of Fife* (Edmonston & Douglas, 1872)

Dr E.B. Ramsay, *Scottish Life and Character* (Gall & Inglis, 1871)

Fatal Casualties at Sea, Lynn Advertiser 1875

George Gourlay, *Fisher Life* (1879)

Kilrounie, *The Kingdom – Handbook of Fife* (Innes, 1882)

The Beggar's Benison of Anstruther (Innes, 1882)

D. Hay Fleming, *Guide to the East Neuk of Fife*, Parts I & II (Innes, 1886)

Geo. Gourlay, *Our Old Neighbours. Folklore of the East of Fife* (1887)

Rev. Walter Wood, *The East Neuk of Fife* (Douglas, 1887)

T. Newbigging Adamson 'Fife Churches', *Trans. Aberdeen Ecclesiological Society*, vol. 3 (1889)

John Geddie, *The Fringes of Fife* (Chambers, 1894)

Dr J. Turnbull, 'The Parish Church of St Monans', *Trans. Aberdeen Ecclesiological Society* No. 3 (1895)

A.H. Miller, *Fife – Pictorial & Historical*, vol. 1 (1895)

Ae. J.G. Mackay, *History of Fife & Kinross* (Blackwood, 1896)

H. Farnie, *Handy Book of the Fife Coast* (Corr, Cupar, 1901)

P. Hume Brown, *A Short History of Scotland* (Oliver & Boyd, 1908)

The Mariners Almanac 1920 (Aberdeen Free Press)

Jas. Wilkie, *History of Fife* (Blackwood, 1924)

H.V. Morton, *In Search of Scotland* (Methuen, 1929)

Jas. Wilkie, *Bygone Fife* (Blackwood, 1931)

J.B. Salmon, *Recording Scotland* (Pilgrims Trust, 1932)

H.V. Morton, *In Scotland Again* (Methuen, 1933)

East Fife Observer 1914–1939

Wm. P. Miller, *Bicentenary of James N. Miller & Sons 1948*, East Fife Observer

Peter F. Anson, *Scots Fisherfolk* (Saltire Society, 1950)

St Monans

Alexander Smith, *Third Statistical Account of Scotland – Fife* (Oliver & Boyd)
'Miller's of St Monans', *The Motor Boat & Yachting*, Nov. 1961
Manning Clark, *A History of Australia* (Chatto & Windus, 1962)
A.R. MacGregor, *Fife and Angus Geology* (Scottish Academic Press, 1968)
Bruce Lenman, *From Esk to Tweed, Harbours, Ships and Men of the East Coast of Scotland* (Blackie, 1975)
Alexander McDonald, *History of Lodge St Monan* (private printing, 1976)
T.D. Drysdale, *Historical Development of the Harbours of the East Neuk of Fife* (Dundee Coll. of Art, 1977)
Jessie Miller, *James N. Miller & Sons, Shipbuilders in Scotland since 1747* (London John, 1980)
'Old St Monans' – Talk by Willie Miller and Tom Ovenstone, Private tape, Jenny MacDonald
The Kingdom of Fife in Days Gone By, Antiquarian, (1980)
W.P. Miller, *History of Boatbuilding over the last 200 years* (Scottish Veteran & Vintage Fishing Vessel Club, 1984)
Billy Kay, *Scots – The Mither Tongue* (Grafton, 1986)
Willie Miller – This is your life (Private publication – Jenny MacDonald)
Forbes MacGregor, *Salt-Sprayed Burgh* (Pinetree Press, 1987)
Joan Clark, *By Boats We Live* (Halcyon Press (New Zealand), 1988)
J. Lewis, 'The Excavation of an 18th Century Salt-pan at St Monance Fife', *Proc. Soc. Antiq. Scot.* 119, 361–370
David Thompson, *Elie Kirk – 350 years – 1639–1985* (Elie Parish Church, 1989)
'How it began', *Believers Magazine* (1989)
Peter Wainwright, 'The Mines and Miners of Goathland, Beckhole and Green End', *Industrial Archaeology of Cleveland*, (1996)
Wm. McNeill, 'The Tung O' Scots', *Lallans 48, Scottish Language Society* 1997
Adrian Cox & Michael King, 'Recent Medieval Metalwork Finds from East Fife', *Tayside & Fife Archaeological Journal*, vol. 3 (1997) pp. 188–203
Tom Weir, 'My Month', *The Scots Magazine*, January 1998
Bill Fyfe Hendrie, 'The Real St Trinians', *The Scots Magazine*, December 1998

Index